Society for Old Testament Study

BOOK LIST 2003

edited by

George J. Brooke

with the assistance of Simon G.D. Adnams

SHEFFIELD ACADEMIC PRESS
A Continuum imprint
LONDON • NEW YORK

© 2003 The Society for Old Testament Study

Published by Sheffield Academic Press (*A Continuum imprint*)
The Tower Building, 11 York Road, London SE1 7NX
15 East 26th Street, Suite 1703, New York NY 10010

www.continuumbooks.com

British Library Cataloguing-in-Publication Data
A catalogue record for this book is available from the British Library

Typeset by Sheffield Academic Press
Printed and bound in Great Britain by Biddles Ltd.

ISBN   0-8264-6668-0

CONTENTS

One copy of the *Book List* is supplied free to all members of the Society.

Copies of this *Book List* may be obtained from:

Orca Book Services
Stanley House
3 Fleets Lane
Poole
Dorset, BH15 3AJ
United Kingdom
Tel: +44 (0)1202 665432
Fax: +44(0)1202 666219
email: orders@orcabookservices.co.uk

Back Numbers of the *Book List* are also available from this address.

Review copies of books for the *Book List* should be sent to the Editor:

Professor George J. Brooke
Department of Religions and Theology
University of Manchester
Manchester M13 9PL
England

PREFACE

The *Book List* continues to develop. In addition to its hard copy this year it is published electronically for the first time. Sheffield Academic Press has hoped that this would be the case for some time and through the editorial skill and hard work of Philip Davies this has now become a reality. Members of SOTS and subscribers to *JSOT* are equally in his debt for this significant step forward.

The reviews in this year's *Book List* are organized under ten headings as in recent years. The large amount of work represented by all these reviews is once again the sign of much time generously given by members of SOTS. I am grateful to them all, but I am especially grateful to those who have taken books at short notice; their swift work in December 2002 and January 2003 keeps the *Book List* as up to date as possible. As last year, I am grateful too for the encouragement and willing assistance from fellow members of the Society who are also colleagues in the Department of Religions and Theology and the Department of Middle Eastern Studies at the University of Manchester. As is customary, thanks also go to several scholars who have brought books to my attention or who have provided reviews from their own personal copies of recently published books; among others, I am especially indebted to Professor L.L. Grabbe, Professor M.A. Knibb, Professor W. Lambert, Professor G.L. Prato, Professor S.C. Reif, Dr W.G.E. Watson, and Dr N. Wyatt.

I am also grateful to the Society for continuing to provide me with funding for assistance in the day-to-day management of the *Book List*. In Manchester I have been very ably assisted by Simon G.D. Adnams; he has taken over and maintained the electronic database established by Julie A. Hughes and has assisted very competently in all the many tasks involved in the preparation of the *Book List*. Sheffield Academic Press is to be thanked for its swift and professional work in the production of the *Book List*; most especially the major contributions of Sarah Norman and Elaine Bingham are noted with appreciation.

The following abbreviations and symbols are employed in addition to those on the basic JSOT list.

ANE	=	ancient Near East(ern)
Bible bibliog.	=	*Bible Bibliography 1967–73: Old Testament* (1974)
BIS	=	Biblical Interpretation Series
B.L.	=	*Book List*
Decade	=	*A Decade of Bible Bibliography 1957–66* (1967)
Eleven Years	=	*Eleven Years of Bible Bibliography 1946–56* (1957)

FAT	=	Forschungen zum Alten Testament
HB	=	Hebrew Bible
HTKAT	=	Herders theologischen Kommentar zum Alten Testament
IOSOT	=	International Organization for the Study of the Old Testament
IZBG	=	*Internationale Zeitschriftenschau für Bibelwissenschaft und Grenzgebiete*
JSJSup	=	Journal for the Study of Judaism Supplement Series
LXX	=	Septuagint/Old Greek Version
MT	=	Masoretic Text
TSAJ	=	Texte und Studien zum antiken Judentum

George J. Brooke
University of Manchester

1. GENERAL

ALTHANN, ROBERT (ed.), *Elenchus of Biblica 1998* (Rome: Editrice Pontificio Istituto Biblico, 2002), pp. 708. n.p. ISBN 88-7653-618-3.

The Elenchus for 1998 is shorter by some 30 pages than that for 1997, but longer by some 230 items. In coverage, coordination, and cross-referencing, it remains beyond challenge. The cooperation in this enterprise between the Pontifical Biblical Institute in Rome and the Department of Biblical Studies in the University of Innsbruck becomes ever closer. And book reviews can be accessed on the Internet, if one chooses BILDI on the menu of the website http://uibk.ac.at (the address http://bildi.uibk.ac.at did not work for this reader).

A.G. AULD

BARBIERO, GIANNI, *Studien zu alttestamentlichen Texten* (Stuttgarter Biblische Aufsatzbände, 34; Stuttgart: Verlag Katholisches Bibelwerk, 2002), pp. 303. €40.90. ISBN 3-460-06341-6.

The dozen articles by B. collected in this volume are all in German, though more than half are translations from Italian. They are divided into three themes. Under 'Individual Passages' are *mamleket kōhᵃnîm* (Exod. 19.6a), *kî 'al kol 'ēlleh* (Jer. 2.34), the MT of Prov. 3.24, 'the love of the daughters of Jerusalem' (Song 3.10b in the context of 3.6-11), and 'the chariots of my noble people' (Song 6.12). Under 'Structural Units' are a synchronic reading of Exod. 33.7-11, 'hear, Israel' (Deut. 6.4-25), the eucharist of the *'ᵃnāwîm* (Ps. 22.23-32), and the tensions in the relationship between the lovers in the Song of Songs epilogue. The last section, on 'Theological Themes', has essays on the young Moses' journey of faith as a summary of the spiritual experience of the Exodus, the foreigner in the Covenant Book and the Holiness Code, and the justice of God and Moses in Exodus 32–34.

L.L. GRABBE

BARR, JAMES, *The Scope and Authority of the Bible* (SCM Classics; London: SCM Press, new edn, 2002), pp. xviii + 154. £9.95. ISBN 0-334-02879-5.

First published in 1980 as Explorations in Theology 7 this book was reviewed in *B.L.* 1981, pp. 86-87. This new edition has a helpful preface by John Barton which makes abundantly clear B.'s determined and constructive effort to establish the meaning of biblical texts as vehicles of theological truth.

P. ADDINALL

BARTON, JOHN (ed.), *The Biblical World* (2 vols.; London: Routledge, 2002), pp. xxiii + 525 (vol. 1); viii + 539 (vol. 2). 94 figures. £130.00. ISBN 0-415-16105-3 (set); 0-415-27573-3 (vol. 1); 0-415-27574-1 (vol. 2).

This is a substantial work dealing with the contents and the social and historical context of the Bible. Edited by B., who supplies a brief introduction, it contains articles from about 50 scholars, mostly from Europe. The first volume begins with an overview of the range of biblical material (OT, Apocrypha, NT) and then goes on to discuss major genres of biblical literature, though it should be noted that, in this section, psalmody and poetry are not actually listed. In a section entitled 'Documents', topics such as the biblical text, Dead Sea Scrolls, inscriptions, Gnostic Gospels and early interpretation are discussed, while the following section deals with thorny problems in history and archaeology. Matters such as language, law, administration and social life offer a fuller understanding of life and culture in Israel and the early Christian church. There are helpful profiles of major figures of the Bible—Moses, David, Jesus and Paul—and treatment of some important religious ideas—salvation, death and afterlife, and purity. The second volume concludes with a look at Jewish and Christian Bible translations and a survey of how the Bible is studied and seen today. These volumes make a useful companion to the *Oxford Bible Commentary* (ed. Barton and Muddiman, see *B.L.* 2002, p. 61), and the substantial bibliographies and full indexes make it an excellent resource for biblical scholarship.

R.B. SALTERS

BEGG, CHRISTOPHER T., *Old Testament Abstracts*, vol. 25 (Washington, DC: Catholic Biblical Association of America, 2002), pp. iii + 636. $26.00. ISSN 0364-8591.

There are 2269 entries in the 2002 volume; the emphasis on abstracting periodicals remains, though the contents of an increasing number of books are also presented.

G.J. BROOKE

BETZ, HANS DIETER, DON S. BROWNING, BERND JANOWSKI and EBERHARD JÜNGEL (eds.), *Religion in Geschichte und Gegenwart: Handwörterbuch für Theologie und Religionswissenschaft*, Band 5. *L–M* (4th, completely rev. edn; Tübingen: Mohr Siebeck, 2000), pp. lxxv + cols. 1704; several illustrations. €214.00. ISBN 3-16-146945-3.

Volumes 1–3 were reviewed in the *B.L.* (1999, pp. 2-3; 2000, pp. 2-3; 2001, pp. 4-6); vol. 4 has so far not been received from the publisher. The following entries are likely to be of interest to readers: Lachen/Weinen; Lachish (N. Na'aman); Lade JHWHs (S. Kreuzer); Lagarde, Paul Anton de; Lagrange, Marie-Joseph; Lakota (religionsgeschichtlich); Lamm (Gottes); Lamparter, Eduard; Land Israel; Landkarten, antike; Landnahme/Landnahmeüberlieferung (E. Otto); Lasterkataloge/ Tugendkataloge; Leben; Lebensbaum; Lebenszyklus; Leeser, Isaac; Lehrautorität; Leib/Leiblichkeit; Leiden; Leontopolis; Leuchter; Levi/Leviten (R. Achenbach);

Levi ben Gerson (Gersonides); Leviathan; Lévy-Bruhl, Lucien; Leydekker, Melchior; Libanon; Libyen; Licht und Finsternis, II Altes Testament (B. Janowski); Liebe; Liebe Gottes und Liebe zu Gott, I Altes Testament (H.-C. Schmitt), IV Judentum; Lieberman, Saul (G. Stemberger); Liḥyānisch/liḥyānische Inschriften; Lilit; Limes (E.A. Knauf); Literarkritik der Bibel; Literarkritische Schule (R. Smend); Literatur und Religion; Literaturgeschichte/Literaturgeschichtsschreibung, II Altes Testament (H. Utzschneider), IV Judentum, 1 Antike (C. Hezser); Literaturwissenschaft, biblisch (C. Hardmeier); Liturgie, VII Judentum (S.C. Reif); Lob, I Biblisch (F.-L. Hossfeld); Lods, Adolphe; Lokale Kulte; Lokalgötter; Löw, Leopold; Lowth, Robert (C. Bultmann); Luria, Isaak; Luther, Martin; Ma'at (J. Assmann); Machaerus; Machsor (S.C. Reif); Madeba (U. Hübner); Magdala; Maggid; Magie; Mahlzeiten, kultische (T. Seidl); Maimonides; Makkabäer (J.W. van Henten); Makkabäerbücher (van Henten); Maleachi/Maleachibuch (H. Utzschneider); Malinowski, Bronislaw; Mammon (P.W. van der Horst); Mampsis; Mamre (Knauf); Manasse (S. Timm); Manasse-Gebet; Mandäismus; Mani; Manichäismus; Mann, II Altes Testament (E.S. Gerstenberger), V Judentum; Mann, Thomas; Märchen; Marduk; Marginalität; Mari (J.M. Sasson); Märtyrer, VI Judentum; Marxismus; Masada (G. Foerster); Maske; Masoreten; Masse/Gewichte; Matriarchat; Medizin, IV Biblisch; Megiddo (B. Halpern); Megillat Ta'anit; Megillot; Melchisedek; Memra; Menahem (Timm); Menora; Mensch, IV Altes Testament (Janowski), VIII Judentum, 1 Antike (Hezser); Menschenopfer, II Altes Testament (J. Day); Menstruation; Mesa (Knauf); Mesopotamien; Messias/ Messianismus; Metapher; Meyer, Eduard; Mezuza; Micha/Michabuch (R. Kessler); Midianiter (Knauf); Midrash; Milton, John; Miqwe; Mirjam (Knauf); Mischwesen, II Archäologisch (C. Uehlinger); Mishna; Mission, III Judentum; Mittelmeerraum (Knauf); Mizwot (Hezser); Moab (Knauf); Moffatt, James; Mohel; Momigliano, Arnaldo; Mond, II Archäologisch (Uehlinger); Monotheismus und Polytheismus, II Altes Testament (H.-P. Müller); Moria (B.J. Diebner); Mose, I Altes Testament (E. Otto), III Judentum; Mosesegen/Moselied (Otto); Mowinckel, Sigmund (M. Sæbø); Muḥammad; Musik/Musikinstrumente, II Geschichtlich, 2 Altes Testament (U. Hübner), 3 Judentum; Mystik, III Geschichtlich, 2 Jüdische Mystik; Mythos/ Mythologie.

L.L. GRABBE

BRIEND, JACQUES and MICHEL QUESNEL (eds.), *Supplément au Dictionnaire de la Bible, Fascicule* 73 (*Sumer–Suse*) (*DBSup*, 13; Paris: Letouzey & Ané, 2002), cols. 257-512. €55.00. ISBN (series) 2-7063-0161-9; (vol. 13) 2-7063-0214-3.

This fascicle has only two entries. Approximately 100 columns are taken up with finishing the entry on Sumer, to make a total of nearly 300 columns for the entire entry—essentially a monograph on the topic (contributors include M.J. Geller and R. Westbrook). The rest of the fascicle is taken up with the first part of the entry on Susa.

L.L. GRABBE

DAVEY, MICHAELA, *Mastering Theology* (Palgrave Master Series; Basingstoke: Palgrave, 2002), pp. xiii + 296. 4 maps. £14.99. ISBN 0-333-61172-1.

'Theology' in this title comprises one-third survey of the Bible, one-third church history, and one-third modern theology split fairly equally between a dozen modern theologians, eight twentieth-century theological movements and ten different approaches to wealth, power, violence, women, family life and sexual matters. The blurb tells us it 'assumes no previous knowledge' and is intended for under-graduates, the laity and ordination candidates. It is difficult to avoid the conclusion that the project was over-ambitious and therefore flawed from the start and there is no doubt that it suffers from the summary and oversimplification inevitable in such a programme. One is constantly wondering 'why this and not that?' Yet despite these (and other) obvious limitations, what we are left with is a very readable and generally reliable piece of work. The biblical section offers a competent history of the biblical period, with due recognition of the skepticism and caveats which much contemporary OT scholarship would wish to insert, followed by a run down of OT, NT and intertestamental literature, in most cases concentrating on information while acknowledging a variety of scholarly opinion, mostly without evaluation and usually (if not always) leaving readers to pursue the matter further and make their own judgment. With so much ground covered superficially, more bibliographical tools would have been an advantage and the author has not been helped by her proofreaders, giving us Boltmann (p. viii), Metyer (p. 115), 'that' for 'than' (p. 250) and the irritating 'centred *around*' on numerous occasions. Despite these and other provisos, however, the book can certainly be recommended for the market for which it is intended.

A. GILMORE

DÁVID, GÉZA (ed.), *Acta Orientalia Academiae Scientarum Hungaricae* Vol. 54.4 (Budapest: Akadémiai Kiadó, 2001), pp. 399-561. n.p. ISSN 0001-6446.

This issue contains nothing concerned with the OT.

J.A. EMERTON

DAVIES, DOUGLAS, *Anthropology and Theology* (Oxford: Berg, 2002), pp. viii + 236. £14.99. ISBN 1-85973-537-1.

D. describes this 'unsystematic' book as a 'conversation between theology and social anthropology', which covers very wide fields in both; the main aim is to use concepts drawn from social anthropology to illuminate theological ideas and, even more, religious experience. It draws its examples primarily from modern Christian practice. There is no direct application to the OT, even though anthropologists working in the field, such as M. Douglas, are referred to. But the book may none-theless have an indirect importance for the study of the OT through its reflection on such topics as sacrifice, gift and charisma and rites of passage. Its main defect appears to me to be its concentration on *religious* practice and experience when both theology and anthropology are concerned with life as a whole.

W.J. HOUSTON

DAVIES, OLIVER, *A Theology of Compassion: Metaphysics of Difference and the Renewal of Tradition* (London: SCM Press, 2001), pp. xxii + 376. £25.00. ISBN 0-334-02833-7.

In this densely argued piece of metaphysical philosophy, several detailed references to OT passages are made to back up the argument. Sections deal with the Divine Discourse (largely Moses and Yahweh at Sinai emphasizing the use of *dābar 'im* rather than *dābar 'el*, and so on), Divine Compassion (key text Exod. 3.14) and Creation, all within a strongly Christian schema.

P. BALLANTINE

DE MOOR, JOHANNES C. (ed.), *The Elusive Prophet: The Prophet as an Historical Person, Literary Character and Anonymous Artist* (OTS, 45; Leiden: Brill, 2001), pp. x + 263. £75.00/$87.00. ISBN 90-04-12160-9; ISSN 0169-7226.

A collection of 14 papers read at the joint meeting of SOTS and Het Oudtestamentisch Werkgezelschap, Soesterberg 2000. An editorial introduction gives a brief overview. The subjects: Jonah (A.A. Abela); Eli, Samuel and David (A.G. Auld); prophets in Chronicles (P.C. Beentjes); Zion (U. Berges); Jeremiah (C. Bultmann); Amos (T.A. Collins); Amos and Moses (M. Dijkstra); prophecy as protest (T.L. Fenton); Jonah's psalm (A.G. Hunter); prophecy, Moses and the Deuteronomic editor (W. Johnstone); the prophetic role in Ezekiel and Jeremiah (H. Leene); Ezekiel's priestly concerns (A. Mein); grammatical person shifts in prophetic texts (L.J. de Regt); Deborah (K. Spronk). There is an inevitable overlap of interest in certain prophetic passages but approaches vary considerably and there is nothing repetitious in the way subjects are handled. Exegesis is in fact informed by remarkable imaginative freedom seeking support in rigorous textual analysis along with much biblical cross-reference and some appeal to extra-biblical sources. Whether the result is demonstration or rationalization readers must judge for themselves, but every paper is thoroughly argued and demands close attention. There is much wide-ranging reference to other scholarly work, not least the influential contributions of Robert Carroll who died during preparations for the meeting. There is a scattering of occasionally distracting misspellings, for example, 'revues' for 'reviews' (p. 142). And there is no valid inference from purely grammatical gender classification to substantive sexual determination (p. 57), a blind alley to be avoided at all costs.

P. ADDINALL

DIETRICH, WALTER, *Von David zu den Deuteronomisten: Studien zu den Geschichtsüberlieferungen des Alten Testaments* (BWANT, 156; Stuttgart: W. Kohlhammer, 2002), pp. 280. €35.50/SwF 61.60. ISBN 3-17-017260-3.

Fifteen studies published between 1976 and 2001 are re-presented in two collections, each in two sections. There are essays on King David and his afterlife in first the Bible and then fiction. And there are essays on Deuteronomistic History-writing, some on sources and some on redaction. Each half of the volume is headed by an additional, previously unpublished essay. The first sets the biblical picture of

David's rule in wider context: it discusses in turn the image of the ANE ruler, David as an ANE ruler, and David as a ruler *sui generis*. The other well illustrates the appropriateness of the overall title of the volume. This discussion of 'kinds of historical presentation in the books of Samuel' reviews in turn David as artist, David as cult-founder, and David as ruler of a dual monarchy. Two of the essays had previously appeared only in English and one in French. It is very helpful to have in one volume such a collection from a commentator on Samuel and Kings and a leading contributor to scholarship on the 'Deuteronomists' over 30 years.

A.G. AULD

ECO, UMBERTO, *Experiences in Translation* (trans. A. McEwan; Toronto: University of Toronto Press, 2001), pp. x + 135. $19.95. ISBN 0-8020-3533-7.

Three lectures given at Toronto in 1998, apparently in Italian, since this is a translation, have been elaborated into two major chapters. In the first, 'Translating and Being Translated', E. uses his own experience as one whose novels and other writings have been translated into many different languages to bring out some of the issues this raises. He stresses that translation requires not only linguistic ability but also intertextual, psychological and narrative competence. The second, 'Translation and Interpretation', is more concerned with technical problems and discusses the complex borderland between translation and interpretation. The views of C.S. Peirce and Jakobson provide the starting-points, but E. ranges widely. There is little here directly concerned with biblical translation (the main exception comes in a discussion of 'Archaic verses Modern', where he looks at different ways of rendering the opening verses of Ecclesiastes), but this lively and witty book should do much to stimulate the imagination of all those engaged in interpretative studies. They will perhaps be encouraged by the Preface, where E. stresses that theoretical difficulties in translation must not obscure common sense.

R.J. COGGINS

GUNN, DAVID M. and PAULA M. MCNUTT (eds.), *'Imagining' Biblical Worlds: Studies in the Spatial, Social and Historical Constructs in Honor of James W. Flanagan* (JSOTSup, 359; London: Sheffield Academic Press, 2002), pp. ix + 336; 29 figures. £75.00. ISBN 0-8264-6149-2.

This Festschrift has two parts. Part I on Spatial Constructs has the following essays: critical spatiality and the construction of the ancient world (J.L. Berquist); social marginality and construction of space (McNutt); Joshua 22 and the ideology of space (D.A. Knight); a virtual temple in Ben Sira 44–50 (C.V. Camp); space and sects in the Qumran scrolls (P.R. Davies); the case for haplography in the transmission of the biblical texts (D.N. Freedman, S.D. Overton); modelling the Mosaic tabernacle (B.O. Long); Michelangelo's *David* and its reception (Gunn); and Derrida and the spectres of Moses (T.K. Beal). In Part II, Social and Historical Constructs, are essays on rethinking the origins of ancient Israel (N.K. Gottwald); the development of the social-scientific approach to the study of the ancient world (J.M. Halligan); the importance of the social context for ritual studies with the red heifer as a case study (F.S. Frick); the Levantine horned altars (L.A. Hitchcock); Bronze Age agriculture in the Dead Sea basin: the case of Bâb edh-Dhrâ', Numeira and Tell Nimrin (D.W. McCreery); when the history of Israel and Judah begins (N.P. Lemche); and the poetics of the history of Israel—shaping Palestinian history (K.W. Whitelam). The editors' introduction gives a précis of the honoree's life and contribution to scholarship, but there is no overview of the essays or what they contribute to the debate.

L.L. GRABBE

HASTINGS, ADRIAN, ALISTAIR MASON and HUGH PYPER (eds.), *Christian Thought: A Brief History* (Oxford: Oxford University Press, 2002) pp. xii + 176. £5.99. ISBN 0-19-280280-1.

Some brief sections from the excellent *Oxford Companion to Christian Thought* with only marginal references to the OT.

P. BALLANTINE

HOLTER, KNUT, *Old Testament Research for Africa: A Critical Analysis and Annotated Bibliography of African Old Testament Dissertations, 1967–2000* (Bible and Theology in Africa, 3; New York: Peter Lang, 2002), pp. vii + 143. £32.00. ISBN 0-8204-5788-4; ISSN 1525-9846.

This work is the fruit of a decade of collecting and analysing doctoral dissertations on the OT from African scholars. The work for some of these dissertations was carried out in Africa (most of them being in Nigeria), the rest in other parts of the world (most of these being in Italy and the USA). All such, and other related matters, are carefully analysed in this work. In Chapter 1, H. focuses on the issues of interpreting the OT in Africa, that African theology is characterized by a certain predilection for the OT, that Africa needs to make its own search for an *interpretatio africana*, but that various difficulties lie in the way of such a search, for example, the lack of resources, and for many Africans the sheer struggle to live. In Chapter 2 there follows an analysis of the 1967–2000 dissertations with annotations, and in particular a brief abstract for each. Chapter 3 has material about academic institutions, networking and publishing, while in Chapter 4 there is a thematic analysis of the material studied in the dissertations, comparative studies (between the African and OT contexts), and exegetical studies. It is H.'s wish that his work will be read by two groups of scholars. The first group comprises African theologians who H. feels tend to neglect African biblical scholarship. The second is the Western biblical scholars about whom, says H., 'In spite of their politically correct talk about the necessity of listening to the supposed margins of the guild, I find that they also tend to neglect African biblical scholarship' (p. 113). It is indeed to be hoped that they will both 'take and read' this timely and challenging work.

M.E.W. THOMPSON

HUNTER, ALASTAIR G. and PHILIP R. DAVIES (eds.), *Sense and Sensitivity: Essays on Reading the Bible in Memory of Robert Carroll* (JSOTSup, 348; London: Sheffield Academic Press, 2002), pp. xix + 480. £65.00. ISBN 0-8264-6049.

Whenever a reader of this *Book List* up to three years ago came across a review that, defiantly thumbing its nose at the requirement to describe the work precisely and economically, launched into a vigorous and entertaining display of wit and erudition, and ended, all the same, by expressing generous enthusiasm for the work, one did not need to look for the signature. It would be 'R.P. Carroll', and it was. Readers of *B.L.* thereby gained some impression of how Robert Carroll delighted, exasperated and illuminated us all, to make no mention of his centrally important contributions to the study of prophecy. This entrancing volume is an appropriate expression of the grief and affection of so many, as well as honouring C.'s memory in the best possible way, by seeking to carry forward his interests and concerns. It shares at least one outstanding characteristic with the honorand: it is never dull. A brief personal memoir by H. opens the volume, and a complete personal bibliography closes it. The 27 contributions are divided, somewhat arbitrarily, between four sections. Part I, 'Reading Robert Carroll', contains just one essay, in which M. Brummitt and Y. Sherwood reflect on the significance of writing in Jeremiah 36 in dialogue with C. himself. In Part II, 'Reading Biblical Texts: Biblical Exegesis', J. Stiebert contrasts the presentation of Esau in the Pentateuch and in the Prophets; J. Blenkinsopp writes on the séance in 1 Samuel 28 with reference to extra-biblical parallels; A.G. Auld considers contrasting ideas of inter-generational responsibility in Kings, Chronicles, Jeremiah and Ezekiel; H.S. Pyper asks questions about the representation of emotion with reference to David's reaction to the death of sons; H.M. Barstad considers ways of understanding the historical Jeremiah based on what we know of prophecy, especially in time of war, in the ANE; A.G. Hunter explores the theme of creation in Jonah in intertextuality with Genesis; P.R. Davies presents Proverbs as a self-portrait of the intellectual class in Judah who created the HB; H.A. McKay casts a suspicious eye on the representation of horses and donkeys in the HB; and J.M. Halligan asks questions about the 'Second Temple', including whether it existed. In Part III, 'Reading the Readers: Ideology and Reception of the Bible', R. Davidson reflects on church and academy as contrasting contexts for the study of the Bible; L.L. Grabbe argues in the face of 'neo-fundamentalism' for maintaining an atmosphere of free discussion; K.W. Whitelam sharply criticizes the way in which so-called 'minimalism' is represented by its opponents; S.C. Reif considers the history of Jewish biblical scholarship in relation to 'Old Testament' studies; J.F.A. Sawyer looks at the significance of the book of Isaiah in the origins of Zionism; F. Landy looks at sexuality in Isa. 8.1-4 and 12.1-6; J. Cook writes on the role of the law of Moses in the LXX and Qumran; R. Setio discusses the dangers of a text such as Deuteronomy 20 in the situation of religious war in Ambon; A. Brenner identifies the significance of the beard (*zaqan*) as the marker of the authority of the 'elder' (*zaqen*); and D.J.A. Clines, similarly, writes on the characteristically masculine aspects of prophecy in the HB. Part IV is entitled 'Reading the Signs: The Bible and Cultural Studies'. D. Jasper reflects on the (im?)possibility of theology in the postmodern condition; S. Prickett argues for the 'polyphonic' character of the Bible with its train of interpretation in Western culture; G. Josipovici studies space and rhythm as essential aspects of biblical interpretation; J. Ashton interprets Browning's *A Death in the Desert* as reactions to Feuerbach's and Renan's views of Jesus; A. Bach writes autobiographically on the feminist movement; the late C. Smith looks at P.G. Wodehouse's use of biblical quotation and allusion; and W. Johnstone examines the interpretation of the biblical text implicit in the frescoes on the north and south walls of the Sistine Chapel, and derived, he shows, primarily from Nicholas of Lyra. This essay is illustrated; the pictures on pp. 432 and 433 have been transposed—not the only, but the worst, typographical disfigurement of this otherwise noble tribute to a fine scholar and a generous man.

W.J. HOUSTON

JOBLING, DAVID, TINA PIPPIN and RONALD SCLEIFER (eds.), *The Postmodern Bible Reader* (Oxford: Blackwell Publishers, 2001), pp. xvii + 381. £15.99. ISBN 0-631-21962-5.

This reader is a collection of 20 essays by literary critics, philosophers, writers and activists as wide ranging as U. Eco, T. Eagleton and J. Derrida, which derives from the work of a group identified as the Bible and Culture Collective. This Collective produced *A Postmodern Bible* in 1995 and this latest work supplements and modifies the earlier volume. It offers a representative sample of the kinds of questions that contemporary readers have brought to the Bible, grouped into three parts—'Rereading the Bible', 'The Politics of Reading', and the 'Conscience of the Bible'—each of which begins with a helpful introduction; and there is a lengthier introduction subtitled 'A Short Course in Postmodernism for Bible Readers', which is aimed at relative newcomers to this subject. Each essay, or extract from a larger work, has its own biographical introduction about the author together with an outline of its content. These are very helpful as the chapter titles give little clue to the subject matter discussed. Taken as a whole this anthology is useful as a basis for discussion with student groups to help them engage with the diversity of this field of scholarship.

J.E. TOLLINGTON

JOHNSON, LUKE TIMOTHY and WILLIAM S. KURZ, *The Future of Catholic Biblical Scholarship: A Constructive Conversation* (Grand Rapids, MI: Eerdmans, 2002), pp. xii + 299. $24.00/£17.99. ISBN 0-8028-4545-2.

Both authors are masters in their field. Johnson is a recognized authority in NT exegesis, with two commentaries in the AB and two in *Sacra Pagina*, with essays in the *ABD*. In the opening chapter, as a Caveat Lector, he gives a brief CV and his present concerns: a seminarian at 13, a Benedictine monk at 19; prayed the Divine Office in Latin for many years, but also did his theological studies in the immediate aftermath of the Second Vatican Council at a school (St Meinrad School of Theology) that had recently revised its entire curriculum within a self-consciously historical paradigm. But he also writes as a Catholic whose professional training as a NT scholar took place at Yale, the very belly of the Enlightenment beast, and whose career as a teacher has been entirely within the framework of the secular academy (ten years at Indiana University's Department of Religious Studies) and Protestant seminaries (six years at Yale Divinity School and ten years at the Candler School of Theology at Emory University). He belongs to what he calls the third generation of Catholic American biblical scholars. The first generation would be those who grew to maturity in the 'old world' of Catholic sensibility, who easily adopted the new historical methods, but for whom the exercise of the historical method was simply a positive addition to a robust and secure identity. The main distinguishing feature of the second generation (to which R. Brown belongs as Kurz notes) is the uncritical acceptance of the dominant historical-critical paradigm, and a style of scholarship that was increasingly directed to other scholars. The third generation are those scholars who underwent the cultural change within Catholicism caused by Vatican II, fulfilled everyone's dream by getting their PhD at Harvard, Yale, Chicago and Vanderbilt, so that they could sit at the table with the best of Protestants and secular scholars and play the game of exegesis as complete equals—who, at mid-life and late career looks around and asks whether the losses have been as great as the gains? The authors are not against the historical method itself and admits the advantage it has been in ecumenical agreed statements. Their critique is that it does not pass beyond this to treatment of the text for the pastoral and theological use of Scripture today. Johnson regrets that more and more seminary professors of both Testaments are lay rather than clerical, and shaped by the academic expectations of the biblical guild: their loyalties and ambitions are directed not to the Church but to the profession. Johnson has an opening statement on what is Catholic about Catholic biblical scholarship and then goes on to speak of rejoining a long Christian conversation on the Bible and Church, with presentation of the premises of premodern and postmodern interpretation. He illustrates earlier dialogue with contemporary culture through Origen and Augustine, and goes on to imagine the world that Scripture imagines. Kurz then responds (with general agreement) to J. and in six chapters takes us beyond historical criticism: with examples on reading John's prologue as Catholics, pre-understandings in applying Scripture (principally on R.B. Hays' *The Moral Vision of the New Testament*) and other NT passages. This very learned book is a further instance of the desire to pass beyond historical criticism to make the Bible the centre of Christian life and the soul of theology. Sentiments that are clearly expressed already by the Second Vatican Council, by Catholic and many other Christian scholars, but not easily achieved.

M. McNAMARA

KALIMI, ISAAC, *Early Jewish Exegesis and Theological Controversy: Studies in Scriptures in the Shadow of Internal and External Controversies* (Jewish and Christian Heritage Series, 2; Assen: Royal van Gorcum, 2002), pp. xvi + 209. €58.99/$52.00. ISBN 90-232-3713-7.

This is a collection of essays on the disputed heritage of the temple and the Aqedah; the polemics surrounding the traditions of those born circumcised; and

Joseph's slander of his brothers, and his relationship to Potiphar and his wife. The final section is an extended treatment of the relationship between OT Theology and the History of Israelite Religion, concluding with a response to R.P. Knierim, *The Task of OT Theology* (1995). The earlier clear and detailed sections are especially important for anyone setting the Hebrew Scriptures in the wider context of the Abrahamic faiths. The final section emphasizes the distinction between the HB and the OT, p. 118 (a matter of some interest to the society), and responds to J.D. Levenson's article 'Why Jews are not interested in Biblical Theology' (in J. Neusner [ed.], *Judaic Perspectives on Ancient Israel*, 1987, pp. 33-61). There is a useful bibliography of Jewish authors in this field.

M. BARKER

KAPERA, ZDZISŁAW J. (ed.), *The Polish Journal of Biblical Research* Vol. 1.2 (Kraków: The Enigma Press, 2001), pp. 155-247. n.p. ISBN 83-86110-50-3.

Vol. 1.1 of this new journal was reviewed in *B.L.* 2002, p. 11. The following articles are to be found in Vol. 1.2: M. Bieniada, 'Factors which Effected Changes in Settlement Pattern and the Character of "Israelite Settlement" during the Transitional Late Bronze and Early Iron Age in Palestine'; B. Poniży, 'Recognition of God according to the Book of Wisdom 13:1-9'; M. Rosik, 'The Meaning and Function of He-Locale'; B.W.W. Dombrowski, 'Another Attempt at Identification of Yahweh and the Ba'al of Ugarit' (review article on book by O. Loretz).

D.M. STEC

KEDOURIE, ELIE (ed.), *The Jewish World: Revelation, Prophecy and History* (London: Thames and Hudson, 2003), pp. 328. 436 illustrations. £19.95. ISBN 0-500-28395-8.

This is the reissue in paperback of the book that was first published in 1979 and not noted in the *B.L.* The illustrations, many in colour, are superb, but although the text still reads surprisingly well, the debates it describes have moved on very considerably. H.W.F. Saggs writes on 'Pre-Exilic Jewry', using Mari and Nuzi to argue, for example, that the beginnings of Israelite culture go back to the first half of the second millennium. Overall his attention to cultural context encourages him to say more about the pre-exilic history of Israel and its institutions than is now clear, but his essay is rescued by his insistence that much is preserved in 'tradition'. H. Maccoby's essay on the Bible sees Deuteronomy (700–650 BCE) as the pivot, the first attempt to create an institutionalized text, and defends the integrity of the Bible as a whole, especially against Christian misreadings. Z. Yavetz writes on the Jews and the great powers of the ancient world, and J. Neusner introduces the Talmud. The majority of the book is taken up with the mediaeval and modern periods.

G.J. BROOKE

KITZBERGER, INGRID ROSA (ed.), *Autobiographical Biblical Criticism: Between Text and Self* (Leiden: Deo Publishing, 2002), pp. xii + 209. $39.95. ISBN 90-5854-019-7.

Provided throughout with extensive footnotes, this collection of essays presents a deep, yet critical account of autobiographical biblical criticism from the minds of a wide range of stellar scholars whose skill can lead the correspondingly empathetic reader into recognition of the sadness possible within exegesis. The rich, explanatory arguments of the essays, prepared originally for a conference session, are interwoven, thus facilitating understanding of the conceptual content of the book as a whole. The contributions are: 'What is Critical about Autobiographical (Biblical) Criticism?' (J.L. Staley); 'Can One Be Critical without Being Autobiographical? The Case of Romans 1.26-27' (D. Patte); 'Perversity, Truth and the Readerly Experience' (Francis Landy); 'Flowing Identities' (Kitzberger); 'The Personal Voice and the Listening Heart' (M.I. Gruber); 'Age and Ageism in the Hebrew Bible, in an Autobiographical Perspective' (A. Brenner); 'Self Criticism, Cretan Liars, and the Sly Redactors of Genesis' (M.G. Brett); '"The Holy Seed Has Mixed Itself with the Peoples of the Lands" (Ezra 9.2): Mestizaje and Ezra? Nehemiah in Black and White' (R.M. Malzonado); 'My Papa was Called Bubba, but his Real Name was Leroy: Violence, Social Location, and Job' (L. Rowlett). Leaning on Caws' 1990 definition, 'outspoken involvement on the part of the critic with the subject matter', the essays argue for the role of the self in every act of criticism, by whatever method, and argue further that it be identified and contextualized; few would disagree. The indexes of names, subjects and biblical references allow ready use of the book for a variety of purposes, and it provides an excellent encounter with the means and outcomes of autobiographical criticism for beginners and established scholars alike.

H.A. MCKAY

LANG, BERNHARD (ed.), *International Review of Biblical Studies*, Vol. 47: *2000–2001* (*IZBG*; Leiden: Brill, 2002), pp. xvi + 539. €110.00/$131.00. ISBN 90-04-12503-5; ISSN 0074-9745.

The previous volume (see *B.L.* 2002, p. 12) was the first to be published by Brill. This volume has a new cover design; and English has become the language of the main title, and also of the headings of the lists of contributors, abbreviations, indices and table of contents. The contributors listed are many fewer, with ten departures and one arrival. There is a considerable increase in entries (to 2115) from the previous two volumes; but the larger increase in length results simply from a larger typeface. Translation required—or was an opportunity for change simply grasped?—that 'Grundlegung' become 'Theological and Exegetical Approaches'. Postmodern exegesis previously shared a section with rhetoric, canonical reading, and intertextuality; but is now part of an additional section that ranges from reader response theory to eccentric exegesis. There is also a short section on digital media. The concentration of this most useful sister-volume is almost exclusively on articles and chapter-length contributions. In this respect the new main title 'Review' may be less transparent than the former 'Zeitschriftenschau'.

A.G. AULD

LEMAIRE, ANDRÉ (ed.), *Congress Volume: Basel, 2001* (VTSup, 92; Leiden: Brill, 2002), pp. vii + 409. 1 plate. €108.00/$126.00. ISBN 90-04-12680-5; ISSN 0083-5889.

The swift publication of the principal papers from the 2001 meeting of IOSOT is most welcome. M. O'Connor writes on discourse linguistics and the exegesis of the HB, arguing that they should be kept apart; S.A. Kaufman outlines the recent contributions of Aramaic studies to biblical Hebrew philology and the exegesis of the HB; A. Wagner puts in a nutshell his positive assessment of the place of speech-act theory in Hebrew and exegesis; E. Ulrich summarizes his thinking on the text of the Hebrew Scriptures at the time of Hillel and Jesus; C. McCarthy considers Aramaic mnemonics, the Qumran tefillin and Deut. 33.2 to illuminate textual issues in Deuteronomy; G. Dorival compares and contrasts the MT and LXX for the psalms, proposing that the LXX reflects the liturgy of Second Temple times better than the MT; H. Weippert presents an ethno-archaeological approach to everyday life in biblical times to allow the voices of women to be heard; U. Rütersworden looks at Deuteronomy 13 in recent research on Deuteronomy; H. Schüngel-Straumann considers feminist exegesis in relation to Genesis 2–3 and notes its significance for interdisciplinary study and inter-religious dialogue; H.M. Barstad finds there is less to say about the Exodus as a motif in Isa. 40.1-11 than is commonly supposed; B. Janowski defends an integrated approach to OT theology as an overtly Christian enterprise; C.L. Meyers argues for the primacy of anthropology (and its use of archaeological evidence) for describing women's religious culture in ancient Israel; J.D. Levenson reflects on the way in which the later doctrine of the resurrection of the dead stands in valid continuity with the promises of life in the Pentateuch and elsewhere and is endorsed by the way personal identity in ancient Israel was constructed; I. Finkelstein reviews the relation between archaeology and text and insists that from an independent point of view 'archaeology must take the lead in writing the history of ancient Israel'; T.C. Römer provides a brilliantly concise overview of 25 years of debate about the Pentateuch; and T. Willi paints a portrait of several Basel Hebraists. The most significant contributions concern various parts or the whole of the Pentateuch, matters of language and socio-linguistics, considerations of text and versions, and assertions about the proper role of archaeology. E. Jenni's presidential address wittily analysed the imperatival forms of בוא by way of making a deferential invitation to the congress. The essays in this volume are made all the more accessible through the inclusion of an index of biblical references.

G.J. BROOKE

MANSER, MARTIN H. (ed.), *Biblical Quotations: A Reference Guide* (New York: Facts on File, 2001), pp. 446. £35.50. ISBN 0-8160-4654-9.

This is a compilation of over 3500 biblical references, drawn from nine different translations, and arranged under 285 themes. There are three indexes, the most useful of which is of key words which appear in themes with a different title. There is a slight preponderance of quotations from the OT and Apocrypha, and it is interesting to note the themes in which OT quotations predominate, such as 'comfort', 'depression', 'food and drink', 'friends', 'gossip', 'justice' (and 'injustice') 'laughter', 'music', 'old age', 'revival', 'sleep' and 'waiting'. There are also highlighted comments on phrases which have become commonplace in English, such as 'weighed in the balance', 'the apple of one's eye', 'no peace for the wicked', 'holier than thou' and 'a fly in the ointment'. These are sometimes illuminating (I did not know that 'at death's door' came from the Prayer Book version of Ps. 107.18), sometimes misplaced ('the patience of Job' is taken from Jas 5.11, not a general inference from the book of Job) and sometimes unclear about what the phrase means now (to put 'the fear of the Lord' into someone is a way of expressing the superlative which has little to do with instilling reverence for God). The major question, however, must be about the intended readership: the scholar and the preacher need a complete concordance, and the ordinary Bible reader is already well served by editions with chain references or thematic indexes. The book is handsomely produced, but its price is out of all proportion to its potential usefulness.

R. TOMES

MOORE, STEPHEN D. (ed.), *In Search of the Present: The Bible through Cultural Studies* (Semeia, 82; Atlanta, GA: SBL, 2002), pp. 195. $19.95. ISSN 0075-571X.

M. wants biblical scholars to think of the red plush of the cinema rather than the dark timber of the pew when studying the Bible. His introduction 'Between Birmingham and Jerusalem' gives an outline of the academic study of popular culture in Britain since the 1960s in order to encourage the biblical scholar to link up to research done in this field. The collection of articles itself is a mixed bag. A powerful piece on OT prophecy is Y. Sherwood's exploration of images such as in Isa. 1.6; 7.20; Jer. 13.22. Inspired by *Sensation*, Charles Saatchi's and Norman Rosenthal's 1997 exhibition at the Royal Academy, the author argues against 'romantic' notions of a prophet and puts a somewhat theatrical emphasis on the 'seedy prophetic underworld'. R. Broadbent traces an ideological bias in one hundred years of writing NT commentaries; J.A. Glancy discusses the relationship between discourses of visuality and textual interpretation; L.E. Donaldson suggests a hermeneutical model of reading as a cross-cultural experience; R. Griffiths looks at the use of the Bible in Thatcherite rhetoric in the light of liberation theology as well as literary theory; and B.E. Brasher writes on millennialism in American film and the global consumer economy. F.C. Black, E. Runions and R. Boer trade in the 'swagger of shock' (as A. Bach observes in her concluding comments on the collection), while A.C. Dowsett contributes a wilfully cryptic and associative analysis of biblical allusions in three popular songs. 'It doesn't take much imagination to relate the appearance of the locusts [in Rev. 9.1-11] to that of a helicopter'—but this exactly may be a problem. Less obvious is I. Hamilton Finlay's play with Judg. 14.14 (and Tate & Lyle's Golden Syrup).

C. BULTMANN

MÜLLER, GERHARD *et al.* (eds.), *Theologische Realenzyklopädie. Band XXXIII: Technik-Transzendenz* (Berlin: W. de Gruyter, 2002), pp. v + 810; 15 plates; 1 map. €198.00. ISBN 3-11-017132-5.

Articles likely to be of interest to readers include the following: Tempel, II Alter Orient und Altes Testament, IV Judentum (V. Fritz, J. Maier); Temple, William; Teresa von Avila; Tertullian; Testamente der XII Patriarchen (M. de Jonge); Testamentenliteratur (M. de Jonge); Teufel, II Altes Testament, IV Antikes Judentum (K. Nielsen, G. Reeg); Textgeschichte/Textkritik der Bibel, I Altes Testament (A. van der Kooij); Theodizee, II Altes Testament, III Judentum (M. Köhlmoos, J. Maier); Theodor von Mopsuestia; Theodoret von Kyrrhos; Theodosius I; Theologie, II Geschichte, II/1 Urformen der Theologie in den biblischen Überlieferungen, II/1.1 Altes Testament (H. Spieckermann); Theologiegeschichte/Theologiegeschichtsschreibung; Theophilus von Antiochien; Theophylakt von Achrida; Theorie und Praxis; Theosophie, II Judentum; Thomas von Aquino; Tier; Tiersymbolik, I Altes Testament, II Antikes Judentum (both by P. von Gemünden); Tischendorf, Constantin von; Tobit (Buch) (B. Ego); Tod, II Altes und Neues Testament, III Judentum (W. Dietrich/S. Vollenweider, G. Stemberger); Tosefta (M. Tilly); Totem/Totemismus; Tradition, I Altes Testament, III Judentum (M. Rösel, T. Kwasman); Traditionskritik/Traditionsgeschichte, I Altes Testament (M. Rösel). There are indexes of biblical passage, names (persons, places, subjects), contributors, and articles by title.

L.L. GRABBE

MÜLLER, GERHARD, *et al.* (eds.), *Theologische Realenzyklopädie. Band XXXIV: Trappisten/Trappistinnen-Vernunft II* (Berlin: W. de Gruyter, 2002), pp. v + 729; 6 plates. €198.00. ISBN 3-11-017388-3.

Articles likely to be of interest to readers include the following: Trauer; Traum; Tritojesaja (R.G. Kratz); Troeltsch, Ernst; Trost, I Bibel und Judentum (G. Stemberger); Tübinger Schulen; Tugend; Typologie; Unsterblichkeit; Unterhaltung; Urgeschichte (E. Blum); Ursprungsmythen; Vaterunser, II Judentum; Vatke, Wilhelm (C. Bultmann); Vaux, Roland de (J. Briend); Vergebung der Sünden, I Altes Testament (A. Schenker), II Judentum (S. Schreiner); Verheissung, I Altes Testament (M. Köckert), IV Judentum (Stemberger).

L.L. GRABBE

PATZIA, ARTHUR G. and ANTHONY J. PETROTTA, *Pocket Dictionary of Biblical Studies* (Downers Grove, IL: InterVarsity Press/Leicester: Inter-Varsity Press, 2002), pp. 128. £4.99. ISBN 0-85111-268-4.

Teachers of biblical studies habitually use terms familiar to them but strange to their students. Patzia and Petrotta have identified over 300 terms which need explaining. They cover terms used for parts of the Bible (e.g., Pentateuch, Psalter, wisdom literature); the basic vocabulary of textual criticism (e.g., emendation, homoioteleuton, Septuagint); terms used in describing the ANE background (e.g., stela, cuneiform, Enuma Elish, Dead Sea Scrolls); Israel's institutions (e.g., cult, levirate marriage, jubilee); events and periods (e.g., exodus, Second Temple Period, Maccabean revolt); people frequently referred to (e.g., Josephus, Wellhausen, Albright); some German terms (*Sitz im Leben, Festschrift*); some Latin ones (e.g., *lex talionis, terminus a quo/ad quem, vaticinium ex eventu*); and some English ones not always understood (e.g., provenance, irony, lexicon). The main critical movements are described, from historical criticism to structuralism, deconstruction, reader-response criticism, and so on. Jewish terms (e.g. Tanak, halakah, Talmud) are well represented. 'Myth' and 'midrash' come with warnings that they are used to mean many things. The definitions are carefully done, and the illustrations are generally apt. The moderately conservative standpoint does not intrude. Students will certainly find the booklet helpful, and teachers who think they can improve on the definitions will at least learn what terms need explaining.

R. TOMES

PHILLIPS, GARY A. and NICOLE WILKINSON DURAN (eds.), *Reading Communities Reading Scripture: Essays in Honor of Daniel Patte* (Harrisburg, PA: Trinity Press International, 2002), pp. xvi + 393. $47.00. ISBN 1-56338-369-1.

Daniel Patte is widely known for introducing French structuralism and semiotics into American biblical study and also for being editor of the journal *Semeia*. This collection has 26 essays under the three headings of Reading, Communities and Scripture. Since a number of them are on NT topics (Patte was primarily a NT scholar) or seem to be a tribute to Patte, those listed here will be those thought of most interest to readers of the *B.L.*: the struggle against mythopoesis (V.P. Gay), teaching as ethics and ethics as teaching (G.A. Phillips), evil and antichrists in a postmodern world (T. Pippin), metaphor as performative (H.C. White), the genesis of Israelite identity, using Ezra 9–10 (D.N. Fewell), Patte's 'tripolar' model for critical biblical studies, with 'Jubilee 2000' as a case (D. Jobling), authority and the rabbinic reading of Scripture (P.J. Haas), and the kingship of Yahweh Psalms (R.C. Culley). An introduction discusses Patte's contribution to scholarship, and Patte himself responds to the essays in a final contribution. A list of his publications completes the volume. There are no indexes, and an annoying feature of the book is the use of endnotes rather than footnotes.

L.L. GRABBE

ROBERTS, J.J.M., *The Bible and the Ancient Near East: Collected Essays* (Winona Lake, IN: Eisenbrauns, 2002), pp. xiv + 434. $42.50. ISBN 1-57506-066-3.

Twenty-six notes and articles written by R. are reprinted here under four main headings: 'Fundamental Issues', 'Themes and Motifs', 'Solving Difficult Problems: New Readings of Old Texts' and, lastly, 'Kingship and Messiah'. They span over 30 years, as the earliest was published in 1970. Some of the earlier essays have not been brought up to date, as is particularly evident in the first in the volume (published in 1985), a survey of 'recent' work that does not go beyond 1980, but they all illustrate the interrelationship between the bible and the ANE. Part 2 also includes the only previously unpublished item on the prophetic texts from Mari. There are 57 texts set out in 100 pages, in transliteration and translation, on facing pages (which is extremely helpful) though no explanatory notes are provided. It is certainly very welcome, as it updates W.L. Moran's 1969 translation (*Biblica* 50, pp. 15-56), and could have stood separately or as an appendix. There are indexes of authors and biblical texts but unfortunately not of the words discussed, many in some detail. P.D. Miller has provided a preface, explaining how the author tends to focus on particular texts rather than on generalities, and this is the strength of this volume.

W.G.E. WATSON

SEKINE, SEIZO, AKIO TSUKIMOTO, TKASHI ONUKI and MIGAKU SATO (eds.), *Annual of the Japanese Biblical Institute*, vol. 25/26 (Tokyo: Japanese Biblical Institute, 2001), pp. v + 153. ¥3000. ISBN 4-947668-46-6; ISSN 0912-9243.

Vol. 24 was reviewed in *B.L.* 2000, pp. 18-19; vols. 25 and 26 have been combined into a single issue. T. Wang writes on 'Family, Law, and Ethos in Leviticus 18: Lessons from and for Asia/Korea'; he argues that Lev. 18.7-16 is the only genuinely original decalogue in the OT, reflecting life in the *bêt 'āb*, and he yearns for the reunification of families in Korea, especially those split apart by the North/South divide, so that the family structures implied in Leviticus can be fully realized in Korean society. Four other studies treat NT topics.

G.J. BROOKE

SEKINE, SEIZO, AKIO TSUKIMOTO, TKASHI ONUKI and MIGAKU SATO (eds.), *Annual of the Japanese Biblical Institute*, vol. 27 (Tokyo: Japanese Biblical Institute, 2001), pp. 173. n.p. ISSN 0912-9243.

This issue contains four essays: giving sense to the statement about loving your neighbour as yourself (Lev. 19.18) (Y. Takeuchi, in French), whether Isa. 6.9-10 is a 'hardening prophecy' (S. Uemura), King Jehoshaphat and his foreign policy in the books of Chronicles (T. Yamaga, in German), and whether Matthew was a Jewish Christian (in German).

L.L. GRABBE

SHEPHERD, LORAINE MACKENZIE, *Feminist Theologies for a Postmodern Church: Diversity, Community, and Scripture* (American University Studies: New York: Peter Lang, 2002), pp. ix + 252. $29.95. ISBN 0-8204-5572-5.

The author is a minister in the United Church of Canada and is responding to debates within that church, particularly in documents addressing issues of sexuality; her goal is to shape a theological response that will embrace concerns for diversity and marginalization, while seeking to remain within the church's distinctive tradition. However, given the ubiquity of these issues in the churches the book is not limited to readers within that denomination. S. starts with a critical analysis of four feminist responses, 'critical modern' (E. Schüssler Fiorenza); 'poststructural' (M. McClintock Fulkerson); 'postcolonial' (K. Pui-Lan); 'postliberal' (K. Tanner), particularly in relation to their attitudes to historicity, to Scripture and doctrine, to personal subjectivity, and to revelation and authority. The theological and hermeneutical approaches of the sexuality documents are then critiqued from the standpoint of a combination of these feminist methodologies. The emphasis here is on method, with little reference to particular scriptural texts. The initial analyses will be accessible to those with a serious but not specialized interest, while the book as a whole will appeal mainly to those exploring the creative use of feminist methodologies within a church context.

J. LIEU

SIRAT, COLETTE, *Hebrew Manuscripts of the Middle Ages* (ed. and trans. Nicholas de Lange; Cambridge: Cambridge University Press, 2002), pp. xvi + 349. 179 illustrations and diagrams. £65.00/$95.00. ISBN 0-521-77079-3.

Although the close study of Hebrew manuscripts long lagged behind equivalent research on Greek and Latin materials, recent years have seen major progress, with the author of this volume playing a leading role in developments during an outstanding academic career in Paris and Jerusalem. Here, in an updated and restructured form of the Hebrew and French editions of 1992 and 1994, she shares with the English-reading public the results of some 40 years of research. All the main aspects of the topic are carefully covered in a lively but thorough treatment that caters for the novice where necessary but also provides sound, detailed and technical data for the specialist. S. demonstrates the importance of Hebrew manuscripts for Jewish literary history, offers clear guidance on how, when and by whom they were written, and traces their fate through the centuries, consistently exemplifying her remarks with a rich variety of well-captioned plates and a generous supply of intriguing data. As an additional treat, she chooses ten manuscript texts and furnishes them with reproductions, transcriptions, translations and background notes. In addition to a characteristically competent translation that only rarely fails to be smooth, de Lange has contributed 'pertinent questions and judicious remarks' and the volume concludes with an extensive bibliography and various indexes.

S.C. REIF

SMEND, RUDOLF, *Die Mitte des Alten Testaments: Exegetische Aufsätze* (Tübingen: Mohr Siebeck, 2002), pp. vii + 279. €29.00. ISBN 3-16-147716-2.

This group of studies by one of the world's leading OT scholars—an honorary member of SOTS who celebrated his seventieth birthday last year—largely reproduces an earlier collection (see *B.L.* 1987, p. 91), with some omissions and additions. There are full indexes. Though all the contents were originally published as long ago as the period 1963–83, they include several influential and still valuable pieces, like the short monographs on 'The Covenant Formula', 'The Centre of the OT', and 'Elements of Historical Thinking in the OT'; and such articles as those on 'Amos's No!', the redaction-history of the Deuteronomistic narrative work, and the Elijah traditions. These, together with seven other essays on such significant subjects as 'The Law in the OT' and 'The History of ןמאה', well display characteristic features of S.'s work: penetrating attention to exegetical and critical detail, sensitivity to big issues about the theological significance of the OT, and the heuristic and creative use of an unrivalled knowledge of the German scholarly tradition. All are lodged firmly within that tradition. Judged as such (without any slight), they represent for me a handful of well-polished and often sparkling gems.

E. BALL

SPARKS, KENTON L., *The Pentateuch: An Annotated Bibliography* (Bibliographies, 1; Grand Rapids, MI: Baker Academic, 2002), pp.160. $16.99. ISBN 0-8010-2398-X.

A wide and genuinely representative range of significant books and articles (predominantly in English, predominantly twentieth century) receive fair-minded summaries, and are helpfully classified according to both text and topic. This complements works such as *OTA*. This new series of IBR Bibliographies looks to be a useful tool for the time-pressed student of the biblical text.

R.W.L. MOBERLY

TILLESSE, CAETANO MINETTE DE (ed.), *Revista Bíblica Brasileira* 18.3 (Fortaleza: Nova Jerusalém, 2001), pp. 183-412; 18.4 (2001), pp. 413-603; 19.1-2 (2002), pp. 1-179. $50.00 p.a.

In Vol. 18.3, T. picks up 'Nova Jerusalém', his work on ecclesiology begun in 1986. He grounds his approach in the cosmic visions of Genesis 28 and Genesis 1 and develops his theme via consideration of the OT theophanies and tent and temple traditions (Chapter 1). His exploratory study of NT ecclesiology (Chapters 2–4) culminates in Chapter 5 with a return to the covenantal dimensions of Genesis 2–11. Vol. 18.4 consists entirely of the annual rich feast of classified reviews, of which pp. 413-503 cover the OT and related areas. In the first issue of the *RBB*'s nineteenth year, a double number, T. resumes his work on the prophets begun in 2001 (*B.L.* 2002, p. 22) with a series of studies on Jeremiah. As always, T. combines traditional approaches with illuminating (and judicious) use of more recent contributions. Not surprisingly, he gives a detailed treatment of the book's Deuteronomistic features, into which he integrates chs. 30–31 (pp. 121-22). He draws interesting parallels between the 'confessions' of Jeremiah, the Book of Lamentations and (especially) the 'Servant Songs' of Deutero-Isaiah (pp. 127-29). There is a lengthy survey of the Deuteronomistic tradition of 'the prophet like Moses', within which Jeremiah too can be situated (pp. 130-79; the Index, pp. 176-77, appears misplaced).

J.M. DINES

ZANK, MICHAEL, *The Idea of Atonement in the Philosophy of Hermann Cohen* (BJS; Atlanta: Scholars Press, 2000), pp. 535. $64.95. ISBN 1-930675-00-3.

The book, an earlier version of which was submitted as a doctoral dissertation at Brandeis University in 1994, offers a substantial study of the philosophical understanding of religion in H. Cohen's writings. The three main sources for this—an essay from the 1890s, published in 1924 only, and two books from 1915 and 1918 respectively—are made the subject of careful discussions. Cohen (1842–1918), who was a professor at the University of Marburg and who also taught for some time at the Jewish Seminary in Berlin, is famous for his place within the philosophical school of so-called Neo-Kantianism around 1900. Z. shows how as a philosopher Cohen sought a transition from moral philosophy to a philosophy of religion. The main argument is that a philosophy which culminates in a theory of ethics can be taken one step further through reflections on the idea of atonement as a specific conceptualization of human self-consciousness and moral agency. Fundamental to this approach is Cohen's understanding of Ezekiel 18 within the framework of the history of sacrifice in Israel; for this he refers to Wellhausen's dating of the sources of the Pentateuch without, however, adopting the latter's judgment about ritual and theology during the Second Temple period. As Z. makes clear, Cohen gave the modern reception of the HB (as well as the Jewish tradition) a direction towards dialogue with rational philosophy. This may be a welcome challenge at a time when much exegetical interest focuses on OT wisdom literature and the prophets as 'dissident intellectuals' (J. Blenkinsopp).

C. BULTMANN

2. ARCHAEOLOGY AND EPIGRAPHY

BIERLING, MARILYN R. (ed.), *The Phoenicians in Spain: An Archaeological Review of the Eighth–Sixth Centuries BCE: A Collection of Articles Translated from Spanish* (Winona Lake, IN: Eisenbrauns, 2002), pp. xv + 304. Numerous figures. $39.50. ISBN 1-57506-056-6.

This collection of essays forms part of the international research project, organized by S. Gitin, concerned with the Neo-Assyrian Empire in the seventh century BCE in terms of centre and periphery. The ultimate purpose of the project is to determine the dynamic of trade during that period. The essays were all translated from Spanish by B. (though some had originally been written in German) and the collection is intended to encourage dialogue between scholars working on the ANE and those working in Spain, since the presence of the Phoenicians in Spain 'is a good example of the effect of Assyrian economic policies on the extended periphery of the empire' (p. ix). The book comprises two parts, dealing in turn with the Phoenicians in the Mediterranean (seven chapters) and the Phoenicians in the Atlantic coastal area (five chapters). A map of all the sites (p. xii) gives an overall view and other maps as well as photographs are provided, though many could be clearer. Also, there is an index of sites and geographical names. While not of direct interest to biblical scholars, the information to be gained in respect of the period in connection with the Assyrian empire provides significant background material.

W.G.E. WATSON

BROSHI, MAGEN, *Bread, Wine, Walls and Scrolls* (JSPSup, 36; London: Sheffield Academic Press, 2001), pp. 312. £65.00. ISBN 1-84127-201-9.

Twenty-three previously published essays are collected together here under four headings. 'Archaeology and History' includes studies on religion, ideology and politics in relation to archaeology, on archaeological museums in Israel, on hill settlements in early Iron Age Palestine, and on the credibility of Josephus. 'Demography and Daily Life' has essays on the population of Iron Age Palestine, on the methodology of population estimates, on the population of western Palestine in the Roman-Byzantine period, on estimating the population of ancient Jerusalem, on the diet in Palestine in the Roman period, and on wine in ancient Palestine. There are three studies on 'Jerusalem': on its expansion during the reigns of Hezekiah and Manasseh, on its character as a capital, and on the role of the temple in the Herodian economy. Chapters on the 'Dead Sea Scrolls' include reconsiderations of the archaeology of Qumran, its status as a monastery, and its daily life, together with essays on various texts and topics: anti-Qumran polemics in the Talmud, visionary architecture (the *New Jerusalem* and the *Temple Scroll*), predestination, marriage and poverty, and hatred. B. has had a rich and varied career which is reflected in the breadth of his hard-hitting writing. He is largely a defender of the so-called consensus view of Qumran, so perhaps it is his demographic studies which are his most significant contributions.

G.J. BROOKE

CAMPBELL, E.F. and G.R.H. WRIGHT, *Shechem III: The Stratigraphy and Architecture of Shechem/Tell Balâṭah*. I. *Text* (by E.F. Campbell; illustrated by L.C. Ellenberger and G.R.H. Wright); II. *The Illustrations* (by G.R.H. Wright in collaboration with E.F. Campbell) (American Schools of Oriental Research Archaeological Reports, 6; Boston, MA: American Schools of Oriental Research, 2002), pp. xxii + 351 (vol. 1); v + 266 (vol. 2). 1 plate; 304 figures (vol. 1); 175 illustrations (vol. 2). $175.00/£125.00. ISBN 0-89757-062-6 (set); 0-89757-058-8 (vol. 1); 0-89757-061-8 (vol. 2).

Finally, 89 years after the end of the original excavations led by E. Sellin (1913–34) and 29 years after the end of the later excavations directed by G.E. Wright (1956–73), the first final report has appeared. It presents the 24 strata on the tell and the fortifications, public buildings and domestic quarters therein from both sets of excavations. It is intended to serve as the backbone of ceramic studies that are still being prepared for publication. Volume 1 contains the write-up of the strata and corresponding photographs, plans, sections, and selected pottery drawings. Volume 2 contains 175 plans, sections and drawings keyed to the text description in Volume 1. Admittedly long overdue, the author has provided the scholarly community with his best interpretation of the records that survived a bombing in Berlin in 1943 from the first excavations and the field reports, notebooks, preliminary reports, and G.E. Wright's popular book from the second set of excavations. He gives a coherent picture of the remains from the 11 fields excavated under G.E. Wright and Sellin's finds, explaining and correcting erroneous descriptions and interpretations in previous publications. These volumes deserve to be in personal and university research collections that specialize in ANE history and archaeology, in spite of the steep price tag. There is plenty of room for debate over the interpretation of the data, but its systematic presentation now allows archaeologists and historians to make independent assessments of the material and Campbell is to be thanked for his dedication and tenacity in the face of multiple hurdles and setbacks.

D. EDELMAN

CASSON, LIONEL, *Libraries in the Ancient World* (Yale Nota Bene; New Haven, CT/London: Yale University Press, 2002), pp. xii + 177. 30 illustrations. $12.95/£8.99. ISBN 0-300-09721-2.

Most of this well-written book is devoted to libraries in the Graeco-Roman world (pp. 17-135), covering questions of literacy, writing materials and forms of books, their copying and circulation, methods of storage and retrieval. Evidence for libraries, public and private, is central, drawn from texts and physical remains. Plans and reconstructions are given of library buildings from that at Pergamum (second century BC) to that at Timgad (third century AD) and ancient illustrations of readers and books. C. states the 'high level of literacy and an abiding interest in intellectual endeavor' of the Greeks who created the 'library as we know it, with shelves full of books on all subjects and doors open to readers with interests in all subjects' (p. 17). Chapter 1, 'The Beginnings: *The Ancient Near East*' notes the Ebla archive and two Sumerian literary catalogues, then passes to Hattusas, citing colophons and catalogues for library organization there. The only 'libraries' from Mesopotamia C. considers are the literary tablets found at Assur, which are mistakenly called the library of Tiglath-pileser I, and Ashurbanipal's library at Nineveh, although he cites colophons from Uruk. Regrettably, he was unaware of O. Pedersen's *Archives and Libraries in the Ancient Near East 1500–300 BC* (1998) and of much specific information. Astonishingly, the Dead Sea Scrolls are not mentioned! For libraries in the classical world and the early Middle Ages, therefore, this is an attractive introduction; for their forerunners in the Near East it is inadequate.

A.R. MILLARD

CHARLESWORTH, JAMES H. (ed.), *The Dead Sea Scrolls: Hebrew, Aramaic, and Greek Texts with English Translation; Pesharim, Other Commentaries, and Related Documents* (Princeton Theological Seminary Dead Sea Scrolls Project, 6B; Tübingen: Mohr Siebeck; Louisville, KY: Westminster John Knox Press, 2002), pp. xxv + 337. €10900/$150.00. ISBN 3-16-147426-0 (Mohr Siebeck); 0-664-22588-8 (Westminster John Knox).

This fourth volume of ten in the Princeton series of editions of texts from the Dead Sea Scrolls (see *B.L.* 1995, p. 25; 1996, p. 24; 2000, p. 25) brings together the pesharim and other texts which can be described as commentaries. M.P. Horgan edits the pesharim. The 'other commentaries' consist of *Commentary on Genesis A* (4Q252) by J.L. Trafton, *Commentary on Genesis B, C* and *D* (4Q253-254a), and on *Malachi B* (4Q253a) by G.J. Brooke; *Commentary on Malachi A* (5Q10) by Charlesworth; *Florilegium* (4Q174) by J. Milgrom; *Melchizedek* (11Q13) by J.J.M. Roberts; *Exposition on the Patriarchs* (4Q464) by Charlesworth and C.D. Elledge; and *Catena A* (4Q177) by Milgrom and L. Novakovic. The 'related documents', and more fragmentary, consist of *Catena B* (4Q182) by Milgrom and Novakovic; Testimonia (4Q175), by F.M. Cross Jr; *Consolations* (4Q176) by H. Lichtenberger; *Midwives to Pharaoh Fragment* (4Q464a) by Charlesworth and Elledge; and fragments identified as 'Unidentified' (4Q464b), and 'Pesher-Like' (4Q183) by Charlesworth and Elledge; and 'House of Stumbling' (4Q173a), by Horgan. These latter are admittedly neither pesharim, nor midrashim, but cite Scripture in some way, which seems to be the reason for their inclusion. This series is a valuable resource for critical editions of the scroll texts.

D.D. SWANSON

DONCEEL, ROBERT, *Synthèse des observations faites en fouillant les tombes des nécropoles de Khirbet Qumrân et des environs* (The Qumran Chronicle, 10; Kraków: Enigma Press, 2002), pp. 114. 21 figures. $50.00. ISBN 83-86110-47-3.

The value of this little book rests in its clear presentation of the work of R. de Vaux on the cemeteries and its reconsideration of his ideas together with those of H. Steckoll, H. Vallois, G. Kurth, K. Kigoshi and O. Röhrer-Ertl. There are also some excellent early photographs from the École Biblique collection. It is unfortunate, however, that most of D.'s work was completed over ten years ago, despite the preface being dated April 2002. The recent very important studies by J. Taylor, J. Zias, S. Sheridan and H. Eshel have provided many valuable insights into the Qumran cemeteries; none of these is mentioned, so that reading D.'s book is like stepping into a parallel universe of discourse. The following are D.'s conclusions: there are graves containing female skeletons; there are graves with two corpses in them which remain unexplained; the relationship between the cemetery and the main building remains uncertain, especially with regard to the unfired bricks found in the graves; the north–south orientation is not systematic; the presence of madder in several of the skeletons requires further consideration; and the Qumran finds must not be discussed apart from the other contemporary cemeteries in the area. D. has shown exemplary caution. The points he makes of ongoing significance need to be integrated with everything else that is now part of the discussion.

G.J. BROOKE

FINCKE, ANDREW, *The Samuel Scroll from Qumran: 4QSam^a Restored and Compared to the Septuagint and 4QSam^c* (STDJ, 43; Leiden: Brill, 2001), pp. viii + 329. 45 plates. ISBN 90-04-12370-9; ISSN 0169-9962.

To begin with, this monograph contains transcriptions of 17 columns of 4QSam^a covering 1 Sam. 1.1–12.19 (cols. 1-11), 24.2–25.3 (col. 24), and 30.24–2 Sam. 4.9 (cols. 30-34); the extant text is indicated by underlining in these columns which are provided merely as a guide. The second section contains a critical apparatus for the same columns together with those that probably covered 1 Sam. 14.14–17.6 (cols. 13-16), 1 Sam. 25.3–28.25 (cols. 25-28), 2 Sam. 4.9–23.17 (cols. 35-52), and 2 Sam. 24.16-20 (col. 54). After short comments on the changes introduced since the earlier publication of some of the material in *RevQ* 76 (2001), pp. 549-606, and more detailed comments on the text divisions in 4QSam^a, there are painstaking plates in handwriting for cols. 1-45. The method followed for the handwritten reconstructions is that used in several publications by É. Puech. The sophisticated calculations of letter dimensions as used in E.D. Herbert's work on the same scroll are not adopted or taken further, though F. acknowledges Herbert's overall contribution to the reconstruction of the manuscript. In the lengthy critical apparatus there is no attempt at helping the reader see what may be the overall significance of the variants for the readings of 4QSam^a in any one place; nor is any comment offered on how the apparatus assists in the reconstruction of the non-extant text. The point of all the painstaking reconstruction work seems merely to be to indicate one possible way the scroll could have looked. There is an immense amount of information here; it will need to be digested by others.

G.J. BROOKE

GITTLEN, BARRY M. (ed.), *Sacred Time, Sacred Place: Archaeology and the Religion of Israel* (Winona Lake, IN: Eisenbrauns, 2002), pp. xii + 228. 7 figures. $29.50. ISBN 1-57506-054-X.

The volume includes papers given in the ASOR program unit, Archaeology and the Religion of Israel, from 1993 to 1996. It has an unusually high number of stimulating and thought-provoking essays for such a collection. Part 1, dealing with the relationship between text and artefact, is standard fare with nothing new. Contributors include J.Z. Smith, W.G. Dever and Z. Zevit. In Part 2, K. van der Toorn proposes that some schematic figurines found in excavations represent teraphim, ancestral figures, while the fertility figurines probably represent Asherah. J.M. Sasson offers a useful, critical response. In Part 3, Z. Zevit and L. Bloch-Smith discuss Solomon's temple, the latter arguing that the interior panel decoration was intended to recreate the Garden of Eden. S. Gitin argues that incense altars are markers of sacred space by nature, regardless of the physical space they occupy. B.A. Levine discusses how presentation offerings were converted to burnt offerings over time. The final two essays in Part 4 offer the most food for thought; W.T. Pitard discusses the many limitations in understanding death and death rituals in ancient Israel. T.J. Lewis tackles the same issue with more positive results. He offers a strong critique of B. Schmidt's rejection of the existence of an ancestor cult in ancient Israel. The volume definitely should be added to university libraries and to the personal libraries of those interested in Israelite religion.

D. EDELMAN

HACHLILI, RACHEL, *The Menorah, the Ancient Seven-Armed Candelabrum: Origin, Form and Significance* (JSJSup, 68; Leiden: Brill, 2001), pp. xxviii + 539 + 92 of plates. Many figures. €150.00/$174.00. ISBN 90-04-12017-3; ISSN 1384-2161.

In this lavishly illustrated volume, H. catalogues known representations of *menoroth* from the Land of Israel and the Diaspora, along with lamps: each item is described in respect of its type, provenance and place of origin (when known); its likely date, site of discovery, and its material characteristics; any inscriptions it might bear; its present whereabouts, and the form of the *menorah* in respect of its base, arms and lamp fittings. This, along with a detailed bibliography, indexes of locations, and the 92 pages of photographs, makes up the second part of the book (pp. 281-539 and plates), and constitutes a first-rate work of reference in its own right. Literary and archaeological testimony to the *menorah* is discussed in the first part of the book: here, its history and origin are explored, along with descriptions of representations of it found inside and outside the land of Israel. Attention is paid to ritual objects which sometimes accompany it in these representations (especially the *shofar*, *lulav* and *etrog*); H. is concerned also to trace use of this symbol among

Samaritans and Christians. The *menorah* seems to have come into its own as a symbol of Judaism from the time of Mattathias Antigonus and the Herodian period onwards; indeed, much of H.'s work is concerned with charting the development of use of this symbol in the post-70 CE period. She does not, however, neglect the Temple *menorah*, and argues that its form in Solomon's Temple was that of a single stand with flared base holding a floral capital with a light, a type of lamp widely attested in the ANE generally. The seven-branched *menorah* familiar to us, she argues, possibly originated in the Hasmonaean period, though this suggestion seems to raise some difficulties, involving as it does the idea that the seven-branched *menorah* was retrojected into the text of Exodus at a time when that book's text had almost certainly assumed its final form. This aside, H. has given us an encyclopaedia of vital information about the *menorah*, temple worship, and the growth and development of Jewish symbols, along with a mass of informed, scholarly 'asides' on Jewish life after 70 CE. In more ways than one, the *menorah* stands for the Jewish people, a fact impressively demonstrated in this book.

C.T.R. HAYWARD

HERMANN, CHRISTIAN, *Ägyptische Amulette aus Palästina/Israel II* (OBO, 184; Freiburg: Universitätsverlag; Göttingen: Vandenhoeck & Ruprecht, 2002), pp.194. 33 plates, numerous illustrations. €189.00. ISBN 3-7278-1381-4 (Universitätsverlag); 3-525-53040-4 (Vandenhoeck & Ruprecht); ISSN 1015-1850.

The present book is Vol. 2 of a much lengthier work with the same title published in 1994 (see *B.L.* 1995, p. 28). The four parts deal in turn with amulets from four sources: Ashkelon, dubbed the 'Amulettmetropole' of the Mediterranean because of the large quantity found there; Akko; other excavations in Israel/ Palestine before 1995 and a private collection in Freiburg acquired from dealers. The descriptions of these amulets are accompanied by drawings and there are 33 photographic plates in black and white, though their quality does not match the high price of the book. A bibliography and brief summaries of the whole book, in German and English, are also provided. As a true student of O. Keel, in his preface the author claims that this material is largely ignored by biblical scholars, whereas it could throw light on biblical texts, and as examples he discusses Ezek. 16.26 and Psalm 91. As the author himself notes, the question to be decided is whether these amulets reflect popular religion or whether they were collected as exotic items.

W.G.E. WATSON

LÖNNQVIST, MINNA and KENNETH LÖNNQVIST, *Archaeology of the Hidden Qumran: The New Paradigm* (Helsinki: Helsinki University Press, 2002), pp. 377. 145 figures. n.p. ISBN 952-91-4958-1.

This book is about much more than archaeology; it is, rather, an attempt at rewriting the history of the religion of the occupants of Qumran. The story begins with the tomb of Jason in Jerusalem: he 'was a Zadokite and an Oniad High Priest, who with his brother Onias lived in exile in Egypt and possibly laid the foundations for the Qumran community' (p. 56). In a journey which takes us from the tomb of

Zadok, via the similarities between some scroll jars from Qumran and those found at Deir el-Medina, the temple of Leontopolis, and Hellenistic mystery cults in Egypt, the reader eventually arrives at Qumran. On the basis of its Hellenistic pottery, the authors claim it was established in the first half of the second century BCE, earlier than R. de Vaux suggested and many decades before the date proposed by J. Magness (see below). They challenge de Vaux's earthquake theory, preferring to see the large crack at loc. 48/49 as the result of earth movement caused by a weight of water; they link this weight with landslides after flooding: 'Qumran was submerged under the salty Dead Sea about 33 B.C. and remained so for several years' (p. 152). Further pointers to Egypt are also described as the Qumran site and its scrolls are examined for astronomical information (both in terms of its alignments and in relation to traditions associated with the sun), magic, healing, burial practices, and the ethnic origin of some of its skeletons. Quite apart from the difficulty of believing that in Roman times the Dead Sea was for a time 70 m above its present level, overall many of the historical connections made in the book remain unconvincing because the authors constantly proceed on the basis of assuming that where two things share certain features, whether in Jerusalem, Egypt or Qumran, the same people must have been responsible for them.

G.J. BROOKE

MAGNESS, JODI, *The Archaeology of Qumran and the Dead Sea Scrolls* (Studies in the Dead Sea Scrolls and Related Literature; Grand Rapids, MI: Eerdmans, 2002), pp. x + 238. 66 figures. $26.00/£18.95. ISBN 0-8028-4589-4.

M. reinforces R. de Vaux's 'Essene monastery' thesis, linking the scrolls and site closely, but gives a different chronology for the history of the settlement. The first three chapters explain archaeological aims and methods, review the exploration of the site and survey the scrolls, asserting their link with the site. Chapter 4, the core of the book, rehearses the buildings and occupational history, first according to de Vaux, then according to M. The remaining chapters focus on aspects of the archaeology, accumulating evidence and arguments for an Essene settlement. These comprise pottery and architecture (challenging theories about the site as a villa); meals, toilet and sacred space (using evidence from the scrolls and Josephus); *miqvā'ôt* and purity in general; women and the cemetery; temple tax, clothing and anti-Hellenizing; and finally the settlements at Ein Feshkha and Ein el-Ghuweir— where in both cases, connections with Qumran are deemed unproven. M.'s plausible periodization of Qumran includes no Period Ia, while Period Ib begins between 100 and 50 BCE and continues after the earthquake of 31 BCE until 9 or perhaps 4 BCE. The Essene identification also remains plausible, though, contra p. 39, they were not necessarily the 'smallest and most marginal' of the 'sects'. Also, de Vaux noted a wall running from Qumran towards Ein Feshkha, possibly enclosing an estate and linking the two sites. Was he wrong? Poor quality illustrations apart, this is an excellent introduction to the archaeology of Qumran.

P.R. DAVIES

SCHWARTZ, MAX, *The Biblical Engineer: How the Temple in Jerusalem Was Built* (Hoboken, NJ: Ktav, 2002), pp. xxv + 166. $17.95. ISBN 0-88125-710-9.

This is a fascinating, large format book full of line drawings, which describes how the Second Temple was built and rebuilt. The author is an engineer, and he deals with practical matters; how did they actually build the Temple? Using both classical and biblical sources, we are introduced to the technology available to architect and engineers of the time, the tools and the techniques. Specialists and others will find this a useful source of information.

M. BARKER

TOV, EMANUEL, with contributions by MARTIN G. ABEGG JR, ARMIN LANGE, ULRIKE MITTMAN-RICHERT, STEPHEN J. PFANN, EIBERT J.C. TIGCHELAAR, EUGENE ULRICH and BRIAN WEBSTER, *The Texts from the Judaean Desert: Indices and an Introduction to the Discoveries in the Judaean Desert Series* (DJD, 39; Oxford: Clarendon Press, 2002), pp. x + 452. £80.00. ISBN 0-19-924924-5.

The indices are in ten sections: (1) the history of the DJD series and its system for the presentation of manuscripts (E. Tov); (2) a list of the texts from the Judaean desert with all their details (Tov, S.J. Pfann); (3) an annotated list of texts classified by content and genre (A. Lange, U. Mittmann-Richert); (4) a list of biblical manuscripts (Tov) and an index of passages in them (E. Ulrich); (5) separate lists of papyri, opisthographs, palaeo-Hebrew texts, Greek texts, Aramaic texts, Nabataean texts and texts in cryptic scripts; (6) a concordance of proper nouns in the non-biblical texts from Qumran (M.G. Abegg); (7) an annotated list of overlaps and parallels in the non-biblical texts from Qumran and Masada (E.J.C. Tigchelaar); (8) a comprehensive list of scribal notations (Tov); (9) a chronological index of the supposed dates of composition of the texts from the Judaean desert (B. Watson); and (10) a list of abbreviations. The publication of the DJD series nears completion; these indices, lists and catalogues make the 38 volumes readily accessible and provide a wealth of other information.

G.J. BROOKE

ZWICKEL, WOLFGANG, *Einführung in die biblische Landes-und Altertumskunde* (Darmstadt: Wissenschaftliche Buchgesellschaft, 2002), pp. 176. SwF33.90/€19.90. ISBN 3-534-15084-8.

In the past, the *Einführungen* have provided its readers with concise and well-informed introductions to a wide variety of topics and the recent contribution by the professor of OT and biblical archaeology at the University of Mainz is no exception. The work will supply its reader with a report on the state of the question of biblical archaeology and related fields. After a brief introduction Z. opens his work with a chapter on the 'land of the bible' (pp. 13-22) addressing questions of terminology and geographical boundaries before giving—in the third chapter—a brief history of biblical archaeology. The fourth chapter is devoted to hermeneutical issues such as the relation between archaeology and exegesis. Here, Z. gives several examples where archaeological evidence can help to illuminate biblical texts. Chapter 5 addresses the problem of chronology and closes with useful charts of the kings of Israel and Judah as well as the monarchs of the surrounding nations. Chapter 6 deals with the land as such, providing an introduction to its geography, climate and so on. The seventh chapter is devoted to a brief overview of current archaeological methods before moving on to historical topography and local customs. The last chapter describes the cultural history. This is a very readable introduction designed for the German student with little or no knowledge of biblical archaeology. The marginal notes allow for quick references and several maps, charts and drawings help to illustrate the information given in the main text. An annotated bibliography concludes the volume.

A.C. HAGEDORN

3. HISTORY, GEOGRAPHY AND SOCIOLOGY

AHLSTRÖM, GÖSTA W., *Ancient Palestine: An Historical Introduction* (Facets; Minneapolis, MN: Fortress Press, 2002), pp. 90. $6.00. ISBN 0-8006-3572-8.

This is the slightly revised version of the introduction to *The History of Ancient Palestine* reviewed in *B.L.* 1994.

P. ADDINALL

BERQUIST, JON L., *Controlling Corporeality: The Body and the Household in Ancient Israel* (New Brunswick, NJ: Rutgers University Press, 2002), pp. xiii + 238. $22.00. ISBN 0-8135-3016-4.

As the subtitle indicates, the stress of this study is upon the relationship between the social construction of the body and the corporeal construction of social structures: 'Over time, there arose a concept of a pure people that began with bodily purity but also involved strong social delineations.' But the cultural differences between the biblical texts and today's reader are vast, making reading problematic. Methodologically, the author takes his greatest inspiration from M. Douglas and M. Foucault. He largely avoids diachronic analysis, taking house structures to be largely unchanged throughout the biblical period, even though they may most directly reflect the realities of the Persian period. Chapter 1 stresses the concepts of wholeness and beauty, including sections on lameness, blindness and deafness, mutilations, and handedness; Chapter 2 deals 'with sexuality and fertility'; Chapter 3 with relations between households, including incest and homosexuality; Chapter 4 with the ageing process (claiming that city dwellers could expect to live roughly three times longer than villagers), including age roles in both the family and wider society; Chapter 5 with 'Foreign Bodies: Reactions against the Stranger', stressing the development of Israelite ethnicity in the Persian period, the fear of foreign bodies, purity and hybridity; Chapter 6 with the nature of the priesthood, including their teaching and medical tasks, and their responsibility to live by higher standards; Chapter 7 with developments in the Hellenistic period, including a section on the problem of adolescence in Ben Sira. The treatment of such a vast range of topics within a book of this size necessarily imposes its own limits. However, many readers will profit from further consideration of the insights deriving from the author's choice of perspectives.

B.S. JACKSON

BOER, ROLAND (ed.), *Tracking* The Tribes of Yahweh; *On the Trail of a Classic* (JSOTSup, 351; London: Sheffield Academic Press, 2002), pp. ix + 205. £50.00. ISBN 0-8264-6050-X.

This began as a Society of Biblical Literature session in 1999 to mark the twentieth anniversary of N.K. Gottwald's *The Tribes of Yahweh* (= *Tribes* below). The editor provides an Introduction which orients the reader to how the essays fit into the wider debate about Gottwald's book. Then follow a series of essays that are both an appreciation of and a critical response to the book: Derrida's *Specters of Marx* and *Tribes* (D. Jobling), *Tribes* in the context of 'second-wave' social-scientific biblical criticism (F.S. Frick), retheorizing earliest 'Israel' (C.L. Meyers), *Tribes* in the trajectory of new directions and models (C.E. Carter), a critique of *Tribes'* Marxist foundation and the unacknowledged use of Talcott Parsons (J. Berlinerblau), the politics of debt, in the spirit of *Tribes* (I. Mosala), the impact of *Tribes* on African biblical hermeneutics (G.O. West), and the importance of Marxism to *Tribes* and to Gottwald's work in general (Boer). The collection ends with a long interview of Gottwald by the editor before the Marxism 2000 conference, and with a response by Gottwald to the contributions in the volume.

L.L. GRABBE

BRAUN, JOACHIM, *Music in Ancient Israel/Palestine: Archaeological, Written, and Comparative Sources* (The Bible in its World; Grand Rapids, MI: Eerdmans, 2002), pp. xxxvi + 368. Numerous illustrations. $30.00/£21.95. ISBN 0-8028-4477-4.

B.'s survey of musical instruments and their uses in this updated and revised translation of *Die Musikkultur Altisraels/Palästinas* (1999) extends from the Stone Age to the early Byzantine period. OT is of basic importance but there are many references to other ancient texts and frequent engagement with modern scholarly work. In particular, 'the most reliable primary source for information about the musical culture of ancient Israel/Palestine is...the archaeological-iconographic evidence' (p. 5) and 'modern research must redirect its attention to the local Canaanite-Israelite-Palestinian musical culture and examine above all the local archaeological-iconographic evidence' (p. 6). Consideration of artefactual evidence is the main theme, well illustrated by photographs and line drawings throughout and supported by a very good bibliography. On the whole an impressive work of scholarship that no one interested in the social aspect of ancient Israelite/Palestinian history, including religious practice, can afford to ignore. One or two qualifications: to assert that David retrieved the ark from the Philistines (p. 20) is a minor slip. More significantly a careful reading of the biblical literature would surely lessen surprise at the absence of archaeological evidence for the Babylonian–Persian period and prevent a merely dismissive attitude to Ezra–Nehemiah–Chronicles (pp. 184-88). While B.'s probable dating of Exod. 28.33-35 to first century CE Judah (p. 195: re Josephus read CE for BCE) raises questions concerning the validity of inferences from the absence of artefactual evidence. The rightful claim of archaeology to monitor textual exegesis must be balanced by a complementary claim in any sound historiographical methodology.

P. ADDINALL

BRIANT, PIERRE, *From Cyrus to Alexander: A History of the Persian Empire* (trans. Peter T. Daniels; Winona Lake, IN: Eisenbrauns, 2002), pp. xx + 1196. $69.50. ISBN 1-57506-031-0.

The original French edition of this work was reviewed in *B.L.* 1998 (pp. 43-44). Although the author intended to update the text for the English edition, the sheer amount of new bibliography overwhelmed him. He indicates how the field has moved on even in six years in his Preface to the English translation, but the text is essentially that of the original edition. Rather than footnotes, references are given in a discussion of sources in a section at the end of the book. This constituted a separate volume in the French edition, which might have been more convenient in certain ways, but having it in the same volume also has its advantages. This reference section contains a wealth of material, and there is little problem in following up individual statements in the text. The text itself is by and large based on primary sources and is a virtual *embarras des richesses*. B. has taken the course of quoting extensively from the original sources, which will be very helpful to most readers, despite increasing the bulk of the text. A.T. Olmstead has long been outdated (even if still frequently quoted by biblical scholars), but none of the recent histories of the Persian empire come close to the completeness and breadth of scholarship of this magnificent work. It is now—and should be seen as—the standard work on Achaemenid history. Note, however, that since writing this book, B. has come to the conclusion that the Gadatas inscription is inauthentic.

L.L. GRABBE

FISCHER, IRMTRAUD, *Gotteskünderinnen: Zu einer geschlecterfairen Deutung des Phänomens der Prophetie und der Prophetinnen in der Hebräischen Bibel* (Stuttgart: W. Kohlhammer, 2002), pp. 298. €20.00. ISBN 3-17-017457-6.

Prophetesses appear relatively infrequently in the OT alongside the more familiar male prophets. Nevertheless they include no less a figure than Miriam, the sister of Moses, Deborah, a major leader among the judges and Huldah, the prophetess whose judgment was sought in Josiah's time as validation for the Mosaic origin of the book of Torah found in the temple. Additionally Isaiah fathered children from a prophetess and gave them mysterious sign-names, while Ezekiel sharply condemns women prophets who claimed authority over issues of life and death. Women with prophetic gifts who are likewise portrayed negatively are the seer-medium of En-Dor, whom King Saul consulted, and Noadiah, who induced fear in Nehemiah. F. traces a development in which, from originally being fully respected alongside male prophets in the pre-exilic era, a major shift occurred in the Persian period. Under growing priestly influence, women with prophetic gifts came to be excluded from all official cultic service and their previously important role denied official approval. This took place in conjunction with the formation of a canon of approved prophecy that acquired formal acceptance as a companion-supplement to Torah. Unashamedly feminist in her approach, F. raises some provocative and challenging perspectives.

R.E. CLEMENTS

FULBROOK, MARY, *Historical Theory* (London: Routledge, 2002), pp. xii + 228. £10.99. ISBN 0-415-17987-4.

A book not written specifically for biblical scholars, yet on a topic of great relevance. F. seeks to moderate between traditional 'source-' and 'evidence'-based empirical historical research and postmodernist claims that there is no 'history', only 'texts about the past'. She upholds something of each position, endorsing the postmodernist claim that there is no theory-free historical research, no single 'master narrative' and thus no single 'past' and no value-free, objective history-writing; but equally arguing that historical sources, and narratives based on them, may impart historical truth. Thus, while different narratives about the past can and will always exist, it is possible to evaluate them by 'mutually agreed criteria' (p. 29). This position many 'traditional' and postmodern historians probably accept, though the criteria may not be easily agreed. F. denies that modern historical reconstructions are either strictly 'fiction' or 'fact'; rather they attempt to 'solve puzzles' (Chapter 4)—to give coherent, empirically supported explanations and accounts of events and circumstances no longer accessible to us directly ('satisfying curiosity', Chapter 7). Can paradigms and perspectives emerge from evidence or are they always imposed (p. 99)? No definitive answer on this; rather, F. proceeds to traverse many aspects of the historian's approach: a necessary relationship with present as well as past, the use of imagination as well as factual representation, the role of 'gatekeeper' and 'tour guide' of the past (pp. 175-80). No startling new perspectives, but an intelligent and well-informed review of current issues and a cogent critique of the extremes of both sides.

P.R. DAVIES

GOTTWALD, NORMAN K., *The Hebrew Bible: A Socio-Literary Introduction* (Minneapolis, MN: Fortress Press, 3rd edn, 2002), pp. xxx + 704. Numerous maps, charts and figures; with CD-ROM. $33.00. ISBN 0-8006-3617-1.

This is the edition of 1986 (reviewed in *B.L.* 1986) which has been updated by use of a CD-ROM using the Libronix Digital Library System and contains both the text of G.'s original book plus study materials by K.C. Hanson. These include study questions, up-to-date bibliography and access to appropriate websites. Whether a student could make easy connections between G.'s text and the newer bibliographies is an interesting point.

P. BALLANTINE

HARDMEIER, CHRISTOF (ed.), *Steine—Bilder—Texte: Historische Evidenz ausserbiblischer und biblischer Quellen* (Arbeiten zur Bibel und ihrer Geschichte, 5; Leipzig: Evangelische Verlagsanstalt, 2001), pp. 217. €50.00/SwF 85.00. IBSN 3-374-01907-2.

This collection is a pertinent addressing of questions of historical methodology, especially the relationship between the biblical and the other sorts of evidence. The essays (all in German) are the following: false dichotomies and a new dialogue between OT literary scholarship and archaeology (Hardmeier), fundamental principles and case studies on iconographic sources and the 'history of Israel' (C. Uehlinger), what archaeology contributes to research into the history of Israel and Judah (H.M. Niemann), the contribution of ancient Hebrew epigraphy to exegesis of the Old Testament and to the secular and religious history of Palestine (J. Renz), photographs as historical documents—a database of historical photographs from Palestine (T. Neumann), the prophet in the Lachish ostraca (U. Rütersworden), and Zerubbabel, the temple and the province of Yehud (A. Meinhold).

L.L. GRABBE

INSTONE-BREWER, DAVID, *Divorce and Remarriage in the Bible: The Social and Literary Context* (Grand Rapids, MI: Eerdmans, 2002), pp. xi + 355. $26.00/£18.99. ISBN 0-8028-4943-1.

The subject of divorce and remarriage is a very live issue within the Church of England, as well as in other parts of the Christian Church, and this book joins a growing corpus of monographs on the subject, and so will be of interest primarily within this on-going Christian discussion. The purpose of this book as stated by the author is 'to understand the meaning of the New Testament teaching on divorce and remarriage as it would have been understood by its original readers' (p. ix). The setting of the social and literary context is what will be of interest to readers of the *B.L.*, however. Beginning with a study of the marriage contract in the ANE, I-B. then turns to the Pentateuch, and finds that what is distinctive in the Pentateuch is not a monogamous ideal, but the greater rights given to women within marriage and remarriage. In the Later Prophets, God is in a typical ANE marriage contract with Israel, but becomes a divorcé with hopes of remarriage. The Intertestamental Period is characterized, via Qumran, Elephantine and Simeon ben Shetah, as one of increasing rights for women, greater marital insecurity, and greater attempts to discourage divorce. This is the setting for the original readers of the NT. I-B. has cast his net widely, and much of what is of interest to readers here will be found in the more academic discussion which goes on in the footnotes. The socio-literary setting argued here has implications for OT students beyond the specific application for which this book is written.

D.D. SWANSON

KING, PHILLIP and LAWRENCE STAGER, *Life in Biblical Israel* (Library of Ancient Israel; Louisville, KY: Westminster John Knox Press, 2002), pp. xxiii + 440. 228 illustrations; 175 in colour. £25.00. ISBN 0-664-22148-3.

The title is a dig at minimalists; this book assumes that the Israel depicted in the Bible is identical with Iron Age Israel as revealed through artefacts. Wellhausen's dating of J, E, D, and P is upheld, yielding reliable written records from the tenth century BCE. Having argued that premonarchic and monarchic Israel covered the full range of the Iron Age, the authors are inconsistent in limiting their range of artefacts to illustrate the culture of this entity to the Iron Age (1200–586 BCE) or to the territory that is claimed to lie within the nation's boundaries in one of the many, conflicting, delineations. This stems in part from Stager's use of finds from his long-running, scantily published dig at Ashkelon to illustrate various parts of every-day life—at least we begin to see something of the finds, though not in context. The book vacillates between focusing on the culture of the Iron Age in Cisjordan and paraphrasing political history as portrayed in the biblical text as though it were 'true'. The result is a hybrid, half-history, half cultural-history volume, which detracts somewhat from its effectiveness. In spite of the inconsistencies, the book provides an excellent discussion of a wide range of aspects of ancient Cisjordanian culture, using artefacts to illustrate biblical words and phrases. It builds on King's earlier, useful work on Amos. It is lavishly illustrated, thanks to outside funding, and is well written. It has occasional repetition of material, which is hard to avoid given the scale of the project. It would make an excellent textbook for a course on Israelite culture, providing a starting point for introducing a number of controversial issues, and should become a standard reference work.

D. EDELMAN

MATTHEWS, VICTOR H., *Social World of the Hebrew Prophets* (Peabody, MA: Hendrickson, 2001), pp. xi + 205. $24.95. ISBN 1-56563-417-9.

This work takes as its starting point the fact that it is important to understand the socio-historical context from which any text in the HB emerged. This is particularly true of the prophets, who were 'primarily concerned with current events, not future happenings' and who 'spoke within their own time, to an audience with a frame of reference very different from ours' (p. 1). The book's intention can be seen from the final sentence of the Introduction. 'Without a sense of what it meant to be a member of Tekoa's hill country farmers and herders or to be an exiled Levite from Anathoth functioning as a prophet in Jerusalem, the reader only skims the surface of the text' (p. 2). But unfortunately the chapter on Amos deals with this only in a limited way, drawing largely on the content of the Book of Amos itself. And the chapter on Jeremiah does not defend the claim that he was an exiled Levite, let alone discuss what that might mean for the reading of the text! After chapters which deal briefly with historical geography and with issues of definition and charac-teristics, the treatment is 'chronological'. A brief chapter on premonarchic proph-etic activity is followed by a more detailed treatment of 'early monarchic prophets' dealing with prophetic figures mentioned in Samuel and Kings. (A separate chapter is devoted to Elijah and Elisha.) Thereafter there are chapters which in the main are on individual books, though 'Prophetic Voices of the Late Seventh Century' and 'Postexilic Prophecy' are dealt with in single chapters. The chapter heading 'The Book of Isaiah' is misleading (since 'Isaiah of the Exile' and 'Isaiah of the Return' are dealt with in the chapter on Postexilic Prophecy) and highlights a problem with the book's 'chronological' approach. Is the chronological sequence that of the pro-phets or that of the books? The book does pay some attention to redactional issues, but this is uneven. For example, it is made clear that the chapter headed 'The Book of Isaiah' is about Isaiah of Jerusalem, but the chapter appears to treat Isaiah 1–39 as a unity reflecting an eighth-century socio-historical context. The work includes a glossary of a number of terms which have been highlighted in the text. (Asherah is surprisingly mentioned as the consort of Baal.) The select bibliography includes details of some online bibliographies which M. has created to assist students.

A.H.W. CURTIS

MORGAN, DONN F., *The Making of Sages: Biblical Wisdom and Contemporary Culture* (Harrisburg, PA: Trinity Press International, 2002), pp. xxv + 182. $22.00. ISBN 1-56338-328-4.

This book is a collection of 12 papers, articles and specially written chapters, which have been brought together with the aim of understanding the nature, functions and message of sages, locating the places where they function, and exploring ways in which the biblical sages may help the Christian Church to address challenges in the field of education. The pieces are grouped in three sections, 'Understanding Biblical Sages', 'Locating Contemporary Sages' and 'Identifying Biblical and Contemporary Sages: Education and Wisdom in Religious Communities'. Several of the papers were originally presented in highly specific situations, such as Hong Kong in the 1990s. While all of them raise interesting questions for the OT specialist, notably concerning the function of the sages in ancient Israel and early Judaism, they perhaps suffer from attempting to relate ancient and modern cultures too closely.

C.S. RODD

PEZZOLI-OLGIATI, DARIA, *Immagini urbane: Interpretazioni religiose della città antica* (OBO; Freiburg; Universitätsverlag; Göttingen: Vandenhoeck & Ruprecht, 2002), pp. xvi + 305. 23 figures. €72.00. ISBN 3-7278-1392-X (Universitätsverlag); 3-525-53041-2 (Vandenhoeck & Ruprecht).

The author, who teaches at the University of Zürich, is concerned in this *Habilitationsschrift* with religious concepts of the city in antiquity. She uses a comparativist approach; mostly Mesopotamian texts dealing both positively and negatively with the city are juxtaposed with Ezekiel's comminations on Jerusalem, the Babylon of the Book of Revelation, 2 Esdras 9–10, and the Qumranic *New Jerusalem* texts (4Q554, 4Q555, 5Q15). Her introductory chapter considers different definitions of the city and theories about urban origins with a view to isolating the peculiar features of the ancient as opposed to the mediaeval or modern city (Fustel de Coulanges, Weber, Childe, Braudel *et al.*). The ancient city is essentially religious both on account of participation in a common cult (de Coulanges) and because it is an essential point of reference in a symbolic system pivoting on the balance between cosmos and chaos. To make the point, she cites hymns of Inanna and Enlil referring to Uruk and Nippur respectively, the Epic of Gilgamesh, the hymn to the city of Arbela home to the goddess Ishtar, the account of the foundation of Khorsabad, *enuma elish*, and the Babylonian *mappa mundi*. Urban models are illustrated with the help of a bilingual (Akkadian-Sumerian) creation myth and, curiously, a selection from the Hippocratic medical corpus. Negative images of the city occupy two chapters featuring city laments and prophetic denunciations of city life. The author took her main prophetic example from Ezekiel 4–5 but missed a golden opportunity with the denunciation of the unnamed city in Isaiah 24–27. Appropriately, the final chapter deals with the visionary city, the city as transcendental cosmos, the heavenly Jerusalem. There is a good bibliography and biblical and analytic indexes.

J. BLENKINSOPP

SKA, JEAN-LOUIS, *Les énigmes du passé: Histoire d'Israël et récit biblique* (Le livre et le rouleau, 14; Brussels: Éditions Lessius, 2001), pp. 144. €15.30. ISBN 2-87299-113-1.

Two conferences held in Rome and Genoa in 1999 were devoted to the debate over history and story in relation to the biblical narrative. S.'s book, translated here from the Italian, is designed to bring the results of these academic proceedings to a much wider public—a laudable enterprise of a kind which the constraints of research assessment have made more difficult for British scholars. As such, the information and arguments here are a synthesis of the scholarly literature rather than an original contribution, but S. is admirably clear, concise and pointed in his summaries as he reviews such topics as the historicity of the conquest and the significance of the Tel Dan stele. In the epilogue to the book, he lays his cards on the table in a more inventive comparison between the biblical narratives and Picasso's *Guernica*. He regards the texts as powerfully evocative works of art that have roots in actual traumatic events but do not seek to reproduce their details naturalistically. Their aim is to 'shape the conscience of a people which seeks to understand what its destiny is in this world' (p. 133) and to invoke the spectator's emotional and moral reaction. Those broaching such subjects with interested and intelligent amateurs or non-specialist students could do worse than structure their teaching around the format and examples chosen in this fine example of responsible popularization.

H.S. PYPER

SMITH, WILLIAM ROBERTSON, *The Prophets of Israel and their Place in History* (with a new Introduction by Robert Alun Jones; New Brunswick, NJ: Transaction Publishers, 2002), pp. cxxii + 446. £26.95. ISBN 0-7658-0748-3.

This volume is a reprint of Cheyne's second edition of S.'s classic work on the prophets with a new Introduction. The latter gives a brief account of S.'s early life, the heresy trial, and his later career and then comments on S.'s views on the prophets and how they related to some other opinions current at the time. Mention is also made of some comments on S. by one recent scholar, since the J.P. Carroll of p. xl proves to be the Society's former president R.P. when the appropriate endnote and select bibliography are consulted. Jones ends his Introduction with the astute observation that although S.'s *Prophets* has to be seen as a work of its own time, it is nevertheless one which 'quite literally made possible the kinds of critique to which it is now subject' (p. xli).

A.H.W. CURTIS

SOGGIN, J. ALBERTO, *Storia d'Israele: Introduzione alla storia d'Israele e Giuda dalle origini alla rivolta di Bar Kochbà* (Biblioteca di cultura religiosa; Brescia: Paideia Editrice, 2nd edn, 2002), pp. 525. €37.00. ISBN 88-394-0637-9.

For reviews of the first Italian and English editions see *B.L.* 1985, p. 41, and for the third English edition see *B.L.* 2001, pp. 38-39. In this second Italian edition the contents and bibliography have been significantly updated, though titles written before the first edition still overwhelmingly predominate in the bibliography. The biggest visible change is the dropping of S.'s hallmark—that of beginning history with the united monarchy. This edition follows canonical order and therefore begins with the patriarchs. The illustrations of earlier editions have been entirely removed.

P.J. WILLIAMS

WESSELIUS, JAN-WIM, *The Origin of the History of Israel: Herodotus' Histories as Blueprint for the First Books of the Bible* (JSOTSup, 345; London: Sheffield Academic Press, 2002), pp. xi + 175. £50.00. ISBN 1-84127-267-1.

Several recent volumes have noted comparisons between Herodotus's *Histories* and the Deuteronomistic History (or what is sometimes called the 'Primary History', meaning Genesis to 2 Kings). W. advances a bold thesis: the author of the 'Primary History' not only knew Herodotus's work but used it as a model for his composition. The main examples used to demonstrate this are a comparison between the Joseph story and Cyrus, Abraham and Cyaxeres, Moses and Xerxes, and the same three-fold structure in Herodotus and the 'Primary History'. Readers will need to see the comparisons for themselves and decide whether they are convincing, but I have to say that I was not persuaded. Most of the similarities involve commonplace motifs that are widely known in ancient literature. W. himself accepts this, at least for some of his comparisons, but argues for a cumulative effect. What he does not do is discuss the differences and the reasons for them, nor the contents in one which have no parallel in the other, if Herodotus was indeed the biblical writer's model.

L.L. GRABBE

ZWINGENBERGER, UTA, *Dorfkultur der frühen Eisenzeit in Mittelpalästina* (OBO, 180; Fribourg: University Press; Göttingen: Vandenhoeck & Ruprecht, 2001), pp. xx + 593. €136.00. ISBN 3-7278-1344 (University Press); 3-525-53994-0 (Vandenhoeck & Ruprecht).

This 1998 Münster dissertation is a comprehensive study of ten early Iron Age (1250–1000) sites: 'Gilo', Hirbet Raddane, Hirbet ed-Dawwara, Et-Tell, Hirbet Selun, Betin, Tell en-Nasbe, Hirbet et-Tubeqa, Ğebel er-Rumede and Hirbet er-Rabud, chosen because they alone provide evidence from the given period and region. The study covers buildings, social life, food and subsistence, clothes, luxury items, contacts with other communities, and religious beliefs as indicated by burial practices and iconography. The archaeological evidence is handled with great caution and with full awareness of how presuppositions can affect its interpretation. An important sub-theme is that of the nature of the Israelite occupation and different theories about this. The results indicate the diversity of the sites in question and suggest that generalizations, for example, about where the inhabitants came from and whether their culture was indigenous or borrowed, are precarious. The lives of the inhabitants of the sites owed much to the particular environments in which they found themselves and in which they had to struggle to survive. Within villages, social structure tended to be centred on the extended family, reaching out to other groups on the model of concentric circles, with likely cooperation between families in food production and some possible small-scale specialization of skills within villages. On issues of wider importance, no evidence for the occupation of the south-east hill of Jerusalem during this period is forthcoming, and Hirbet Seilun (Shiloh) does not appear to have been a sanctuary. The sparser and later development of the Judaean section of the middle-Palestinian hill country compared to that further north is also apparent. This is a very informative and exceptionally thorough piece of work.

J.W. ROGERSON

4. TEXTS AND VERSIONS

BONS, EBERHARD, JAN JOOSTEN and STEPHAN KESSLER (eds.) with the collaboration of PHILIPPE LE MOIGNE, and general introduction to the Twelve Prophets by TAKAMITSU MURAOKA, *Les Douze Prophètes, Osée* (La Bible d'Alexandrie, 23.1; Paris: Les Éditions du Cerf, 2002), pp. xxiii + 194. €27.00. ISBN 2-204-06901-9.

This addition to La Bible d'Alexandrie is the product of a team of scholars making their debut on the project. The meticulous notes which accompany the French translation of the Greek are mainly textual and linguistic, but there are also exegetical points, so that the LXX can be appreciated as a version in its own right. A comprehensive introduction sets out the overall characteristics of the translation. It is on the whole a faithful rendering. It enhances the themes of knowledge of God and education, but interpretative changes are few—to counter misunderstanding of imagery (e.g., Hos. 4.12), to save God's omniscience (Hos. 8.4), or for the sake of religious consistency (e.g., Hos. 3.4). A notable feature of both introduction and commentary is that the history of the reception of Hosea in the Dead Sea Scrolls, the Targum, the NT (especially 1.10, 6.1-6, 11.1, 13.14), and the Church Fathers is taken into account. Modern commentators are also well represented, but there is a lacuna concerning the writings of feminist scholars on Gomer's alleged prostitution. There is an additional introductory survey by Takamitsu Muraoka of the LXX of the Minor Prophets as a whole, which, following H. St J. Thackeray (1903), is argued to be the work of a single translator. The volume provides an essential point of reference not only for LXX studies, but also for all future Hosea scholarship. The use of Greek and Hebrew in transliterated form (except in Muraoka's chapter) also gives it a degree of wider accessibility.

A.K. JENKINS

CLARK, DAVID J. and HOWARD A. HATTON, *A Handbook on Haggai, Zechariah, and Malachi* (UBS Handbook Series; New York: United Bible Societies, 2002), pp. xi + 501. n.p. ISBN 0-8267-0147-7.

Since the 1960s the United Bible Societies have been engaged in a major project aimed at establishing the most satisfactory text-form of the OT and then of providing helps for translators who might have little or no knowledge of Hebrew. The first part of the project is enshrined in the series of volumes *Critique textuelle de l'Ancien Testament*, which have appeared from 1982 onwards in the series OBO;

the second part in the series 'Helps for Translators', mainly in a series on 'UBS Handbooks' devoted either to single biblical books or to two or three shorter books, but also with several accompanying 'Technical Helps for Translators'. It is perhaps useful to set out this background as a way of evaluating both the strengths and the limitations of the volume here reviewed. Though some more general concerns (exegetical, historical and linguistic) are raised, they are almost always in the context of the provision of appropriate guidance for the translator. Two versions (RSV and TEV) are set out in full, and frequent reference is made to other recent translations, with proposals relating to the characteristics of different receptor languages; the appropriate OBO volume is referred to when textual difficulties are acute. The main distinctive feature of this particular volume is the stress on discourse analysis, perhaps not surprisingly as C. has written extensively on the topic. The whole is rounded off by a bibliography and a glossary of terms relating to translation and exegesis.

R.J. COGGINS

DE MOOR, JOHANNES C., *A Bilingual Concordance to the Targum to the Prophets*, Vols. 9–11, *Isaiah I (ז–א), Isaiah II (ס–ח), Isaiah III (ת–ע)* (Leiden: Brill, 2002), pp. vi + 348 (vol. 9); iv + 375 (vol. 10); iv + 486 (vol. 11). €114.00/$133.00 (each vol.). ISBN 90-04-12636-8 (vol. 9); 90-04-12637-6 (vol. 10); 90-04-12638-4 (vol. 11).

The first three volumes of this massive undertaking were reviewed in *B.L.* 1997, p. 51. The format was fully described there, and it has been maintained since. Five more volumes were noted in 1998, pp. 60-61, and a further six in 2000, pp. 59-60, so that the whole is now getting close to completion; only the 'minor prophets' remain. For these volumes on Isaiah, the project director himself resumes primary responsibility, as he did for the first volume on Joshua. In his brief preface, he pays a handsome tribute to the pioneering bilingual concordance to the *Targum of Isaiah* by J.B. van Zijl, even while contrasting his own work with it. He points out correctly that any such concordance involves a subjective element and that the justification for the decisions made cannot be included in the work itself; the value of a new concordance is thus obvious, especially since D. assumes double, or even triple, translations more often than van Zijl did. The final volume helpfully concludes with a Hebrew-Aramaic index of the whole.

H.G.M. WILLIAMSON

GREENBERG, GILLIAN, *Translation Technique in the Peshitta to Jeremiah* (Monographs of the Peshitta Institute Leiden, 13; Leiden: Brill, 2002), pp. xiii + 242. €64.00/$75.00. ISBN 90-04-11980-9; ISSN 0169-9008.

This detailed and thoughtful study of the translation technique of Peshitta Jeremiah, by a student of the late Michael Weitzman, is divided into 15 chapters, the three longest of which concern 'Additions' (vis-à-vis MT), 'Duplicate Passages', and 'Difficult Hebrew: Influence from the LXX' (strong evidence for such influence is limited to four passages; elsewhere, polygenesis is the preferred explanation for agreements). Throughout it is assumed that MT was 'a close enough approximation to the Vorlage (sc. of the Peshitta) to justify its use' as the yardstick for comparison. Since Jeremiah has not yet appeared in the Leiden *Vetus Testamentum Syriace* series, the study is based on 7a1, although collations of other manuscripts have been made available to the author, and readings of 9a1 are usefully discussed in a separate chapter. There are three appendices: a list of seven interesting cases where Aphrahat rather unexpectedly supports 7a1 against 9a1 = MT; a discussion of the relationship between Peshitta and *kethib/qere* readings; and details concerning the various renderings of *ṣade* in the Peshitta.

S.P. BROCK

GRYSON, ROGER (ed.), *Vetus Latina: 46. Arbeitsbericht der Stiftung; 35. Bericht des Instituts* (Freiburg: Herder, 2002), pp. 52. n.p.

This report of the Vetus Latina Institute contains a short note to honour W. Thiele's 50 years of involvement with the Institute, a brief in memoriam for R. Schnackenburg and reports on the ongoing editorial work on Ruth (B. Gesche), Tobit (J.-M. Auwers), Judith (P.-M. Bogaert), Esther (J.-Cl. Haelewyck), Song of Songs (E. Schulz-Flügel), and Sirach (W. Thiele), as well as on some NT books.

G.J. BROOKE

HENGEL, MARTIN, *The Septuagint as Christian Scripture: Its Prehistory and the Problem of its Canon* (Old Testament Studies; Edinburgh: T. & T. Clark, 2002), pp. xvi + 153. £25.00. ISBN 0-567-08737-9.

The indefatigable H., in part summarizing, in part developing earlier publications, considers why and how the Church came to accept as scriptural a larger collection of writings than that found in the Hebrew canon. Successive chapters trace the appropriation of the Septuagint by the Church (with special attention to the role of the—developing—translation-legend in controversy with Jews), the consolidation of its place there (and the discussion about the differing degrees of significance attached to books found or not found in the HB), the origin of the Septuagint as a Jewish work, and, finally, its use as a whole within the early Church (beginning with the NT writers). H. rightly sees puzzles in the story and emphasizes the often tentative nature of his explanatory observations. In particular, 'the question of *why* the Old Testament attained in the church precisely the form present…in the great codices of the fourth and fifth centuries is essentially insoluble' (p. 112), though he suggests the reason may be the books' edifying and instructional character, and wonders whether Christian–Jewish links in Rome from the first century on may initially have stimulated their fuller Christian reception. That this book is packed with extensive learning and judicious exposition will surprise no one. There are minor errors and inconsistencies in the English presentation, but the translation (by M. Biddle) generally reads well. It is a little surprising to see no reference to the work of J. Barton and of M. Müller, and I would myself have valued more reflection on the hermeneutical and theological significance of the Septuagint's role in the

Church; but the book offers a very useful compendium of material and comment from which all will learn.

E. BALL

HERBERT, EDWARD D. and EMANUEL TOV (eds.), *The Bible as Book: The Hebrew Bible and the Judaean Desert Discoveries* (London: British Library/Oak Knoll Press, 2002), pp. x + 360. 8 illustrations. £40.00. ISBN 0-7123-4726-7 (British Library); 1-58456-083-5 (Oak Knoll).

The conference from which these papers came was titled 'The Bible as Book: The Text of the Bible in Light of the Discoveries in the Judean Desert'. The title of this volume reflects the way in which the conference itself could remain within the bounds of text-critical issues, but had to ask prior questions about which texts are 'biblical' and which are not. This is a matter not only of the textual diversity of the Qumran texts, but of the 'rewritten' Scriptures, among others. S. Talmon's essay, 'The Crystallization of the "Canon of Hebrew Scriptures" in the Light of Biblical Scrolls from Qumran', gives a clue to much of what follows from A. Lange, G.J. Brooke, J.C. VanderKam, and P.S. Alexander under the headings of 'Canonical Development' and 'Rewritten Scriptures at Qumran'. T.H. Lim, S. Metso, E.J.C. Tigchelaar, J. Høgenhaven, and S. White Crawford discuss 'The Bible as Used and Quoted in the Non-Biblical Texts from Qumran'. Text and text-critical questions still form the largest section of the book, with essays by E. Tov, A. van der Kooij, E. Ulrich, E.D. Herbert, D.W. Parry, M.G. Abegg Jr, and P.W. Flint. Finally, S.C. Daley and H.P. Scanlin look at the influence of the scrolls on the modern English Bible and the public's view of the Bible. Discussion of 'canon', the relative 'authority' of different texts, and what is 'Scripture' at Qumran, has moved on rapidly in the short time since these papers were given; in this volume one can see how the lines were laid down early in the discussion.

D.D. SWANSON

MORRISON, CRAIG E., *The Character of the Syriac Version of the First Book of Samuel* (Monographs of the Peshitta Institute Leiden, 11; Leiden: Brill, 2001), pp. xvi + 173. €66.00/$81.00. ISBN 90-04-11984-1; ISSN 0169-9008.

After an introductory chapter, this sensitive and careful study approaches the subject from two main angles: 'Characteristics of the Syriac Version', and 'The Relationship between the Syriac Version and other Biblical Versions'. A short final chapter deals with 'Implications and Conclusions'. Three appendixes supply: a list of 'Non-exclusive agreements' (of Peshitta with other ancient witnesses, against MT); a list of readings that appear in secondary witnesses to LXX; and a discussion concerning whether the Syriac translator was Jewish or Christian (no firm conclusion is possible). This is a very helpful contribution to Peshitta studies.

S.P. BROCK

MORTENSEN, B.P. and PAUL V.M. FLESHER (eds.), *Newsletter for Targumic and Cognate Studies*, 28.1 (Laramie, WY: University of Wyoming, 2001), pp. 10. $15.00. ISSN 0704-59005.

The items listed under 'Targum' continue to suggest a very broad definition of the term, nevertheless these issues bring together a good number of useful studies in (principally) related fields. All four issues have lists of reviews of books coming within the general scope of the *Newsletter*.

R.P. GORDON

PETIT, FRANÇOISE, *La chaîne sur l'Exode, Édition intégrale*. IV. *Fonds caténique ancien (Exode 15,22–40,32); Texte établi* (Traditio Exegetica Graeca, 11; Louvain: Peeters, 2001), pp. xiv + 359. €95.00. ISBN 90-429-0993-5 (Peeters Leuven); 2-87723-561-0 (Peeters France).

Publication of this second volume of the *Catena* on Exodus (for the first volume, see *B.L.* 2002, p. 57) completes P.'s critical edition of excerpted patristic comments on this text. The extracts preserved here derive mainly from Cyril of Alexandria and Gregory of Nyssa, although some Hexaplaric items find a place: these last are likely to be of interest to readers of the *B.L.* Otherwise, some comments transmitted in the names of Origen and Didymus the Blind are preserved, and P. is able to show how other, anonymously transmitted material often originates with Diodore of Tarsus. The Church Fathers displayed less interest in the latter part of Exodus than in its early chapters: little discussion of the chapters on the tabernacle and its service survives, and the textual witnesses to Catena for this part of Exodus are confused and often of poor quality. As ever, P. excels in bringing order to textual witnesses, tracing sources, and providing tables which co-relate the manuscript evidence with those sources. There is much fine detective work here.

C.T.R. HAYWARD

POLAK, FRANK and GALEN MARQUIS, *A Classified Index of Minuses of the Septuagint*, Part I: *Introduction*, Part II: *The Pentateuch* (Computer-Assisted Tools for Septuagint Study, 4-5; Stellenbosch: CATSS Project, 2002), pp. xiv + 93 (Part I); xviii + 414 (Part II). ISSN 0-7972-0886-0 (Part I); 0-7972-0887-9 (Part II).

This new research tool has been produced using the CATSS database of the Septuagint and Hebrew texts. The first volume provides information on the rationale of the project, the sigla used, the choices made in selecting evidence and suggestions for use of the material. The second volume provides the evidence itself (i.e. 'the Index') from the Greek Pentateuch; further volumes are expected to cover the remaining books of the Bible. The Index is a listing of passages with Hebrew and Greek quotations in which a word or phrase of the MT (using *BHS*) is not represented in the Greek (using Rahlfs'). Each passage quoted has sigla to represent the features of the minus, as well as the likelihood of it being a minus in the text rather than the translator's interpretative choice. The editors have chosen not to include those cases where the minus is probably a result of semantic or syntactic difference, or the limits imposed by translation itself. The Index, therefore, first and foremost provides evidence for the early state of the biblical text. The passages are, however, categorized according to the type of word, phrase or clause that is not represented allowing for research into the frequency of certain minuses. From this one may understand better the varying textual traditions. It might then also be used for the study of translation technique, allowing one to see how certain phrases are rendered or if there is a textual tradition in which the said phrases are omitted. Given the uncertain state of the biblical text in antiquity, the information provided in these volumes is indispensable. Nevertheless, each instance will have to be considered on its own merit, even if the editors have at least noted differences between the editions they use (Rahlfs' and *BHS*) and respectively Göttingen and Qumran. These carefully prepared volumes provide an impressive array of evidence that should enhance all future work on the Septuagint and the textual history of the HB.

J.K. AITKEN

SHEAD, ANDREW G., *The Open Book and the Sealed Book: Jeremiah 32 in its Hebrew and Greek Recensions* (JSOTSup, 347; The Hebrew Bible and its Versions, 3; London: Sheffield Academic Press, 2002), pp. 316. £50.00. ISBN 1-84127-235-3.

S. uses Jeremiah 32 as a way of testing out the relationship between the Hebrew (MT) and the Greek text (LXX). Choosing a single chapter has the advantage of studying all variants systematically, as opposed to some other studies that have picked examples from all over the book. S. tries to steer a 'middle path' between those who see the LXX as a literal translation of its *Vorlage* and those who see most variants as the result of translation technique. Being rather sceptical that the LXX is a more original text than the MT, he accepts that the LXX is often shorter than the MT because of revisions of the latter; however, he also argues that the LXX suffers a good deal from haplography, so that its shorter text in such cases is not superior to the MT. S. is rightly critical of some of the shibboleths so often bandied about and the rather narrow range of possibilities for interpretation sometimes put before the reader. The relationship between the LXX and the MT is often more complicated than some of the simplistic statements made about it. Yet his own conclusion that 'the assumption that we are dealing with two "books" or recensions—which the results of the present study do nothing to alter—gives to each text its own integrity, the violation of which is not lightly undertaken', is not adequately supported. It is still possible to make a critical judgment that one recension is superior to another.

L.L. GRABBE

SIQUANS, AGNETHE, *Der Deuteronomiumkommentar des Theodoret von Kyros* (Österreichische Biblische Studien, 19; Frankfurt am Main: Peter Lang, 2002), pp. 381. £30.00. ISBN 3-631-38868-3; ISSN 0948-1664.

Theodore of Cyrrhus (late-fourth to mid-fifth century CE) is important both as an eminent Antiochian exegete with a taste for Alexandrian typology, and as a prime witness to the Lucianic or (better) Antiochian text. In her thorough and scholarly study of Theodoret's exegetical method, S. covers both aspects. Exegetically,

Theodoret is shown to belong within well-established traditions, but with the ability to adapt them to the concerns of his own time. The 'Quaestiones in Deuteronomium (QD)' forms part of Theodoret's late work, the 'Quaestiones in Octateuchum'. The genre is not strictly speaking that of a commentary, but S. defends her use of the term because of Theodoret's systematic treatment of the text of Deuteronomy, and the length and complexity of some of his 'answers' to the textual and exegetical 'questions' posed. Her starting point is her own German translation of the Greek text, keyed line by line to the 1979 critical edition by N. Fernández Marcos and A. Sáenz-Badillos. This makes for rather awkward reading but is useful for cross-referencing in the diverse and meaty discussions that follow. She ends with a number of helpful statistical analyses and other summaries. These enable the reader to situate the QD, and its author, within the wider context of the 'Quaestiones' genre and of patristic exegesis in general. S. has made a valuable contribution to a growing area of interest, that of the early history of the biblical text and its interpretation. It shows what can be done once critical editions are available for scholarly use.

J.M. DINES

TREMBLAY, P. HERVÉ, *Job 19,25-27 dans la Septante et chez les Pères grecs: Unanimité d'une tradition* (Etudes Bibliques, 47; Paris: Gabalda, 2002), pp. 571. €75.00. ISBN 2-85021-140-3; ISSN 0760-3541.

It has become popular in recent years to read the text of the LXX as a Greek text, without reference to the Hebrew. This position is also argued at length by T. who notes that the LXX was the Bible of both the Alexandrian Jewish community and the early Christian church. Much of the book is taken up with an analysis of the Greek text of the passage from several perspectives, including the relationship of the passage to the *Testament of Job*. Arguing that the early Greek patristic writers might be important witnesses for the meaning of the text, he also does a complete survey of their exegesis. He thinks that the Hebrew text might envisage a resurrection, but he is certain that this is the unanimous (hence, the subtitle) intent of the Greek text. This also shows that the Alexandrian community of the second century BCE believed in the resurrection. T. does not believe that the Hebrew text translated by the LXX in this passage was substantially different from the MT.

L.L. GRABBE

VAN STAALDUINE-SULMAN, EVELINE, *The Targum of Samuel* (Studies in Aramaic Interpretation of Scripture, 1; Leiden: Brill, 2002), pp. xiv + 767. €139.00/$162.00. ISBN 90-04-12164; ISSN 1570-1336.

This lengthy volume offers broad overviews on several topics related to the study of Targums generally as well as *Targ. Sam.* in particular. Beginning with a summary of previous work on *Targ. Sam.* (Chapter 1), a discussion of the text of *Targ. Sam.* (Chapter 2), an overview of the exegetical and translational features of *Targ. Sam.* (Chapter 3), as well as a series of semantic studies in *Targ. Sam.* (Chapter 4), S. demonstrates an impressive breadth of engagement with literature that discusses this Targum. S.'s awareness of ideas concerning *Targ. Sam.*, however, does not produce a rigorous consideration of the conceptual issues they raise; she tends to repeat what has already been stated concerning *Targ. Sam.* with little critical interaction. As a result, her commentary chapters (Chapters 5 and 6) say little that is new, though she does make some very helpful observations concerning similarities and differences between *Targ. Sam.*, other Samuel texts, and their interactions with biblical and rabbinic traditions. Despite these helpful insights, S. does not incorporate them into any overall thesis. Consequently, this volume will serve as an excellent general introduction to Targum scholarship as well as to *Targ. Sam.*, but those wishing to find new ideas concerning the Targum will have to seek them elsewhere.

S.G.D. ADNAMS

VINEL, FRANÇOISE, *L'Ecclésiaste* (La Bible d'Alexandrie, 18; Paris: Cerf, 2002), pp. 186. €25.00. ISBN 2-204-06903-5; ISSN 1243-1982.

LXX Ecclesiastes is an exceptionally 'literal' translation that displays affinities with the *kaige* tradition and has been asserted by some to be the work of Aquila. It is probably the latest book of the LXX, of Palestinian provenance. There are no traces of an earlier Greek version, but there are some fragments of a different translation attributed to Aquila. In her introduction Vinel agrees that the version was made by Aquila or in his school. She surveys in turn the differences between the Greek and the extant Hebrew, various stylistic features, intertextuality, and the main themes of the book, before addressing the history of interpretation: midrash and targum on the Jewish side and patristic readings, from Gregory Thaumaturgus to Jerome, on the Christian (not neglecting the patristic comments preserved in the various catenae), with a glance at later expositors such as Sa'adya and Isho'dad of Merv. Such are the authorities cited in the copious notes that accompany the French translation. A careful and sensitive treatment of a difficult text.

N.R.M. DE LANGE

ZENGER, ERICH (ed.), *Der Septuaginta-Psalter: Sprachliche und theologische Aspekte* (Herders Biblische Studien, 32; Freiburg im Bresgau: Herder, 2001), pp. vii + 347. n.p. ISBN 3-451-27623-2.

This is the fifth volume in as many years to deal wholly or in part with the Greek Psalter. This Septuagint book has attracted attention in the light of its complex textual history, its possible origins in Palestine, its possible theological exegesis (despite being a 'literal' translation) and its date. Accordingly many of the essays in the current volume discuss these key issues. A. Aejmelaeus opens the volume with discussion of where we might find interpretative elements in the Psalms, criticizing in particular the work of J. Schaper, *Eschatology in the Greek Psalter* (1995) and its lack of attention to translation technique. S. Oloffson also considers method in his study of law, but concentrates on the theological motif of lawbreaking (the only English language essay in the volume). The problems of identifying interpretative features is also discussed by M. Roesel in his study of Psalm headings (a subject also discussed by R. Stichel), by A. Cordes on Psalm 76 LXX and by H. Gzella in an account of the renewed interest in the book. Such problems underlie many of the studies discussing theological themes: the renaissance of earlier myth (J. Schaper), angels (A. Schenker), the portrayal of God (E. Zenger), the messianic unicorn (H. Gzella), Torah/Nomos (F. Austermann) and theological motifs in LXX 1 Chronicles and Psalms (S. Seiler). Finally, essays on features of the translation of the 'fourth book' of Psalms (F.-L. Hossfeld), the textual history of the book (A. Cordes), its textform at the time of the NT (U. Ruesen-Weinhold), and rabbinic attitudes to the LXX and Aquila (G. Veltri) provide discussion of further key issues. Inevitably in a collection of essays the contribution of each varies, but overall the standard here is high, and, given its frequent engagement with current debates, this collection will remain of importance for all engaged in Septuagint studies.

J.K. AITKEN

5. EXEGESIS AND MODERN TRANSLATIONS

BARTON, JOHN, *Joel and Obadiah: A Commentary* (Louisville, KY: Westminster John Knox Press, 2001), pp. xxi + 168. £25.00. ISBN 0-664-21966-7.

This commentary, on two books which have suffered from the 'relative neglect' (p. ix) which has affected some of the so-called Minor Prophets, is a welcome and worthy addition to the OTL series. B. places his work within the historical-critical tradition and, while not ruling out the possibility of synchronic and holistic readings, defends the view that 'commentaries should seek the original location of the book so far as is possible' (p. x). Attention is therefore paid to the possible stages of development of each book. It is argued that Joel comprises (a) two parallel cycles of oracles about the state of the country (1.2-20 and 2.1-17) each involving details of the disaster which has befallen, a call to lament, and the lament itself, and (b) several short pericopes which are secondary additions. With regard to Obadiah, B. somewhat hesitantly terms 15a, 16-21 as 'Deutero-Obadiah' (p. 118). Select bibliographies for Joel and Obadiah are followed by the commentary on each book, comprising an introduction and then a detailed section-by-section treatment. The translation given within the text is B.'s own, though based on NRSV. B. notes with approval the suggestion that a feature which links the two books is their re-use of earlier oracles. Commendable attention is paid to the key theological themes of books which, each in its own way, seek to say something about God's purposes for the world.

A.H.W. CURTIS

BASSETT, FREDERICK W., *Love: The Song of Songs* (Brewster, MA: Paraclete Press, 2002), pp. 48. $14.95. ISBN 1-55725-298-X.

By cleverly selecting from the original text some of the more erotic passages, rearranging them into 17 passionate utterances of more or less equal length, avoiding textual and literary critical issues and interspersing the pages with bucolic line drawings (the work of Valenti Angelo, a professional illustrator who died in 1982), the author has succeeded in producing 'an ideal token for that special soulmate'. Perhaps that is why there is no suggestion in text or drawing that the lovers are unlikely to have been of European stock or that the ups and downs of their sexual desire may be a mirror of the relationship between the believer and his god.

M.E.J. RICHARDSON

BENNETT, HAROLD V., *Injustice Made Legal: Deuteronomic Law and the Plight of Widows, Strangers, and Orphans in Ancient Israel* (Grand Rapids, MI: Eerdmans, 2002), pp. xiii + 209. $28.00/£19.99. ISBN 0-8028-3909-6.

'Who benefits from the Deuteronomic relief laws? The widows, strangers and orphans they purport to help or the legislating elite?' In this provocative study B. attempts to answer these questions. Utilizing critical theory of law, B. reads Deut. 14.22-29; 16.9-15; 24.17-22 and 26.12-15 from the perspective of those the law claimed to relieve. The book proceeds in a clear and methodical manner. After an introduction the Hebrew terms for widow, stranger and orphan are examined, followed by a detailed exegesis of the relevant texts. Having established that legal texts may conceal socio-political interests and though well-intentioned may intensify exploitation of the poor, B. indicates in the fourth chapter the ways in which the Deuteronomic law resulted in oppression. While claiming to help the most vulnerable in society, it was nothing more than an attempt to fleece the Israelite peasant farmer. The fifth chapter concludes the book's argument with the thorny questions of authorship. On the basis of descriptions of Israel under the Omrides from the Deuteronomistic History, Bennett argues that this is the most likely period for the economic oppression of the peasantry. Where the monarchy used physical coercion to extract goods from local farmers, officials of the Yahweh-alone cult developed ideologies for the same purpose. This is an engaging and readable study, though it raises a number of problems besides the obvious questions about an Omride dating for the laws. First, there is a tension in the book between well-intentioned legislation that in maintaining the status of the elite actually intensifies oppression (Chapter 4), and a deliberate policy to exploit the peasantry (Chapter 5). Secondly, the problematic question of how straightforward it is to read the Deuteronomic law against a putative historical background, when the logic of the laws in their present canonical context presupposes a (largely) classless society, is never addressed.

N. MACDONALD

BERLIN, ADELE, *Esther: Introduction and Commentary* (in Hebrew) (Mikra Leyisra'el; Tel Aviv: Am Oved Publishers; Jerusalem: The Hebrew University Magnes Press, 2001), pp. xii + 164. n.p. ISBN 965-13-1422-3.

In keeping with the perspective of the series to offer a 'scientific commentary' (*peirush madda'i*) B. concentrates on digesting the findings of modern scholarship on the philology, history, realia, literary structure, origins and development of the Book of Esther. There is some reference as to how Esther was read within Jewish tradition: short sections in the introduction are devoted to the LXX, to Josephus, and to the interpretations of *Hazal*, and here and there in the textual notes we find specific references to the Mishnah, Bavli, Yerushalmi, Mekhilta deRabbi Ishmael, Rashi and other classic authorities, but traditional Jewish exegesis is drawn upon only perfunctorily. This is a pity, since one might have expected a series such as this, by Jewish scholars in modern Hebrew, to be less locked into the modernist approach, and to recognize that many of the assured results of modern critical and historical study of the Bible were anticipated by the early modern and mediaeval commentators, and even by the *darshanim* of late antiquity. However, this is perhaps a quibble. The notes are clear, knowledgeable and incisive, the production values excellent. This is one of the best commentaries on Esther to appear for some time (for the English version see *B.L.* 2002, p. 62).

P.S. ALEXANDER

BERNARD of CLAIRVAUX, *Talks on the Song of Songs* (ed. B. Bangley; Christian Classics; Brewster, MA: Paraclete Press, 2002), pp. xiv + 155. $14.95. ISBN 1-55725-295-5.

In the twelfth century there was a great renewal of interest in the Song of Songs, particularly on the part of the Mystics, among whom undoubtedly the most important was Bernard of Clairvaux (1090–1153) who devoted 18 years to his 86 Sermones in Cantica Canticorum. He exhaustively treated every line of the Song up to Chapter 3.3, regarding the work as allegory and aiming to purge it of any suggestion of carnal lust. In a short introduction Bangley reminds us that Bernard used his sermons as a springboard for a major exposition of Scripture and for a detailed analysis of the spiritual life. Bernard found God incarnate in each word of the Bible, with inspiration in every nuance. Bangley regrets that Bernard's complete work has never been attempted in the style of this edition, and thus it is strange that his own paraphrased excerpts from all 86 sermons include only some 20 percent of the original text. He admits that he risks imposing his own ideas and imagination upon his source, with the dangers involved in selecting subjectively from it. The edition contains 19 short endnotes and a limited bibliography for further reading. Bangley claims to have kept in mind both the specialist and the general reader. It is debatable whether he satisfies either, neither or both.

J.D. BAILDAM

BLENKINSOPP, JOSEPH, *Isaiah 40–55: A New Translation with Introduction and Commentary* (AB, 19A; New York: Doubleday, 2002), pp. xvii + 411. $45.00. ISBN 0-385-49717-2.

This, the second of three volumes on the Book of Isaiah, has been dedicated by B. to his colleagues in SOTS in gratitude for his appointment as President in 2000–2001. It continues the meticulous scholarship displayed in the first volume and again both the translation and the comments reflect attention to the ancient texts and the history of their interpretation. The translation conveys the succinct, forceful, style of the MT effectively and B. has combined well-known traditional language with new phraseology throughout in a way that emphasizes his own fresh insights into the meaning of the text. The comprehensive introduction covers the whole spectrum of textual, literary, canonical, theological and interpretative issues in a clear and structured way; and concludes with a considered justification of the historical-critical method that is adopted. Each section contains a thorough discussion of relevant scholarship and ends with the conclusions that B. applies throughout the commentary. In brief he demonstrates the complex relationship between the three parts of the Book of Isaiah and argues for chs. 34–35 and 56–66 as exegetical developments on both Isaiah 1–33 and 40–55. He notes the change in focus from Jacob/Israel in 40–48 to Zion/Jerusalem in 49–55 and the difference in usage of the term *'ebed* in the two sections. B. argues that Cyrus is to be identified in 42.1-9 whereas the other three Servant texts have been inserted into 49–55 by a Trito-Isaianic editor, whose hand can also be seen more widely in these chapters. The servant is now the prophet who took over the task originally assigned to Cyrus, a task that resulted in him being abused, and then soon after the prophet's death 52.13–53.12 was composed as a panegyric. With regard to the vexing question of where Isaiah 40–55 was composed B. concludes that the balance of evidence just supports the view that the core of 40–48, at least, originated in the Babylonian dia-spora. The debates on Isaiah 40–55 will continue but this volume makes a signifi-cant contribution to the dialogue. Highly recommended.

J.E. TOLLINGTON

BRIDGES, CHARLES, *Proverbs* (Crossway Classic Commentaries; Wheaton, IL: Crossway Books, 2001), pp. 286. £10.99. ISBN 1-85684-210-X.

Charles Bridges (1794–1869) was an Anglican evangelical clergyman. His devo-tional and spiritual commentary on Proverbs was published in 1846. Pre-critical (and therefore not anti-critical), its aim is to expound the 'literal meaning', although some allegorizing is found (wisdom's house in Proverbs 9 is the church), and Christ is the key to the whole of Scripture. The elegant style makes this an attractive work that will be of interest not only to the intended readers of the series but also to those studying the afterlife of the text.

C.S. RODD

BROWN, RAYMOND, *The Message of Numbers: Journey to the Promised Land* (The Bible Speaks Today: Old Testament; Leicester: Inter-Varsity Press, 2002), pp. 308. £9.99. ISBN 0-85111-491-1.

The aim of this series is to make the Bible useful and relevant to the contemp-orary reader. Such a goal is especially important with books like Numbers, which as the author admits, are not high on Bible readers' priority lists. The thrust of the volume is therefore expository rather than exegetical. The exposition, however, is in the hands of a skilled practitioner (a former Principal of Spurgeon's College), and is based on careful exegesis. This keeps the text well balanced, covering the entire book, and not just the narrative parts. The application of the content of Numbers to modern life and its demands is made on analogical rather than allegorical principles, so that the exposition is both sane and challenging. It will be useful for individual readers and for study groups, and may also serve to help those who have to deal with this book at a purely academic level also to engage with its message.

D.J. CLARK

BRUEGGEMANN, WALTER, *David's Truth* (Minneapolis, MN: Fortress Press, 2nd edn, 2002), pp. xx + 153. $15.00. ISBN 0-8006-3461-6.

The first edition of this work was found 'at once infuriating and enthralling' in *B.L.* 1986, p. 65. Another reviewer 17 years on has sympathy with that judgment. The main text is very little changed, and some errors remain. A substantial new preface (pp. ix-xvi) offers an overview of selected studies of David and the books of Samuel in the period between the editions. A few of the endnotes have been extended. And the bibliography, author index and Scripture index are welcome additions. The new select bibliographies are right up to date, and yet make some strange choices: Polzin's *David and the Deuteronomist* (on 2 Samuel) is listed, but not *Samuel and the Deuteronomist* (on 1 Samuel); and the first two volumes of Fokkelman's quartet (the second should be dated 1986) are there, but not the third.

A.G. AULD

BRUEGGEMANN, WALTER, *Testimony to Otherwise: The Witness of Elijah and Elisha* (St Louis, MO: Chalice Press, 2001), pp. xi + 140. $19.00. ISBN 08272-3640-9.

B. uses a selection of OT texts as the foundation for preaching a radical alternative to ways of life based on governmental power, wealth and technology and the blinkered, self-centred greed associated with them. 'Imagination' is a key word, displayed in the stories concerning Elijah and Elisha and essential for the modern appreciation and exposition of them. Elijah and Elisha embodied the radical 'alternative' in their own day, bringing nourishment and life to the needy by means of miracle, the 'otherwise' transforming the world in a manner which mere earthbound reason cannot envisage. B. does not shrink from naming modern examples of persons embodying this 'otherwise', and his book is directed to serious current need; but this makes his assertion, '[t]he prophetic narratives…are not relevant to our lives and no effort is made here to make them relevant' (p. 127) somewhat difficult to grasp. B. imagines that the first tellers and hearers were themselves baffled by such stories but found in them a means of escape from a world which 'had become unbearably wearying' (pp. 127; 1-2). Regrettably, if understandably, B. dismisses questions regarding the truth of the stories, since 'Old Testament claims for God finally do not appeal to historical facticity' (p. 12). For B. the canonical authority of Scripture is of fundamental importance but he confesses inability to see how this was achieved by the stories in question (pp. 1-2). This inability is, however, unsurprising in view of B.'s rhetorical vagueness, indifference to fact and fine disregard for consistency.

P. ADDINALL

CALVIN, JOHN, *Genesis* (Crossway Classic Commentaries; Wheaton, IL: Crossway Books, 2001), pp. xvi, 384. £11.99. ISBN 1-85684-209-6.

It is not surprising given C.'s emphasis on the sinfulness of human nature, that it is his commentary on Genesis that has been selected for the Crossway Classic

Commentaries. Produced between 1550 and 1554 from transcribed lecture notes (except perhaps for the early chapters), its focus on the literal and historical sense shows how far interpretation had moved from the dominant mediaeval concern with the spiritual meaning that was still being advocated by Erasmus in the 1520s. The commentary is also grounded in the Hebrew text rather than the Vulgate. C., for example, rejects Jerome's derivation of Moriah (Gen. 22.2) from *rāhāh* (*sic*) 'see' in favour of 'the land of divine worship' from *yārēh* 'fear, reverence'. C. displays many fine and sensitive insights—the pathos, for example, of Abraham's readiness to sacrifice Isaac, the bearer of the promise of salvation—but the way he deals with the ambiguities inherent in narrative and characterization tend to be governed by his theological convictions. Despite J.I. Packer's adulatory Preface, the commentary is of more interest for what it reveals of C.'s theology than for its exegesis. The translation seems to be a modernization and simplification by the series editors of John King's English translation of 1847, in order to make it more accessible to lay Christians, students and ministers. It reads well, but it is regrettable that the translator is not specified, nor the edition on which the translation is based.

A.K. JENKINS

CHRISTENSEN, DUANE L., *Deuteronomy 1:1–21:9* (WBC, 6A; Nashville, TN: Thomas Nelson, 2001, 2nd edn), pp. cxii + 1-460. $39.99. ISBN 0-7852-4220-1; *Deuteronomy 21:10–34:12* (WBC, 6B; Nashville, TN: Thomas Nelson, 2002), pp. li + 461-915. $34.99. ISBN 0-8499-1032-3.

Volume 6A represents a completely revised and updated second edition of C.'s earlier 1991 first edition. Although these two new volumes each contain the same abbreviations list, and the same extensive bibliography of some 22 pages (that of 6B being slightly longer to include some more recent publications), they nevertheless need to be taken together for a number of basic reasons. For example, 6A contains essential introductory material concerned with the text and versions of Deuteronomy, a review of critical research, and a detailed outline of Deuteronomy, together with a presentation of C.'s fundamental approach in seven excursuses, whereas 6B contains indexes relating to both volumes of the Deuteronomy commentary (these include a comprehensive index of biblical and other ancient texts, and indexes of modern authors cited, principal topics discussed, and key Hebrew words). C.'s approach differs from the traditional understanding of Deuteronomy as a compilation of three sermons followed by three appendixes in that he proposes that 'Deuteronomy is best explained as a didactic poem, composed to be recited publicly to music in ancient Israel within a liturgical setting' (p. lxxxiv). He understands the Song of Moses (Deuteronomy 32) as the basic kernel of the book, embedded in the much larger 'Song of Moses' which we now call the book of Deuteronomy (arguing that Deuteronomy 32 is 'the most archaic material in the book'). C. relies heavily (perhaps too heavily one could argue) on concentric structural patterns found, he would maintain, at virtually all levels of analysis. For him 'the system of counting morae is foundational to the present analysis of the Hebrew text of Deuteronomy' (p. lxiii), and 'it is by this means that the prosodic units were determined as well as the boundaries between them' (p. lxxxiii). To determine the rhythmic structure C. also makes use of the syntactic accentual method of the Polish linguist Jerzy Kurylowicz, and finds the two approaches (of counting morae and identifying syntactic accentual stress units) complement each other. He then summarizes the rules for both approaches. The translation of the text and the body of the commentary reflect this approach, where the numbers in the first column accompanying the translation indicate the mora count in the Hebrew text for that line, while those in the second column indicate the syntactic-accentual stress units. Each textual unit is presented structurally, complete with its respective stress units and numerical data, and to one not fully convinced of the validity of this detailed structural analysis, it could be somewhat off-putting. There is a wealth of information in the two commentaries, but at times essential connections between the Hebrew text itself and the comment offered on the respective translation or paraphrase are not explained. One such example occurs at Deut. 21.12b–13a. The MT verbs are in the third fem. ('she shall shave her head, pare her nails, put off her captive's garb'), yet the commentary on p. 473 appears to follow the LXX's second sg. rendering of these three verbs ('when you see…and desire to take her…shave her head, pare her nails and keep her for a full…') without explanation or rationale.

C. MCCARTHY

CONIDI, FRANCESCO (ed.), *Weisheiten der Bibel* (Gütersloh: Gütersloher Verlagshaus, 2002), pp. 127. €9.95. ISBN 3-579-02331-4.

The body of this book is made up of short extracts from the biblical wisdom books cited from the 1984 revised edition of the Luther Bible, including the wisdom books of the Apocrypha. The extracts are grouped under the following headings: wisdom, folly, fortune and misfortune, wealth and poverty, good and evil, right and wrong behaviour, speech, friends and enemies, life, general exhortations and advice. Though conceived as a guide for right living today, C.'s brief introductory comments show that he has tried to be faithful to the significance of the sayings in their original contexts and his well-tempered remarks might encourage his readers to seek for further illumination about the texts themselves.

G.J. BROOKE

CORRAL, MARTIN ALONSO, *Ezekiel's Oracles Against Tyre: Historical Reality and Motivations* (Biblica et Orientalia, 46; Rome: Editrice Pontificio Istituto Biblico, 2002), pp. xiv + 249. €16.00/$16.00. ISBN 88-7653-349-4.

This monograph is a revised version of a doctoral dissertation completed in 2000 within the Skirball Department of Hebrew and Judaic Studies at New York University, under the supervision of Baruch Levine. Thirty-five years ago, in 1968, there appeared in the same series a volume by H.J. van Dijk bearing a very similar title, namely *Ezekiel's Prophecy on Tyre (Ez. 26.1–28.19): A New Approach*. C. is, of course, well aware of this and in part defines his own task in contrast with it. Whereas van Dijk's was a philological and syntactical study, employing Northwest Semitic parallels in a manner much influenced by Dahood, the present work is a study of the historical reality and motivations of the Tyrian oracles. It argues that economic and political reasons are the main causes for the condemnation of Tyre. There is much impressive research represented here, for example on Judah's lack of metal resources and its consequences. The study provides a new interpretation of Ezek. 26.2, namely that the text describes the situation that resulted from Nebuchadnezzar's destruction of the Philistine ports at the end of the seventh century. It is argued that Tyre anticipated a major trade shift to her own ports that would mean Judah's economic ruin. It would be good to be told more of the role of the Tyrian oracles within the context of the foreign nations section as a whole (chs. 25–32). More especially, although C. interestingly proposes a connection between Tyre's religion and her economic activities, the book is somewhat thin on the theological function of this material within Ezekiel. Nonetheless, this monograph is to be welcomed as a valuable addition to the critical literature on Ezekiel.

P.M. JOYCE

DALLMEYER, HANS-JÜRGEN and WALTER DIETRICH, *David–ein Königsweg: Psychoanalytisch-theologischer Dialog* (Göttingen: Vandenhoeck & Ruprecht, 2002), pp. 256. €28.00. ISBN 3-525-01624-7.

The idea of a collaborative work on David which involves a psychoanalyst and a biblical scholar is calculated to make some practitioners of either brand of the dark arts shudder, but to others will seem a fruitful, if problematic, approach to texts of lasting and disquieting cultural resonance. In this case, however, the result is rather bland and the insights into the biblical text are not particularly startling. The book confines itself to a reading of what the authors call the 'David-Roman': effectively the books of Samuel. There is little discussion of textual issues. The use of psychoanalysis wavers between a rather old-fashioned enquiry into the motivations of the character David and a somewhat more interesting reading of the structure of Samuel in mythic terms drawn ultimately from the work of Otto Rank. As is to be expected, this issues in what is formally a brand of allegorical reading with psychoanalytic categories jostling with theological ones in the decoding of the text. To the relief of some readers, but the disappointment of others, the writers seem to take no account of the developments of psychoanalytic criticism stemming from Lacan and beyond. The books of Samuel are a rich enough mine to reward any intelligent reading and there are interesting insights in what is a nicely produced book, although the use of different type faces, some of which are quite small, to differentiate sections is in the end irritating rather than helpful.

H.S. PYPER

DOBBS-ALLSOPP, F.W., *Lamentations* (Interpretation: A Bible Commentary for Preaching and Teaching; Louisville, KY: John Knox Press, 2002), pp. xiv + 159. £14.99. ISBN 0-8042-3141-9.

This commentary is part of a series which aims to provide a contemporary expository commentary for students, teachers, ministers and priests. The Introduction presents Lamentations as originating in Palestine soon after 586 BCE, and possibly the work of one poet. It is seen as drawing on a number of literary genres, most notably the city lament and the work is categorized as lyric poetry. Lamentations exhibits 'a complex, chainlike unity, wherein each poem is joined to some subset of the other poems in a multiplicity of overlapping ways' (p. 23). Particularly important among the book's theological themes are those of theodicy/antitheodicy, the visual confronting of suffering, and the notion of divine violence. It is suggested that the book is not without hope. 'Hope is implicated above all in the fact of survival, for these poems are pitched towards survival' (p. 46). The Commentary is based around the book's five poems, each treated according to its major subsections rather than verse by verse. The commentary on the text is punctuated with helpful excursuses on the personified Zion, allusions to the Egyptian captivity, the Everyman, conventional language, the choral lyric, and the silence of God. The last of these includes an apt comment which is, in a sense, a summary of what is argued for the book; the poet 'confronts God's silence straight on and navigates the silence as best he can…in an effort to remain faithful to the God he cannot hear' (p. 154). The work combines a commendable concern to understand the overall theology of Lamentations with much detailed comment on points of linguistic and exegetical interest.

A.H.W. CURTIS

FISCHER, IRMTRAUD, *Rut* (HTKAT; Freiburg im Breisgau: Herder, 2002), pp. 277. €55.00. ISBN 3-451-26811-6.

This refreshing commentary on the book of Ruth is clearly laid out, with marginal headings for each paragraph to indicate the content. The print is a pleasure to read, and Hebrew words are in Hebrew script (sometimes vocalized). F. sees a clear structure to the book in which each chapter follows the same structural outline, with the whole book also having its own integral pattern (see the helpful table on p. 25). The book is dated to the Persian period and its contents interpreted in this context; for example, it is seen as a riposte to the edicts against mixed marriages in Ezra–Nehemiah and Deuteronomy. The book is unusual in that female characters dominate (despite the forceful presence of Boaz, the structure of the book centres on the women). There is nothing against a female author, though F. does not assume that this is so. Unlike some German commentators, even in recent times, F. is fully cognizant of work being done in English-speaking scholarship.

L.L. GRABBE

FISHER, LOREN, *Who Hears the Cries of the Innocent? Job 3–26* (Willits, CA: Fisher Publications, 2002), pp. 124. $20.99/€39.00. ISBN 1-4010-4025-X.

This is a book about Job 3–26 (F. calls it Job II), a poem which F. sees as covered up by the ancient story of Job (Job I) the viewpoint and text of which he describes in Part I (pp. 19-45). In Part II (pp. 46-101) F. attempts to uncover Job II and let it speak for itself, especially in relation to the question 'Who hears the cries of the innocent?' as that question needs to be posed after 11 September 2001 about 'powerful leaders…who oppress the poor and cause the suffering of the innocent for profit (or oil)' (p. 13). The Job of Job II is the 'realistic story of a good man, who was impatient; a good man who would finally make a strong case for a trial with God, even though he knew that there was no justice' (p. 46). Job 4.7 represents the perspective which Job II rails against. In fact the God of Job's opponents does not exist; and to talk of any other God means very little since he barely discloses himself in a whisper (Job 26.14). Throughout the fresh translation is provided with brief informative notes based on years of experience with ANE texts. In the end, faced with this theological minimalism, F. lets Job's wife provide a way forward in her simple yearning for a hopeful song of love and support.

G.J. BROOKE

FONTAINE, CAROLE R., *Smooth Words: Women, Proverbs and Performance in Biblical Wisdom* (JSOTSup, 356; London: Sheffield Academic Press, 2002), pp. xv + 296. £60.00. ISBN 0-82646-024-0.

F. examines the book of Proverbs from an explicitly feminist viewpoint, and in particular what response someone committed to the 'hermeneutic of resistance' should make. F. has published widely on ANE and other parallels to Proverbs and draws on this material. In her first of two long chapters, she explores the female roles used in the text such as the positive roles of mother, wife and teacher and negative ones including scold, adulteress and prostitute. She considers women were sages and healers, as Canaanite evidence suggests, and is critical of the male bias of the final redactors. There is also an interesting comparison with the generally patriarchal portrayal of women in the Norse sagas. In the second chapter, F. explores women using the wisdom they have, drawing on biblical examples such as the wise women of 2 Samuel. The portrayal of Jerusalem as female in Ezek. 16.1-45 (printed in full) is discussed, and other examples include an extensive discussion of the cultural history of the Queen of Sheba. A short chapter consists of modern proverbs prepared by F.'s own students, including a male version of Prov. 31.10-31. This book does not engage extensively with traditional scholarship. Rather it presents an alternative reading, supported by wide-ranging examples.

R.H. MORTIMORE

FRANKEL, DAVID, *The Murmuring Stories of the Priestly School: A Retrieval of Ancient Sacerdotal Lore* (VTSup, 89; Leiden: Brill, 2002), pp. x + 385. €102.00/ $119.00. ISBN 90-04-12368-7; ISSN 0083-5889.

This is a redaction-critical examination of four narratives of murmuring that belong to the priestly tradition—Exodus 16, Numbers 13–14, 16–18, and 20—in the hope eventually of shedding further light on the process of Pentateuchal development as a whole. F. argues that contrary to scholarly opinion the narrative portions of P reflect not only late material but also contain early traditions, and that this is particularly true for the four P murmuring stories, all of which are notoriously complex in terms of their composition. Beginning with a survey of the Pentateuchal murmuring tradition as a whole, F. argues that the earliest elements in murmuring stories showed how the people's legitimate fears about their survival in the wilderness were met by divine provision, and that the picture of the people's complaints as arising from incorrigible sinfulness is a later development. In light of this, F. then undertakes a detailed textual examination of each of the four priestly murmuring narratives, and argues that each consists of not only an early non-priestly version of the material but also an early priestly version, together with a variety of (often priestly) editorial material that supplements both the non-priestly and the priestly narratives. Priestly material was therefore a significant factor in the early stages of Pentateuchal development as well as in the later ones. A thorough and detailed piece of work, that despite the inevitable subjectivity of the approach offers much food for thought.

D. ROOKE

FRYDRYCH, TOMAS, *Living under the Sun: Examination of Proverbs and Qoheleth* (VTSup. 90; Leiden: Brill, 2002), pp. xv + 255. €68.00/$79.00. ISBN 90-04-12315-6; ISSN 0083-5889.

This slightly revised PhD thesis (Edinburgh, 2000; supervised by Peter Hayman) is certainly worthy of being brought to a wider audience of those interested in biblical wisdom literature (and also those interested in OT theology, on which F. makes a number of observations). The presentation is marred somewhat by poor copy-editing/proofreading—although occasionally the infelicities are amusing (e.g., 'the tail of Caesar's new clothes' [p. 64] or 'worth than being dead' [p. 160])—and the translations of the biblical material are at times a little wooden, but the interpretation is invariably skilful and interesting, and the arrangement of the discussion under such categories as 'general worldview', 'epistemology', 'cosmology', 'anthropology' and 'ethics' works well. The two wisdom writings under examination show many similarities, in that they both stem from the same human/Israelite quest for self-understanding and self-realization, but their major differences are seen to arise from divergent socio-economic circumstances: Proverbs emerges from the self-contained world of the village where family and long-standing tradition are of the utmost importance, whereas Ecclesiastes speaks of a society oppressed by intrusive and unjust royal administrative structures; accordingly, the former presents a picture of *homo docilis* while the latter sketches *homo limitatus*. The study concludes that the two books cannot be reconciled with each other, because their worlds are so different, and poses the question of whether the formative influences of their respective external environments may be of greater theological significance than the particular perspectives of Proverbs and Ecclesiastes *per se*.

J. JARICK

FYALL, ROBERT S., *Now My Eyes Have Seen You: Images of Creation and Evil in the Book of Job* (New Studies in Biblical Theology; Downers Grove, IL: Inter-Varsity Press, 2002), pp. 208. £10.99. ISBN 0-85111-498-9.

This is not a full commentary on Job but is nevertheless an interesting and informative contribution to an understanding of it. The MT is the basic text upon which F. comments. The book is treated as a unity composed by a single author whose inspired message we try to grasp. This view is argued for over against very different approaches. F. shows continual sensitivity to the linguistic details as well as the outstanding literary quality which serve as vehicles for the work's theological content. There is careful comparison with other biblical passages and relevant reference to Canaanite literature. F. takes into account a fair range of scholarly opinion in making his judgments, not least that of D. Clines who sees Job in a somewhat different light. F.'s presentation is clear and reflects something of the 'live' quality attaching to oral communication in lecture room and pulpit. His study of Job deserves a wide readership and will be particularly helpful to those needing an informed introduction to the book. For those interested in the nature of myth (p. 26) one would have expected reference to the work of J. Rogerson. The famous quotation from Kant (p. 58) comes from the Critique of *Practical* Reason, and opens the conclusion to the second part. And this philosopher's essay on the inevitable failure of theodicy demands inclusion in any reading list for those attempting to fathom one of the world's greatest pieces of literature.

P. ADDINALL

GREENBERG, MOSHE, *Ezechiel 1–20* (trans. M. Konkel; HTKAT; Freiburg im Breisgau: Herder, 2001), pp. 445. €70.00. ISBN 3-451-26842-6.

Greenberg's commentary on Ezekiel, the third volume of which (on chs. 38–48) is awaited, has become a distinctive landmark in modern Ezekiel studies, with its holistic approach to the text. It is in Germany that a very different emphasis, typified by the elaborate redactional theories of Pohlmann, has remained most influential. And so the appearance of this first volume in German is a significant event. M. Konkel has translated Greenberg's AB volume on Ezekiel 1–20, which appeared in English two decades ago and was reviewed by R.E. Clements in *B.L.* 1984, pp. 52-53. Physically, the volume is beautifully presented, a great improvement on the somewhat rough-hewn 1983 original. There is a short foreword by Erich Zenger and a valuable updated bibliography.

P.M. JOYCE

HANEY, RANDY G., *Text and Concept Analysis in Royal Psalms* (Studies in Biblical Literature, 30; New York: Peter Lang, 2002), pp. xix + 244. £40.00. ISBN 0-8204-5048-0; ISSN 1089-0645.

Royal psalms have stimulated a wide range of diverse interpretations since the abandonment of the traditional understanding that they represent a form of messianic prophecy. The form-critical studies of H. Gunkel and the cult-historical studies of S. Mowinckel have shown that they require to be interpreted against a background of ANE royal ideology. H.'s dissertation divides into an outline history of modern research, beginning with a detailed review of the work of these two pioneering scholars. This is followed by much briefer surveys of more recent (1975–99) attempts at modifying and extending these approaches. The second part of the study provides detailed exegesis of three of the most significant royal psalms, Psalms 2, 110 and 132. Primary attention is given to the concepts used to express the status, function and achievements of the king, arguing firmly that these are based on ideological and mythological images of royal power, and not on historical situations. Overall the dissertation affirms the rightness of the cult-historical approach, as supported by comparative studies of Ugaritic and related evidence. It will be valued for its careful exegetical arguments and the up-to-date bibliography of such a central theme.

R.E. CLEMENTS

HOFFMAN, YAIR, *Jeremiah: Introduction and Commentary*. I. *Chapters 1–25* (in Hebrew) (Mikra Leyisra'el; Tel Aviv: Am Oved Publishers; Jerusalem: Hebrew University Magnes Press, 2001), pp. xxi + 512. n.p. ISBN 965-13-1493-1.

HOFFMAN, YAIR, *Jeremiah: Introduction and Commentary*. II. *Chapters 26–52* (in Hebrew) (Mikra Leyisra'el; Tel Aviv: Am Oved Publishers; Jerusalem: Hebrew University Magnes Press, 2001), pp. xiii + 513-911. n.p. ISBN 965-13-1493-1.

This commentary follows a standard format. The first volume contains a detailed and important introduction of ten parts: (1) short comments on the place of Jeremiah in the canon; (2) for the first time in a modern commentary extensive details of the fragments of Jeremiah from Qumran as well as comments on the LXX; (3) a survey of the historical background in the context of the weakening of Assyrian rule in Israel, the emergence of the Babylonian empire, the destruction of Jerusalem, and the exile; (4) a portrait of the life and character of Jeremiah according to a range of sources; (5) an important overall assessment of the language and style of the book in general and in particular (concerning the book's unity and typical features, especially in relation to the psalms); (6) a description of the various literary genres in Jeremiah; (7) an assessment of the book's composition and redaction with a clear list of what can and cannot be attributed to the prophet himself; (8) an outline of the teaching of Jeremiah on the destruction and exile with comments on eschatology; (9) comments on the principles of interpretation; and (10) a select bibliography. In the commentary proper the Hebrew text is presented, in prose or poetry as suitable, and there are detailed notes; some sections also have introductory comments or fulsome excurses.

G.J. BROOKE

HOLLAND, MARTIN, *Das erste Buch Samuel* (Wuppertaler Studienbibel, Altes Testament; Wuppertal: R. Brockhaus Verlag, 2002), pp. 320. €20.00. ISBN 3-417-25238-5.

This and its (remarkably different) sister commentary on 2 Samuel by K. vom Orde (see p. 72) appear to be the first volumes noted in *B.L.* from the Wuppertaler Studienbibel, Altes Testament (H.'s 1995 volume with Steinhoff on Judges and Ruth was not reviewed). In each section, a fairly literal working translation is followed by brief notes on the text chosen for translation, fuller verse-by-verse commentary, and then a summary statement of conclusions and questions which often concludes in Christian assertions not easily related to the passage as discussed. A short introduction (pp. 14-22) is organized in three sections, of which the first and third seem oddly titled: 'historical context' includes a summary account of Saul's kingship; 'chronology' does speak for itself; then 'the origin of 1 Samuel' ends with a presentation of the message of the book. H. concludes that 1 Samuel is a textbook for guilt for which no one begs forgiveness, while 2 Samuel provides pictorial instruction of where it leads if someone does beg God for forgiveness and God responds in love. Neither Fokkelman nor Polzin rates a mention, nor even Stoebe's substantial contribution to the KAT. Gunn's *Fate of King Saul* is the only non-German title in the short Bibliography. 1 Samuel proves a difficult book for this Christian commentator.

A.G. AULD

HOOKER, PAUL K., *First and Second Chronicles* (Westminster Bible Companion; Louisville, KY: Westminster John Knox Press, 2001), pp. x + 295. £9.99. ISBN 0-664-25591-4.

This series of commentaries is intended for the use of Protestant Christian lay people, primarily American. The present volume is a no-nonsense contribution, working through the text on a paragraph-by-paragraph basis. While there is no engagement with other scholarship, the author is abreast of the main conclusions of current moderate opinion on these books. His discussion is always positive, seeking to draw out what he sees as the Chronicler's purpose for his contemporaries in theological terms, and sometimes making allusion to ways in which these principles might find current application. The style is far from homiletic, however. The intended readers will no doubt be educated (if they can be persuaded that Chronicles is a valuable book for them to study), though they will still have quite a lot of work to do if they wish to move from education to edification.

H.G.M. WILLIAMSON

HORINE, STEVEN C., *Interpretive Images in the Song of Songs: From Wedding Chariots to Bridal Chambers* (Studies in the Humanities: Literature, Politics, Society, 55; New York: Peter Lang, 2001), pp. xviii + 235. n.p. ISBN 0-8204-5156-8; ISSN 0742-6712.

H. specifically engages J.M. Munro's study, *Spikenard and Saffron: The Imagery of the Song of Songs* (*B.L.* 1996, p. 65) which, although 'a groundbreaking work' (p. 63), 'fails to identify the central metaphor of the Song' (p. 3), namely, the bridal chamber. In fact, using literary analysis in terms of the imagery used, he makes a reasonable case for the view that Song is set within marriage, although occasionally the argument seems forced. In particular, his explanation of the famous crux in 6.12, based on ANE texts and pictorial evidence of early Greek wedding customs, is certainly plausible and in general there are some quite sharp observations on imagery and style. As a complete translation of Song is provided, as well as an excellent bibliography, the book could almost be considered a commentary and no doubt would provide stimulating material for a series of seminars.

W.G.E. WATSON

HOSSFELD, FRANK-LOTHAR and ERICH ZENGER, *Die Psalmen II: Psalm 51–100* (Die Neue Echter Bibel Altes Testament, 40; Würzburg: Echter Verlag, 2002), pp. 319-530. €24.50/SwF 44.50. ISBN 3-429-02359-9.

This concise commentary largely follows the established pattern of the Neue Echter Bibel series, offering an introduction to each psalm, the translation of the *Einheitsübersetzung*, some textual notes based on that translation and a brief commentary. Yet, while other volumes in the series display the translation at the top of the page with the commentary at the bottom, in the present volume the commentary follows the translation of the psalm, which is first laid out in full. The authors have also produced an extensive commentary for the new Herders theologischer Kommentar zum Alten Testament series, so the present volume presents their conclusions in briefer form. The introductions to the individual psalms cover the psalm's theme, genre, thematic development (which is presented in comparison with the structure suggested in the *Einheitsübersetzung*) and time of origin as well as its place and function in the book of Psalms. The exposition and commentary follow the structure suggested in the *Einheitsübersetzung* even when the authors disagree with it. Being the second part of the psalms' commentary, the volume does not have a general introduction but does feature an extensive and up-to-date bibliography on Psalms 51–100. It admirably fulfils the aims of the series, offering a great deal of information in a concise form accessible to a wide readership.

K. MÖLLER

HOULDEN, LESLIE and JOHN ROGERSON (eds.), *The Common Worship Lectionary: A Scripture Commentary Year B* (London: SPCK, 2002), pp.viii + 286. £20.00. ISBN 0-281-05326-X.

This volume provides a commentary on each of the Sunday readings in Year B and on the readings for a selection of major holy days according to the Anglican version of the Revised Common Lectionary. This is valuable because most of the available resources are based on the American version of the Revised Common Lectionary, from which the Anglican lectionary differs in a number of places. Some of the commentaries on NT passages have been taken directly from *Texts for Preaching Year B*, published by Westminster John Knox Press. This volume does not attempt to provide ready-made sermons, rather it provides the background knowledge essential for interpreting the texts. It is written from the perspective of modern academic scholarship, without conforming to any particular school of biblical interpretation. Each passage is put in its literary and theological context. Key issues arising from it are discussed along with points to note about the text itself, such as comments on the literary structure and the vocabulary used. There are also suggestions as to the message within the text and how it might speak to the church today. This book provides plenty of food for thought in sermon preparation —it is a very useful resource.

S.A. GROOM

JAPHET, SARA, *1 Chronik* (trans. D. Mach; HTKAT; Freiburg im Breisgau: Herder, 2002), pp. 472. n.p. ISBN 3-451-26816-7.

J.'s commentary on the books of Chronicles, reviewed in *B.L.* 1994, p. 63, is recognized as the leading work in its field by the foremost international specialist on these books. Granted that (somewhat surprisingly) the Herder commentary series is willing to include translations, it was thus an obvious choice. There are some slight changes with regard to the English original. Apart from the fact that the work will be published in two volumes, the format has been accommodated to that of the series, so that the text has been broken up into more titled sections, marginal headings have been added and each section now includes its own bibliography. In addition, there has been some slight abbreviation (mainly in the introductory sections to each chapter), some sections which were originally treated separately have now been joined (e.g., 1 Chronicles 11–12 and 28–29), and there has been some updating of the bibliographies, though this has apparently not resulted in significant rewriting of the text itself. The translation, by D. Mach, is by no means slavish, but seems accurately to convey the sense of the original, and indeed we are assured that J. was actively and frequently consulted at all stages. While one might suppose that those who are able to benefit from this commentary would already be able to read English, the greater availability and convenient access to this work will serve only to enhance further J.'s already established reputation.

H.G.M. WILLIAMSON

JOHNSON, RICHARD and TRICIA JOHNSON, *Discovering Genesis: Crossway Bible Guide* (Crossway Bible Guide; Leicester; Crossway Books, 2001), pp. 187. £4.99. ISBN 1-85684-202-9.

Crossway Bible Guides are designed as brief aids for evangelical groups and individuals wanting to study the Bible. After the expected prolegomena a few pages are allocated to each section of Genesis (normally around a chapter). A sentence states the (or a?) 'point', a few sentences give a more descriptive summary, then the section is briefly discussed. Occasionally issues that might trouble the reader are treated in a little more detail—for example, one page on 'How long is an everlasting covenant?' in the discussion of ch. 17. Finally there are three questions relating to possible applications of the text. These questions are often stimulating, though sometimes more help in identifying some of the relevant considerations might be welcome. The book assumes conservative perspectives on most matters, but within those boundaries attempts to be nuanced: the flood's essential historicity is taken for granted, but whether it was global or local is left open; the discussion of ch. 22 cites Heb. 11.19 but doesn't allow it to control the exegesis. Those who share the book's theology and want an initial way into the text may well find it helpful.

K. GRÜNEBERG

KEEL, OTHMAR and URS STAUB, *Hellenismus und Judentum: Vier Studien zu Daniel 7 und zur Religionsnot unter Antiochus IV* (OBO, 178; Freiburg: Universitätsverlag; Göttingen: Vandenhoeck & Ruprecht, 2000), pp. xi + 147. €39.00. ISBN 3-7278-1321-0 (Universitätsverlag); 3-525-53992-4 (Vandenhoeck & Ruprecht).

Each of the four articles in this volume presents a clear view on one of the contentious issues in a historical interpretation of the influence of Seleucid politics and Hellenistic culture in Judah. In an article which was first published in 1978, U. Staub makes a strong case for recognizing the image of an elephant, known through the Seleucid armies, behind the fourth beast in Dan. 7.7. Keel argues that there never was an altar at Modein and that for this and some other reasons 1 Maccabees 2 should be read as a purely ideological chapter which aims at justifying the Hasmonaeans' claim to the high priesthood. In a revised version of his contribution to a conference in Ljubljana in 1996, Keel elucidates Antiochus IV's motivation for his interference with the Jerusalem cult: against the background of Greek philosophical contempt for ritualistic distinctions, the Jewish prohibition to sacrifice swine was to be abolished. Thus the *šiqqûṣ šōmēm* is explained as a structure on top of the altar which served for sacrificing swine. The impact of Greek thought on second-century religious literature is further explored in an article on Daniel 2–7. Keel tries to demonstrate that the core concept which underlies the representation of Nebuchadnezzar in these chapters is a Greek (Aristotelian and Stoic) view of the contrast between animals and human beings. The volume makes fascinating reading.

C. BULTMANN

KESSLER, JOHN, *The Book of Haggai: Prophecy and Society in Early Persian Yehud* (VTSup, 91; Leiden: Brill, 2002), pp. xx + 334. €97.00/$113.00. ISBN 90-04-12481-0; ISSN 0083-5889.

The specific aim of this study is to examine the vision of prophecy and society portrayed in the book of Haggai set against the social context in which the book was produced. K. argues that not only the oracles of Haggai are sixth century but that the framework was also composed during this general period of time; that is, the entire book was redacted before 500 BCE. Part of the argument depends on the temple having been completed in 515 BCE, a date often cited without recognizing that it is far from secure. K. also argues that Haggai should be seen as independent of Zechariah 1–8, not as part of a single or even composite work. The central theme of the book is the effectiveness of the word of Yahweh as mediated by the prophet Haggai. Against a number of other interpretations, K. argues that the image of Haggai is in the same mould of 'typical prophet' as Amos or Jeremiah. Haggai also provisionally accepted Persian rule; he was not fomenting rebellion or making anti-Persian statements, even in coded form, but trying to smooth over any conflicts in society. K. stresses that Haggai is a much more complex prophet than often assumed, especially in the creative way that he uses past Israelite religious traditions to get across his message in a new and greatly transformed situation. By his skilful use of the Jeremiah tradition, for example, he is trying to convey his message to both the returnee exiles and those of the non-exiled population.

L.L. GRABBE

KOOLE, JAN L., *Isaiah III* (Historical Commentary on the Old Testament, Isaiah III, 3, Isaiah 56–66; Leuven: Peeters, 2001), pp. xxi + 531. €50.00. ISBN 90-429-1065-8.

The first two parts of this commentary were reviewed in *B.L.* 1998, p. 85 and *B.L.* 1999, p. 73. The present volume completes the commentary on the same lines, consisting entirely of comment on the individual sections of the text, without any material of an introductory nature. For such material the reader needs to turn to the Introduction to the whole book in the first volume, where pp. 19-33 are devoted particularly to these chapters. The tentative conclusion there is that a possible early exilic nucleus has been the object of redactional revisions, which may also have to do with the incorporation of these chapters within the book of Isaiah as a whole. It is good that K. was able to complete this commentary before his death in 1997, and that the whole is now available in English translation.

A. GELSTON

KWAKKEL, GERT, *'According to My Righteousness': Upright Behaviour as Grounds for Deliverance in Psalms 7, 17, 18, 26, and 44* (OTS, 46; Leiden: Brill, 2002), pp. 342. €100.00/$116.00. ISBN 90-04-12507-8.

A translation of the author's dissertation, a thesis thorough in its analysis and judicious in its judgments. K. offers an exegesis of five psalms with explicit confessions about upright behaviour towards God and man; he seeks to demonstrate that the psalmists are motivated not by their own sense of self-righteousness but rather by a belief that God, who promises life and prosperity to all who are faithful to him, must show himself to be righteous by intervening to bring them out of crisis. In this reading, K. questions whether cultic interpretations (whereby the psalmists, being admitted into the Temple liturgy, are pronounced righteous on account of their standing within the community) are necessary. K. gives close attention to issues of text, exegesis, composition, setting, function and date, with a final assessment of what the psalmist's assertions about his upright behaviour might mean. The book is strong in historical-critical exegesis, yet avoids any hypothetical contextualizing. It is a shame that there was no engagement with the literary context of the psalms—the placing of Psalm 17 between 16 and 18, and Psalm 18 between 17 and 19, Psalm 26 between 25 and 27, and Psalm 44 between Psalms 42–43 and 45. Furthermore, given the theological interest in the issue of innocent suffering and the pleas for God to be gracious, little is made of the similar literary and theological devices used in confessions in Jeremiah or the laments in Job. But as a focused exegesis of the five most pertinent psalms to claim God's help on the basis of the psalmist's self-righteousness, this is an important contribution to other larger issues.

S.E. GILLINGHAM

LEONHARD, CLEMENS, *Ishodad of Merv's Exegesis of the Psalms 119 and 139-147: A Study of His Interpretation in the Light of the Syriac Translation of Theodore of Mopsuestia's Commentary* (CSCO, 585: Subsidia Tomus, 107; Leuven: Peeters, 2001), pp. vi + 307. €75.00. ISBN 90-429-0960-9; ISSN 0070-0444.

Theodore of Mopsuestia's influential *Commentary on the Psalms* survives only in parts, in the Greek (Psalms 32–80), Latin (Psalms 1–40) and Syriac (Psalms 119, 139–147); of these the Syriac was only published (by L. van Rompay) in 1982, from a nineteenth-century manuscript in Cambridge originating from Urmi. Against the backdrop of these sections of Theodore's *Commentary* preserved in Syriac L. examines how the ninth-century East Syriac commentator, Isho'dad of Merv, approaches the same passages and what use he makes of Theodore, the exegete *par excellence* for the East Syriac tradition: this turns out to be surprisingly little, but in the process of demonstrating this L. has thrown much valuable light on the interests underlying, and the sources of, Isho'dad's exegesis. A helpful introductory chapter sets out the wider background.

S.P. BROCK

LIMBURG, JAMES, *Psalms for Sojourners* (Minneapolis, MN: Fortress Press, 2nd edn, 2002), pp. xiii+ 128. $9.00. ISBN 0-8006-3466-7.

This is a slim, inexpensive revision of L.'s 1986 edition, drawing from his recent commentary in the Westminster Bible Companion Series (2000) and the article 'The Book of Psalms' in *ABD*, V (1992). Using mainly the NRSV and TEV, and explaining terms such as 'Messiah' and 'Festivals' in a non-technical way, L. writes for a non-theological lay audience. In six chapters he offers a pastoral and semi-autobiographical reading of the wisdom psalms and royal psalms, the psalms of lament, trust, pilgrimage and praise, and the hymns of creation. Psalm 127 is 'A Word for Worriers and Workaholics'; Psalm 8, 'Midway between the Apes and the Angels'; and Psalm 150, 'From King David to Duke Ellington'. With an eye to 'the strength, passion and fire' within the psalms, L.'s appeal is for those who enjoy an easy-to-read interpretation replete with contemporary (often American) illustrations.

S.E. GILLINGHAM

LINDEN, NICO TER, *Die schönsten Geschichten der Bibel* (Gütersloh: Gütersloher Verlagshaus, 2002), pp. 157. €9.95. ISBN3-579-01332-7

Since 1995, when he left his preaching position at the Westerkerk in Amsterdam, the author has devoted himself to the task of retelling the biblical narratives in a very distinctive way, which has attracted the attention of scholars working in libraries as well as the more general newspaper-reading public (he is a regular columnist for the respected Dutch daily *Trouw*). His selection of passages from the Torah appeared in Dutch in 1995, in German in 1998 and in English a year later (see *B.L.* 2000, p. 81); those from the Former Prophets in Dutch in 1999, and a year later in German and English (see *B.L.* 2001, p. 70). What we have here is a selection of the best-known parts of those two earlier German editions presented as a pocket-sized paperback and intended as a foretaste of what can be found in the two previously published larger volumes. No corresponding Dutch anthology seems to have appeared. The gift of amalgamating spiritual insight with informed scholarship, which previous reviewers have noted so obviously has been granted to this author, does much to strengthen the bridge between the pew and the pulpit and the podium.

M.E.J. RICHARDSON

LUCAS, ERNEST, *Daniel* (Apollos Old Testament Commentary; Leicester: Apollos; Downer's Grove, IL: InterVarsity Press, 2002), pp. 359. £19.99. ISBN 0-85111-750-5.

The aim of this series is to 'provide not only tools of excellence for the academy, but also tools of function for the pulpit' (p. 7). The latter is achieved mainly in 'Explanation' sections at the end of pieces of commentary that also comprise a new translation, textual notes, notes on form and structure, and comment. This volume also includes translations, with brief introductions, of the 'Additions'. The brief Introduction concentrates on textual and form-critical matters, together with a 'historical context' section that reviews Jewish history from Neo-Babylonian to Seleucid times. Within the commentary section, while opinions regarding literary disunity or historical error are usually explained carefully, the verdict always discourages the reader from such options. Nevertheless, on the questions of dating the book and on pseudonymity, often the litmus test of conservative-evangelical orthodoxy, L. argues that these problems should not be theological issues for the modern Christian reader, and broadly accepts the generally held view about the origin and history of the book. As a tool for the student or pastor, this commentary is rather good. It engages with critical scholarship, and is well written in a way that commentaries often are not. Non-religious readers may disagree on what the book should mean to a modern reader, but that is a question that non-confessional commentaries unfortunately do not even bother to raise.

P.R. DAVIES

MACCHI, JEAN-DANIEL and THOMAS RÖMER (eds.), *Jacob: Commentaire à plusiers voix de Gen. 25-36; Mélanges offerts à Albert de Pury* (Le monde de la Bible, 44; Geneva: Labor et Fides, 2001), pp. 399. SwF 60.00. ISBN 2-8309-0987-9.

For once a Festschrift has been produced in which the editors have taken control and directed the contributors to write in their own style and from their own perspectives on short sections of the Jacob cycle (Genesis 25–36). The result must please A. de Pury greatly. The contributors and the pericopae for which they have been responsible are as follows: J.-L. Ska (Gen. 25.19-34), A. Marx (Gen. 26.1-14a), J. Vermeylen (Gen. 26.14b-25); T. Naef (Gen. 26.26-35); F. Smith (Gen. 27.1-40), P. Guillaume (Gen. 27.46–28.8), M. Rose (Gen. 28.10-22), F. García López (Gen. 29.1-14), H.-P. Mathys (Gen. 29.15-30), A. LaCoque (Gen. 29.31–30.24), A. Bühlmann and E. Jurissevich (Gen. 30.25-43), A. Schenker (Gen 31.1-25 and Exod. 21.7-11), J.-D. Macchi (Gen. 31.24-42), J.-G. Heintz (Gen. 31.43–32.1), T. Römer (Gen. 32.2-22), W. Dietrich (Gen. 32.23-33), K. Schmid (Gen. 33.1-11),

E. Blum (Gen. 33.12-20), J. Van Seters (Gen. 34), P. Gibert (Gen. 35.1-5), B.J. Diebner (Gen. 35.6-15), J. Briend (Gen. 35.16-22a), M. Bauks (Gen. 35.22b-29) and E.A. Knauf (Gen. 36.1-43). In addition C. Uehlinger considers male relationships in the Joseph cycle, H. Seebass looks at Jacob in the Pentateuch without Genesis, S.L. McKenzie reviews Jacob in the prophets, P. von Gemünden investigates Philo's treatment of Jacob, J.A. Soggin discusses the sources of Heb. 11.17-19, E. Starobinski-Safran comments on classical and mediaeval Jewish interpretations of Gen. 28.12-13, and G. Sed-Rajna looks very briefly at visual interpretations of Jacob's dream at Bethel. An overall bibliography on the Jacob cycle would have made this valuable collection even more appealing.

G.J. BROOKE

MAIER, CHRISTL, *Jeremia als Lehrer der Thora: Soziale Gebote des Deuteronomiums in Fortschreibung des Jeramiabuches* (FRLANT, 196; Göttingen: Vandenhoeck & Ruprecht, 2002), pp. 422. €64.00. ISBN 3-525-53880-4.

How did it come about that Jeremiah, a prophet of divine judgment, was seen and presented as a teacher of the Torah in the book that bears his name? This Berlin *Habilitationsschrift* seeks to answer this question by examining the passages in Jeremiah where the Hebrew word 'torah' occurs, and in particular Jer. 7.1–8.3, 26.1-24, 11.1-17, 17.19-27, 22.1-5, and 34.8-22. A section entitled 'use and function of the term torah in Jeremiah' discusses other passages, ending with 31.31-34. The enlargement of the Jeremiah tradition in the formation of the book presents him in various roles, including as social teacher and mediator between God and the people. In this process, the model of what was regarded as the prophet *par excellence*, Moses, played an important role.

J.W. ROGERSON

MANDOLFO, CARLEEN, *God in the Dock: Dialogic Tension in the Psalms of Lament* (JSOTSup, 357; London: Sheffield Academic Press, 2002), pp. x + 222. £50.00. ISBN 0-8264-6200-6.

M. claims that her 'dialogic critical method' represents a new approach to psalms study. She considers 11 laments (Psalms 4, 7, 9, 12, 25, 27, 28, 31, 55, 102, 130) and two thanksgivings (30, 32) where she notes evidence of 'a didactic voice'—a tonal shift from first to third person. This socio-rhetorical and theological study raises several critical issues. One is whether the shifts represent a more spontaneous oral stage in psalmody or a more formal written composition. Another is the role of the cultus: the 'voice', if not that of the supplicant, mediates (through a 'didactic horizontal discourse') God's retributive justice, along the lines of Deuteronomistic theology, and this suggests a prophet, a Levitical priest, or a director of the liturgy. Perhaps the most important issue, which is explored in the latter part of the book, with some interesting references to M.M. Bakhtin, is the extent to which these psalms reflect the conflicts between questioning of established tradition (through the supplicant) and offering of orthodox answers (through the 'didactic voice'). At times too many universal assertions are made from an analysis of just 13 psalms;

and too much emphasis is sometimes placed on the 'didactic voice', which often plays a minor part within each of these psalms; furthermore, M. writes more of the conflict between just two voices (the supplicant and the 'DV') than of the interchange between several voices in the same psalms (the audience, and God, for example, as well as the supplicant and the 'didactic voice'). But her claims illustrate the boldness of her assertions, and suggest the book has implications beyond a study of the psalms in question. This is undoubtedly a fresh and stimulating work.

S.E. GILLINGHAM

MCCONVILLE, J.G., *Deuteronomy* (Apollos Old Testament Commentary, 5; Downers Grove, IL: InterVarsity Press; Leicester: Apollos, 2002), pp. 554. £21.99. ISBN 0-85111-779-1.

M.'s commentary offers a theological interpretation of the canonical text. Utilizing a format familiar from the WBC series, each passage of the text receives a translation, textual notes, observations on form and structure, comment and explanation. The remarks on form and structure focus on structure and rhetoric more than form-critical questions of the passage's *Sitz im Leben*. The explanation section explores the significance of the passage in the context of the rest of the OT and makes moves towards the NT. Throughout the commentary there is evidence of M.'s distinctive contribution to the interpretation of Deuteronomy. This is particularly true of the introduction where, after a succinct and insightful summary of the critical debate, he offers a pre-monarchic date for the book. This view is based on M.'s interpretation of Deut. 16.18–18.22. In his opinion, it offers an approach between a statist (pre-exilic) and utopian (exilic or postexilic) view of the book. Thus, 'though the religious-political ideology of Deuteronomy must be embodied in real arrangements in space and time...the programme carries deeply within itself the capacity to critique such arrangements' (p. 36). M. has continued to voice an engaging alternative in the current discussion about the interpretation of Deuteronomy. It is unfortunate that many of the interesting critical issues raised by such a theory (such as the relationship to the Book of the Covenant) are largely unaddressed.

N. MACDONALD

MURRAY, PAUL, *Journey with Jonah: The Spirituality of Bewilderment* (Dublin: Columba Press, 2002), pp. 69. Illustrated. €5.99. ISBN 1856-07363-7.

This very brief volume (the NAB text of Jonah comprises almost an eighth of the text) is by an Irish Dominican who is best known for his writing on Christian literature. This expertise is evident in an eclectic and stimulating range of quotations from the Christian and Jewish interpretative tradition. The author himself gives us a meditation on the prophet's own spiritual and emotional response to the events of the story. Jonah is 'a religious bigot' (p. 53), and the purpose of the book is for us 'like Jonah, to undergo the grace and mystery of bewilderment' (p. 61). The notion is interesting, but it is only loosely based in the text, and the reading of Jonah's character hardly does justice to the subtlety of the story. The brevity and meandering character of the book makes it hard to recommend, but the literary references are of interest.

P. JENSON

NEDERLANDS BIJBELGENOOTSCHAP, *Tehiliem: Twintig psalmen uit de Nieuwe Bijbelvertaling* (with illustrations by Lika Tov; Heerenveen: Uitgeversgroep Jong bloed, 2002), pp. 64. €29.50. ISBN 90-6126-850-8.

This beautifully produced book will appeal to anyone interested in the psalms and, especially, in illustrations of biblical texts. Beginning with Psalm 1 and ending with Psalm 50, it contains a range of literary types (praise, thanksgiving, lament, supplication, etc.) selected to illustrate the richness and beauty of the Hebrew poetry, each with a stunning illustration by an artist whose remarkable sensitivity to the contours and nuances of the biblical text is evident in her choices of what features of the text to represent. The illustrations are full of detail and, like the psalms they illustrate, they are thought-provoking and rich in interpretative possibilities. All of them—whether conveying a spirit of joy and celebration or an atmosphere of seriousness or despair—are done with a light touch; they are never overly reverential or sentimental, as biblical illustrations often can be. The new Dutch translation from which these 20 psalms are taken is a joint project of the Catholic Bible Foundation and the Dutch Bible Society due to appear in December 2004 (the translations here have not yet been finalized). The book includes brief textual notes and a list of verses from the psalms that served as the chief inspiration for the illustrations. The publisher is to be commended for an attractive design with its ideal blend of text and illustration.

J.C. EXUM

O'CONNOR, KATHLEEN M., *Lamentations and the Tears of the World* (Maryknoll, NY: Orbis Books, 2002), pp. xvi + 156. £20.00. ISBN 1-57075-399-7.

The author is a Jeremiah scholar who has recently made herself a specialist in Lamentations. Coming hard on the heels of her commentary (2001) in the *New Interpreters Bible*, this book should probably be read alongside it, at least for maximum effect. The book is divided into two major sections. Part I, entitled 'Commentary: Who Will Comfort You?' consists of a commentary on the five chapters of Lamentations, about 80 pages in length, while Part II, entitled 'Reflections: A Theology of Witness' is some 66 pages long. The commentary begins with a short chapter in which the author states her position on several introductory matters—the book is a work of art, authorship, the acrostic is deeply symbolic, chapter three is not the only significant material, God's missing voice. She then proceeds by dividing the chapters into units and offering a translation before commenting, and she does this by interweaving the translated text with her observations. O. writes with admirable lucidity and insight, hence although this is not a substantial work, there is nothing trivial or unimportant in what she says. Her reflections in Part II have to do with Lamentations as 'a resource for the work of reclaiming our humanity, for breaking through our denial, personal and social, and for teaching us compassion'; and it is, perhaps, in this section that the author is at her best. The book is an important contribution to the study of an important part of the HB.

R.B. SALTERS

ORDE, KLAUS VOM, *Das Zweite Buch Samuel* (Wuppertaler Studienbibel, Altes Testament; Wuppertal: R. Brockhaus Verlag, 2002), pp. 320. €20.00. ISBN 3-417-25240-7.

This and its (remarkably different) sister commentary on 1 Samuel by M. Holland (see p. 61) appear to be the first volumes noted in *B.L.* from the Wuppertaler Studienbibel, Altes Testament (vom Orde's 1997 volume on Ezra and Nehemiah was not reviewed). In each section, the literal working translation is followed by a verse-by-verse commentary in which explanation and evaluation are combined. Text-critical discussion is handled in footnotes. The short introduction (pp. 15-22) covers similar material to the sister-volume, but is much more clearly organized in seven sections. O. insists that, while an interpretation of Samuel directed towards the NT is legitimate and possible, a reading of the book in its own terms is also useful for the Christian reader. The bibliography is very much more detailed than in Holland's *1 Samuel*. R. Polzin and H.J. Stoebe have their place, though not J.P. Fokkelman; and several non-German titles are included. This commentary is much easier to commend than its sister; however, 2 Samuel may also be a more congenial book.

A.G. AULD

OTTO, ECKART and ERICH ZENGER (eds.), *'Mein Sohn bist du' (Ps 2,7): Studien zu den Königspsalmen* (Stuttgarter Bibelstudien, 192; Stuttgart: Verlag Katholisches Bibelwerk, 2002), pp. vi + 258. €23.90. ISBN 3-460-04921-9.

This collection comes from a symposium in the year 2000 at the University of Munich on the theme, 'The Royal Psalms between Egypt and Assyria'. The essays (all in German) are the following: the king as son of God in Egypt and Israel (K. Koch), ruler legitimation in Psalms 2 and 18 in their ANE context (Otto), redaction critical observations to Psalm 72 and to the programme of the 'messianic Psalter' (Psalms 2–89) (Zenger), Psalm 72 and the Judahite royal ideology (B. Janowski), Psalm 72 in its ANE contexts (M. Arneth), Psalm 89 and the fourth 'book' of Psalms (Psalms 90–106) (F.-L. Hossfeld), and the form-critical proximity of Ps. 89.4-5, 20-38 to texts from the Neo-Assyrian court (H.U. Steymans).

L.L. GRABBE

PICKETT, BRIAN, *Songs for the Journey: The Psalms in Life and Liturgy* (London: Darton, Longman and Todd, 2002), pp. x + 197. ISBN 0-232-52384-3.

P. believes that the psalms 'can lead us, in company with others, across the threshold of new relationships…into a fuller vision of ourselves in the world'. This is an imaginative survey of the mystical quality of psalmody, as preserved through different liturgical traditions. He takes ten different aspects of psalmody related to pilgrimage themes, and quotes widely from the Talmud, Jewish prayer books, Greek Orthodox and Syrian Orthodox offices, Armenian, Coptic and Ethiopic liturgies, the Roman Missal and Divine Office, as well as a number of Anglican and Episcopal prayer books and worship books from Iona, Corrymela and Taizé. This is a rich tapestry which illustrates the transformation of the psalms in their earliest Jewish setting into myriads of other liturgical and personal settings over the years. P.'s book is more about the ways in which other believers have used the psalms than about the psalms themselves; but it works, as the universal appeal of psalmody shines through.

S.E. GILLINGHAM

PIKOR, WOJCIECH, *La comunicazione profetica alla luce di Ez 2–3* (Tesi Gregoriana, Serie Teologia, 88; Rome: Editrice Pontificia Università Gregoriana, 2002), pp. 316. €20.00/$21.00. ISBN 88-7652-940-3.

This monograph is a revised version of a doctoral dissertation completed by a Polish scholar within the Gregorian University in Rome, under the supervision of P. Bovati. The study combines effectively close study of two key chapters with a broader treatment of prophetic communication within Ezekiel. P. considers the position of the chapters within the book, and then the structure of Ezekiel 2–3 as a whole, before moving in for a close analysis, which equips him to discuss the communication process as evidenced in these two chapters. P.'s treatment highlights two complementary perspectives, the prophet's relationship with the deity, perceived as the source of his communication, and the verbal aspects of his relationship with his audience. This ends the first section of the work, to be followed by a much shorter second section broadening out the study to consider these questions in the context of the book as a whole, giving particular attention to 12.21–14.11; 24.15-27; 33. This is a competent study, reflecting a close familiarity with the international scholarly debate.

P.M. JOYCE

PIRSON, RON, *The Lord of the Dreams: A Semantic and Literary Analysis of Genesis 37–50* (JSOTSup, 355; London: Sheffield Academic Press, 2002), pp. xi + 168. £50.00. ISBN 0-8264-6200-X.

Based on a University of Tilburg, Netherlands, dissertation (supervisor E. van Wolde), this study seeks to answer the questions: Why is Joseph hardly ever mentioned outside Genesis? Why does Joseph not receive a portion of the land promised to his ancestors? How did he come to lose his special position to Judah? In order to answer these questions, P. does a synchronic analysis of this entire section of Genesis. The reader (envisaged as a scholarly person who has read the text several times) is seen to play a major part in the process of interpretation. P.'s reading finds both positive and negative sides to Joseph in the narrative, and gives a different interpretation to aspects of the story than is normally done (e.g., the brothers did not sell Joseph to Egypt). P. has made an interesting case, but it seems to me P.'s claim that 'the reader' plays a major part in the interpretation is unfounded: what we have is P.'s reading of the text. Other readers might well interpret it differently.

L.L. GRABBE

PRESSLER, CAROLYN, *Joshua, Judges, and Ruth* (Westminster Bible Companion; Louisville, KY: Westminster John Knox Press, 2002), pp. xii + 312. $24.95. ISBN 0-664-25526-4.

Several volumes in the Westminster Bible Companion for lay users were reviewed in *B.L.* 2000 and 2001. The (explicitly American) scholarly consensus on a Deuteronomistic History composed in two stages, before and after the exile, is assumed as the background against which to read Joshua and Judges. Ruth is separately introduced, but its composition is set in the same central period of the development of the OT. Throughout the treatment of Judges and Ruth, as generally in the series, the biblical text (NRSV) is printed in full early in each section of comment: the comment occupies little more space than the text, and directs the reader to the principal issues at stake. However, within Joshua 12–21, very little text is set: only 13.1-7; 14.1-15; 20.1-6; and 21.1-3, 43-45. Pressler writes crisply and to the point; and the intended readership should find this a useful addition to the series.

A.G. AULD

REINMUTH, TITUS, *Der Bericht Nehemias: Zur literarischen Eigenart, traditions-geschichtlichen Prägung und innerbiblischen Rezeption des Ich-Berichts Nehemias* (OBO, 183; Fribourg: University Press; Göttingen: Vandenhoeck & Ruprecht, 2002), pp. xiii + 383. SwF 75.00. ISBN 3-7278-1377-6 (University Press); 3-525-53998-3 (Vandenhoeck & Ruprecht).

R. begins with the statement that things have become quiet on Nehemiah, despite a lot of activity around the book(s) of Ezra–Nehemiah. This dissertation at the Humboldt University in Berlin (supervisor Peter Welten) aims to reverse this trend by a study of the first-person narrative in Nehemiah. The first main result is that the first-person narrative is made up of two major and distinct strands: the 'narrative of wall building' and the 'Nehemiah Memorial'. (This may seem slightly confusing in that the term 'Nehemiah Memorial' has often been used of the whole First-Person Narrative, but R.'s discussion is clear.) The first was written at a time more or less contemporary with the repair of Jerusalem's walls and shows no internal conflict; the second was written after his activities in Judah, in the last quarter of the fifth century, in the wake of internal opposition to a number of his reforms. The wall-building narrative is now roughly in Neh. 1.1-4, 11; 2.1-20; (3.1-32—this list was not composed by Nehemiah but incorporated into his narrative); 3.33–4.17; 6.1-19; 7.1-5; 12.31-32, 37-40. The Nehemiah Memorial is preserved approximately in Neh. 5.1-19; 13.4-17, 19-25, 27-31. At least two redactions revised and expanded the first-person account with small additions. This thorough study refines rather than revolutionizes our understanding of the Nehemiah first-person narrative.

L.L. GRABBE

RILETT WOOD, JOYCE, *Amos in Song and Book Culture* (JSOTSup, 337; London: Sheffield Academic Press, 2002), pp. 249. £50.00. ISBN 1-84127-244-2.

To say of this study that it emerges from a Toronto PhD under Brian Peckham, though true, would give a seriously limiting impression. A major theory as to the development of Amos, and, by implication, other prophetic collections, is here put forward. The oldest part of the book is held to be a series of seven interrelated poems, a tragic vision of the day of the Lord. They were composed by Amos himself for dramatic oral performance at a *marzēaḥ*. A comparable role is envisaged for other prophets down to the time of Jeremiah; in many of them allusions to Amos can be traced. In the Second Temple period these traditions were developed through a deliberate editorial process into the book as we know it. The tragic vision of the earlier poems has now become comic—both terms being used, of course, in their techical sense, with appropriate links made with the Greek literary world from Homer onwards; an extended comparison is made between Amos and the seventh-century Greek poet Archilochus. Finally, in a chapter entitled 'From Song Culture to Book Culture' particular attention is paid to intertextual questions, especially the complex inter-relation between Amos and the Deuteronomistic History. There is much here which others will question, but on any showing this is a major and positive contribution to the complex problem of the development of the prophetic material.

R.J. COGGINS

RÖDDING, GERHARD, *Die Schöpfungsgeschichte: Wie ich sie heute verstehen kann* (Gütersloh: Quell, 2002), pp. 144. €12.95. ISBN 3-579-06020-1.

About half this book presents in a popular, though somewhat sermonic, form much of what has been the standard fare among biblical scholars concerning the creation account in Gen. 1.1–2.4a. Before the exegesis of Genesis there are short sections on the creation accounts of Babylon and Egypt and comments on Israel's context, as well as an introduction to the sources of the Pentateuch. The exegesis of Genesis itself is a careful retelling with significant topics highlighted, such as the way in which God creates through command; it is a pity that the general reader is not presented with more on the recent form-critical insights into the text. There are several references to the NT along the way. The second half of the book considers how the modern reader should appropriate the meaning of the creation account. Those tempted towards the opinions of creationism will find a far better alternative here with much common sense (if they are able to recognize it as such). There are sections on Marcion and Luther, on human responsibility, on creation and the natural sciences, on the problem of evil, and on the relationship between humans and other creatures.

G.J. BROOKE

ROFÉ, ALEXANDER, *Deuteronomy: Issues and Interpretation* (Old Testament Studies; Edinburgh: T. & T. Clark, 2002), pp. xiv + 258. £30.00. ISBN 0-567-08754-9.

This volume collects 15 essays on Deuteronomy by R. from 1971 to 1999: 'The Book of Deuteronomy: A Summary'; 'The Monotheistic Argumentation in Deuteronomy 4.32-40: Contents, Composition and Text'; 'Deuteronomy 5.28–6.1: Composition and Text in the Light of Deuteronomic Style and Three *Tefillin* from Qumran (4Q128, 129, 137)'; 'Qumranic Paraphrases, the Greek Deuteronomy and the Late History of the Biblical אשׂנ'; 'The End of the Song of Moses (Deuteronomy 32.43'; 'The Arrangement of the Laws in Deuteronomy'; 'The Tenth Commandment in the Light of Four Deuteronomic Laws'; 'The Strata of the Law about the Centralization of Worship in Deuteronomy and the History of the Deuteronomic Movement'; 'The Organization of the Judiciary in Deuteronomy'; 'The History of the Cities of Refuge in Biblical Law'; 'The Laws of Warfare in the Book of Deuteronomy: Their Origins, Intent and Positivity'; 'Family and Sex Laws in Deuteronomy and the Book of the Covenant'; 'The Covenant in the Land of Moab', 'Methodological Aspects of the Study of Biblical Law'; 'Review of M. Weinfeld, Deuteronomy and the Deuteronomic School'. Many of the essays concern the Deuteronomic law, and all show R.'s careful attention to textual criticism, literary history and Deuteronomy's theological vision. The collection of these studies is to be welcomed, especially since they have been given full subject, author and source indices.

N. MACDONALD

ROSS, ALLEN P., *Holiness to the Lord: A Guide to the Exposition of the Book of Leviticus* (Grand Rapids, MI: Baker Academic, 2002), pp. 496. $32.99. ISBN 0-8010-2285-1.

The subtitle is to be understood exactly: the object is to offer guidance to those giving expository preaching on Leviticus (if such there be!), not to provide a commentary on every detail. R.'s standpoint is Christian and conservative; he strives to understand the underlying theological principles of each section, and in every case to show how the principles are expressed in the NT in the light of the fulfilment of the Law in Christ. Each section includes a detailed outline (the text is not given), suggestions on how an exposition might be organized, R.'s own exposition, either in the order of the text or arranged topically, concluding observations which always include a one-sentence theological summary, and a bibliography. An introduction also emphasizes Christian hermeneutic, but does not neglect a historical discussion leading to the expected conservative conclusion; there is also a substantial general bibliography. The bibliographies include all the best literature on Leviticus; they are not confined to conservative works. R. himself is learned, judicious and admirably clear in his style. Many issues are discussed seriously, even if one may feel that in many cases the result is a foregone conclusion—for example, the substitutionary effect of the hand-leaning in 1.4. For the intended readership the book could hardly be improved on.

W.J. HOUSTON

RUPPERT, LOTHAR, *Genesis: Ein kritischer und theologischer Kommentar, 2. Teilband: Gen 11,27–25,18* (FzB, 98; Würzburg: Echter Verlag, 2002), pp. 657. €36.80/SwF 65.50. ISBN 3-429-02461-7.

In the substantial introduction to this commentary, R. sets out his understanding of this part of Genesis and discusses various questions arising from it. His approach is primarily critical, but it is also theological; it is primarily diachronic rather than synchronic. Unlike scholars such as R. Rendtorff and E. Blum, he adopts a form of the traditional source analysis: J (tenth century), E (eighth century), and P (a source not just a redaction, c. 550–510); the Jehovist is dated in the late eighth century, and a redaction is postulated in the reign of Josiah. The length of the commentary gives R. scope to discuss many subjects, and there are 11 excurses. Particular attention may be drawn to R.'s theory about Genesis 14, in which he finds a *Grundschicht* from the late eighth century, in which Chedor-laomer stands for Tiglath-pileser III and Sargon II; three expansions are postulated, the last of them c. 520. The commentary ends with a consideration of the figure of Abraham in Genesis, in the rest of the OT and the NT, and in Christian thought.

J.A. EMERTON

RYKEN, LELAND, *The Word of God in English: Criteria for Excellence in Bible Translation* (Wheaton, IL: Crossway Books, 2002), pp. 336. $15.99. ISBN 1-58134-464-3.

This book is a challenge to the widely accepted principle of 'dynamic-equivalence' in Bible translation. R. argues that the 'essentially literal' approach exemplified in the KJV and RSV is a more satisfactory approach for serious Bible readers than the dynamic equivalence found in such versions of the Bible as the NIV, GNB or NLT. R. argues that precise use of language is expected in all important communication, whether it be a great novel, legal documents, or instruction manuals. Dynamic equivalence sits light to precise renderings of the original. R. then tackles some of the fallacious arguments used to justify dynamic equivalent translations, that the Bible is simple, that only its ideas matter, that they can be easily transposed into modern dress, that we should translate meaning rather than words, that readability is the ultimate goal in translation, that Bible readers have poor reading ability, need short sentences, cannot understand or learn to understand technical or theological terminology. Having questioned the common arguments for dynamic equivalent translation, R. then proceeds to spell out the principles that should characterize a good 'essentially literal' translation. As an English literature specialist R. is not concerned solely with fidelity to the original Hebrew and Greek, but with the translation sounding like powerful natural English. In this regard he shows how many modern versions are not simply inexact in their renderings of the original, but often banal and unrhythmical to boot. R. argues that a good translation should allow the literary qualities of the different books of the Bible to be fairly represented, not reduce them all to colloquial everyday speech. Modern translations often fail badly in the poetic books. Poetic images should be retained, not replaced by abstractions (e.g. 'fortress' by 'protection'). Bible translations should allow the ideas of the biblical world to be appreciated, not impose modern equivalents on the reader. Where the original is ambiguous and can be interpreted more than one way, the translation ought, if possible, to preserve the ambiguity. R. concludes his book by an appeal for a sympathetic translation of Bible poetry. He wants love poetry to sound like love poetry and proverbs to sound like proverbs. He pleads that everywhere natural English speech rhythms should characterize translations designed for public reading. Countless examples from modern translations show how these principles have been widely ignored. A review cannot do justice to the detailed argument of this book. Though not all may share R.'s enthusiasm for the KJV and its successors, he raises issues too long ignored that ought to be taken into account in choosing versions for use in church or classroom.

G.J. WENHAM

SCHWAB, GEORGE M., *The Song of Songs' Cautionary Message Concerning Human Love* (Studies in Biblical Literature, 41; New York: Peter Lang, 2002), pp. xviii + 221. £38.00. ISBN 0-8204-556-0; ISSN 1089-0645.

In contrast with most of the recent studies of the Song of Songs, this monograph argues that there is a strong element of 'negativity' in the Song that warns against free love, since 'the Song does in fact seek to persuade the reader to regard love as a mixed blessing, something one should be cautious when approaching' (p. 41). Much of S.'s argument rests on the phrase 'do not stir up love' in Song 2.7; 3.5; 8.4 and the passage Song 5.2-8. Without discussing other scholarly opinions, S. moves from the detected 'negativity' in Song of Songs to a comparison with other biblical texts that display—in S.'s view—a similar negative attitude towards sexuality. Here the author uses a broad spectrum of comparative texts and includes deutero-canonical writings as well as the NT. A look into the bibliography reveals that S. has not consulted any of the major foreign language commentaries (e.g. G. Gerleman, H.-P. Müller, O. Keel) and one wonders why this has been the case. This study is an interesting proposal, but the reader is left with the impression that the argument is a bit forced; for example, it never occurs to S. that Song 2.7b might be addressed to the daughters of Jerusalem not to interrupt the love of the couple. If the 'love' in this phrase is really the 'uncontrollable power that is best left asleep' (p. 45) it is more than questionable. Despite the many valuable insights offered in the book, the author seems far too concerned to bring the Song of Songs in line with the ethical teaching on sexuality in the NT and that he feels uneasy about the Song's celebration of human sexuality.

A.C. HAGEDORN

SEDLMEIER, FRANZ, *Das Buch Ezechiel, Kapitel 1-24* (Neuer Stuttgarter Kommentar, Altes Testament, 21/1; Stuttgart: Verlag Katholisches Bibelwerk, 2002), pp. 336; 9 illustrations. €28.90. ISBN 3-460-07211-3.

WERLITZ, JÜRGEN, *Die Bücher der Könige* (Neuer Stuttgarter Kommentar, Altes Testament, 8; Stuttgart: Verlag Katholisches Bibelwerk, 2002), pp. 364; 1 map; 14 illustrations. €30.90. ISBN 3-460-07081-1.

This commentary series aims to be scholarly based but written in a language understandable to lay people. The two volumes here seem to fulfil that goal. The introductions in both appear to be clearly written. Werlitz, for example, gives a helpful table and examples of the 'framework formula' (*Rahmenformular*) found widely in Kings. His discussion of the different forms of the Deuteronomistic

History theory is clear but somewhat brief, and one wonders what the lay person seeing it for the first time would make of it. He also has a quite balanced treatment of the question of using 1 and 2 Kings for historical reconstruction. Interestingly, his strictures seem to be ignored by Sedlmeier who gives an overview of the history of Israel that looks to be simply a paraphrase of the biblical text. Sedlmeier also has a rather simplistic excursus on 'false prophets'. Both books have a number of excursuses and appendixes that aim to address specific questions such as chronology, the list of kings, and theological themes. An advertised feature of the series is attention to reception history (*Wirkungsgeschichte*). Werlitz devotes more than 20 pages to this topic; Sedlmeier has only one, but he notes that he is saving a fuller treatment until his final volume. Both volumes have some helpful illustrations and suggestions for follow-up reading. A disconcerting feature of this series (judging from these two volumes) is the practice of referring to other volumes in the series by volume number only, but since no list of the volumes is to be found anywhere in the book, one does not know which particular biblical book is being commented on.

L.L. GRABBE

SEVILLA JIMÉNEZ, CRISTÓBAL (ed.), *Jonás* (Asociación Bíblica Española, Reseña Bíblica, 33; Estella: Editorial Verbo Divino, 2002), pp. 72. €7.81/$10.00. ISSN 1134-5233.

Reseña Bíblica is a cross between an academic journal, a monograph and a popular magazine. Apart from the final six or so pages, which contain announcements and reviews, Jonah is the theme of the whole issue. Despite some rather large print and copious black and white pictures strewn throughout the text (mostly early depictions of Jonah and the fish, given without date) much of the comment is academically profitable. There are five essays: 'Was the Prophet Jonah Swallowed by a Whale?' (A. Álvarez Valdés), 'From the Sea to Terra Firma' (Sevilla Jiménez), 'The Story of a Conversion' (R. Tadiello), 'Jonah and the "Difficult" Mercy of God' (G. Antoniotti), and 'The Sign of Jonah' (V. Mora). These cover historical and theological aspects of the book, and include some very suggestive readings, the final one arguing that the 'sign of Jonah' can be found in all four Gospels. There then follows the first Spanish edition of the Midrash on Jonah (M. Pérez Fernández). The treatment of Jonah concludes with discussion of how Jonah might be used in Catholic catechesis (pre-school to adult). With some adaptation much of the text could profitably be translated into English and used for introducing Jonah to students.

P.J. WILLIAMS

SHERWOOD, STEPHEN K., *Leviticus, Numbers, Deuteronomy* (Berit Olam: Studies in Hebrew Narrative and Poetry; Collegeville, MN: The Liturgical Press, 2002), pp. xviii +306. $39.95. ISBN 0-8146-5046-5.

S.'s work is a discussion of narrative art in Leviticus, Numbers and Deuteronomy. Each book is given a detailed introduction and notes. The introduction begins by explaining the name of the biblical book. Its interest to Christian (Roman Catholic) readers is indicated by listing NT citations and its use in the lectionary.

This is followed by a consideration of the delimitation of the book and its language. Observations follow on 'time (pace and order), plot (especially tension and resolution), structure, characterization, voice, symbolism and imagery, reading position (the manipulation of knowledge by the narrator), and point of view' (p. xiii). The notes on the text are not an exhaustive commentary, but a collection of observations on the literary art of the text by S. or other commentators. The effect is similar to that found in Ehrlich's *Randglossen*. Attention to the literary art and symbolism of these books, too easily characterized as mere laws, is to be welcomed. Nevertheless, at points more (in some cases, any) analysis of the graphs, tables and long lists of verses would have been desirable.

N. MACDONALD

SICRE, JOSE LUIS, *Historia Josué* (Nueva Biblia Española, Comentario teológico y literario, Historia; Estella: Editorial Verbo Divino, 2002), pp. 520. €28.90. ISBN 84-8169-488-6.

S. has prepared an excellent opening volume to a projected commentary on the books Joshua–Kings. His introduction (pp. 21-76) opens with the book likened to a television series on Joshua, the impact of each episode heightened by the efforts of a succession of editors: apart from the 36 anonymous casualties at Ai, the only Israelite who dies during the conquest is Achan. Then, in turn, he discusses the name of the book and its protagonists; content and structure; author and date of composition; relationship with Deuteronomy; additions of priestly origin; text; moral problems raised; book of Joshua and history; and presents a useful and up-to-date bibliography. Translation and commentary follow in the familiar three parts (Joshua 1–12; 13–21; 22–24), except that the opening divine speech to Joshua (1.1-9) is set apart as an introduction. Each portion is furnished with its own bibliography; and the translation and commentary offer equally careful readings of the MT and of a wide range of scholarship. Seven themes are accorded separate treatment each in an excursus, four of these relating to Josh. 3.1–5.1 (the distinct terms for the ark, the history of the ark, the lists of conquered peoples, and distinct approaches to Joshua 3–4). It is in these overviews that this reader finds in concentrated form the problem which is present, if often less obvious, throughout this able and well-informed study. Translating and commenting on MT, except in the few cases where it can be improved on the basis of other ancient witnesses, is an excellent exercise, and possibly preferable to basing commentary on a reconstructed, eclectic text. But using MT, with little reference to LXX, as a starting-point for analyses of the history of tradition is another matter, and unnecessarily hazardous.

A.G. AULD

SKA, JEAN-LOUIS, *L'argile, la danse et le jardin: Essais d'anthropologie biblique* (Connaître la Bible, 27; Brussels: Lumen Vitae, 2002), pp. 77. €9.00. ISBN 2-87324-173-X.

This collection, translated from the Italian, derives from three talks on biblical themes given by S. to groups of young people attending retreats at the monastery of

Camaldoli in Tuscany. The talks are framed by an introduction and an epilogue. They are good examples of how S. puts into practice his conviction that the concrete and undogmatic tone of the Bible can communicate to all sorts of hearers. They do not pretend to be contributions to scholarship, but they are well crafted and insightful. In the first essay, S. treats the story of the flood as a reflection on the inevitable presence of violence in the world, a violence which God can use as a creative power. He reflects on David's dance before the ark in the second essay and relates the story to Hindu mythology. David's participation in sacred dance represents the forces of fertility as opposed to the sterility of Michal's disdainful rejection. The third essay discusses some NT passages concerned with the resurrection. *B.L.* readers who are faced with similar audiences will find a good model of how intelligent reading can be made engaging.

H.S. PYPER

SYKES, SETH, *Time and Space in Haggai-Zechariah 1–8: A Bakhtinian Analysis of a Prophetic Chronicle* (Studies in Biblical Literature, 24; New York: Peter Lang, 2002), pp. xiv + 172. £33.00. ISBN 0-8204-4596-7.

S. follows W.A.M. Beuken's 1967 study in reading Haggai–Zechariah 1–8 as a unity in the chronistic genre, and applies Bakhtinian principles so as to bring out the significance of that genre. The key term is 'chronotope', proposed as a means of analysing the socio-historical settings of literary works. After establishing the unity of Haggai and Zechariah 1–8, S. offers an extended analysis of the world-view presented by numerous Babylonian Chronicles, with particular attention to the understanding of the ideal king from the standpoint of the Esagil priesthood. The Judaean and Israelite chronicles referred to in 1 and 2 Kings are claimed to be similar in presentation, and the final chapter argues that Haggai–Zechariah 1–8 transforms this genre into a prophetic form, which also originates from a temple scribe, perhaps Zechariah himself. Whereas earlier studies have maintained that Haggai and Zechariah set out to maintain the established socio-political order (an ideological understanding), the claim is here made that they wished to subvert that order (a utopian understanding), by showing Yahweh rather than the Persian ruler to be the true king. The study certainly challenges some conventional assumptions; it would have benefited from stricter editing. There are repetitions and at least one footnote which simply repeats what has just been said in the text.

R.J. COGGINS

WALLACE, RONALD S., *Hannah's Prayer and Its Answer: An Exposition for Bible Study* (Grand Rapids, MI: Eerdmans, 2002), pp. xiv + 113. $14.00/£9.99. ISBN 0-8028-6068-0.

This short book comprises what was originally a series of expositions printed in the quartely magazine *Evangel*. We are told that they were rewritten for this book, the intended readership of which is those involved in individual or group Bible study. It is certainly those individuals and groups who will benefit from it, rather than those who come to the opening chapters of 1 Samuel in more academic ways.

One of the main purposes of the narrator at the beginning of 1 Samuel, according to W., 'was eventually to bring home to us the importance and efficacy of prayer' (p. xiii). Whatever may be the truth of that, clearly one of the main purposes of W. is to bring home to his readers the importance and efficacy of prayer. The work is attractively written, with considerable reference being made to the NT. What is less in evidence is corresponding reference to the contemporary world, and help for those who have difficulty in seeing the presence of God in that world, and who perhaps ask questions as to what does happen when they pray. For the benefit of group Bible study, some questions at the end of each of the seven chapters into which the book is divided might have served to tease out a contemporary understanding of God's action in and involvement with the world of today.

M.E.W. THOMPSON

WILDBERGER, HANS, *Isaiah 28–39* (trans. Thomas H. Trapp; A Continental Commentary; Minneapolis, MN: Fortress Press, 2002), pp. xvi + 781. $75.00. ISBN 0-8006-9510-0.

This is the third and final volume of Trapp's translation of W.'s Isaiah commentary in the BKAT series. The standard of translation of the first two volumes was rather severely criticized in *B.L.* 1993, p. 70, and 2000, pp. 92-93, though of course the value of having this great work made available to a wider circle of readers was acknowledged. This final volume not only includes the commentary on the chapters indicated, but also W.'s 'introduction' to the book, covering in some 200 pages such topics as the textual history of the book, the formation of Isaiah 1–39, the prophet and his relation to the religious traditions of his people, his theology and that of the later writers whose work is included in these chapters, as well as their language and speech forms. The translator has put us further in his debt by supplying more than 30 pages of additional bibliography covering the period since W. wrote, down to 2001; though he admits that this is not exhaustive, it is certainly extensive, and it usefully follows W.'s own headings and subdivisions so that it can be properly used alongside his commentary. There is a sense in which W.'s commentary marks the culmination of a once dominant phase in the long history of the study of Isaiah. It is not possible to conceive now of a work of this kind which does not take account of the place of these chapters within the book as a whole, whether in terms of a synchronic reading or with a concern for an overarching diachronic redaction-critical analysis. While scholarship thus moves inexorably forward, the conclusion of the translation of this important work of abiding value will be widely welcomed and appreciated.

H.G.M. WILLIAMSON

6. LITERARY CRITICISM AND INTRODUCTION
(INCLUDING HISTORY OF INTERPRETATION, CANON AND SPECIAL STUDIES)

ALBANI, MATTHIAS and MARTIN RÖSEL, *Theologie Kompakt: Altes Testament* (Calwer Taschenbibliothek, 92; Stuttgart: Calwer Verlag, 2002), pp. 176. 7 figures. €11.90. ISBN 3-7668-3754-0.

This little introduction covers an immense amount in its few pages in an interesting and balanced way. With the addition of the names of a few English-speaking scholars, it deserves to be published in an English version as soon as possible. An introductory chapter sets the scene. Following chapters cover the history of Israel (in which issues surrounding the land and the periodization of history are addressed), the variety of the biblical books, the history of research on the OT (which opens by tackling the issue of Mosaic authorship and ends with positive comments on feminist exegesis), the methods of modern research, crucial themes (covenant, decalogue, temple, kingship, creation, Yahweh), the OT as part of the Christian Bible, and an exemplary exegesis for the beginner of Genesis 1–3.

G.J. BROOKE

ALEXANDER, T.D., *From Paradise to the Promised Land: An Introduction to the Pentateuch* (Carlisle: Paternoster Press; Grand Rapids, MI: Baker Academic, 2002), pp. xxvii + 339. 4 maps and diagrams. £19.99. ISBN 1-84227-136-9.

The first edition was reviewed in *B.L.* 1996. This second edition adds Part I, a discussion of contemporary academic approaches to the Pentateuch.

P. ADDINALL

BARRICK, W. BOYD, *The King and the Cemeteries: Toward a New Understanding of Josiah's Reform* (VTSup, 88; Leiden: Brill, 2002), pp. xiii + 274. 1 map. €73.00/ $85.00. ISBN 90-04-12171-4; ISSN 0083-5889.

B. offers a thorough re-analysis of the presentation of Josiah's reform in Kings and Chronicles, claiming that the 'ascendency of synchronic analysis...has not obviated the validity of or need for diachronic study of this material' (pp. 4-5). The brief opening chapter questions some earlier assumptions concerning the relationship between Judah and Assyria, the connection between Josiah's law-book and Deuteronomy, and the security of the Deuteronomistic History hypothesis. Then, in

Chapters 2–6, B. examines the reports of Josiah's reform and other passages believed to be closely related, with particular emphasis on their likely compositional history. One interesting suggestion is that the original form of the reform report '[i]n terms of content and style...resembles a royal memorial inscription such as Mesha's' (p. 141). In Chapters 7–10 he examines the material as a potential source for reconstructing the history of the period, bringing into the discussion archaeological and extra-biblical textual material. The intriguing possibility with which we are confronted at the very end of the book is that Amos and Hosea were both buried in Jerusalem and 'commemorated by a funerary monument which Josiah took pains to preserve' (p. 220). B. points out that the nine main chapters of the book are 'by design, neither exhaustive nor definitive' (p. 15). They are, however, in the main closely argued, packed with a wealth of detail, and provided with copious footnotes. (But this reader prefers to reserve judgment on the Amos and Hosea suggestion!)

A.H.W. CURTIS

BARTON, JOHN and MICHAEL WOLTER (eds.), *Die Einheit der Schrift und die Vielfalt des Kanons/The Unity of Scripture and the Diversity of the Canon* (BZNW, 118; Berlin: W. de Gruyter, 2003), pp. v + 307. €84.00. ISBN 3-11-017638-6.

The ongoing cooperation between Bonn and Oxford has produced this intriguing set of essays on canon within Christianity. Barton argues that the diversity within Scripture should be seen as a positive advantage, not least in undermining any kind of authoritarianism that insists on a uniform reading; H. Seebass expresses hermeneutical dislike for the view that the OT should be designated First Testament, because the designation seems to limit the universality of God; M. Wolter reverses the collection's title and writes on the diversity of Scripture and the unity of the canon, stressing the role of reception in appreciating the character of canonicity; M. Ludlow considers the 'criteria of canonicity' in the early church; J. Webster suggests that the suitable dogmatic location of the canon is as part of the history of divine judgment and mercy ('as a knife at the church's heart'); P.S. Fiddes ponders profoundly the boundaries of canon in relation to thoughts about revelation; R. Morgan looks at the NT canon with a view to showing that Christian identity should depend upon discipleship to the crucified Jesus, rather than on any attempt to overcome the diversity of the NT; C. Schröder-Field discusses the different expectations of the canon in biblical theology and Protestant dogmatics; G. Sauter enquires ecumenically about the relationship between canon and church; and G. Bader comments on how the character of canons changes according to their function. While the unity and the diversity of the canon are addressed creatively and openly, the diversity of the Church, particularly beyond the confines of Anglicans, Baptists and Lutherans is barely considered. The essays come across as making a valuable theological step in the right direction for some kinds of Christian.

G.J. BROOKE

BECKMANN, KLAUS, *Die fremde Wurzel: Altes Testament und Judentum in der evangelischen Theologie des 19. Jahrhunderts* (Forschungen zur Kirchen- und

Dogmengeschichte, 85; Göttingen: Vandenhoeck & Ruprecht, 2002), pp. 400. €64.00. ISBN 3-525-55193-2.

The negative attitude of the young Schleiermacher to the OT is well known, deriving as it did from his conviction that the heart of Christianity lay in an awareness of God mediated through encounter with Christ. Although Schleiermacher modified this view later, this negative assessment of the OT has cast a long shadow over systematic theology ever since. Not all German theologians in the nineteenth century shared this view, however, and this Bonn dissertation considers the attitude towards the OT of C.I. Nitzsch, J.A.W. Neander, D.F. Strauß, E.W. Hengstenberg and J.C.K. von Hofmann, in addition to that of Schleiermacher. Of these, only Hengstenberg was an OT scholar, and his strongly orthodox position took the OT to bear prophetic witness to the coming of Christ. Hofmann believed that the OT contained God's self-revelation through history, culminating in the coming of Christ. Strauß is particularly interesting because he believed that the NT was deeply anchored in Jewish mythology. This is more of a book for theologians than for biblical scholars, and it touches only marginally upon issues that concern the latter. Wellhausen is mentioned only once, in a footnote!

J.W. ROGERSON

BRENNER, ATHALYA (ed.), *Prophets and Daniel* (A Feminist Companion to the Bible, Second Series, 8; London: Sheffield Academic Press, 2001), pp. 317. n.p. ISBN 1-84127-163-2.

Several of the studies in this volume are published in their first English translation or are reprinted directly from elsewhere. The collection opens with a major essay on the Queen of Heaven by J.M. Hadley. In a section on female prophets E. Fuchs writes on prophecy and the ambiguous or clearly derogatory construction of women, R. Jost looks briefly at women prophets in Ezek. 13.17-21, and R. Kessler considers Miriam and the prophecy of the Persian period. A third section contains studies on 'the Pornoprophetic(?) "Marriage" Metaphor' which especially develop the theme of violence: G. Baumann looks at the disappointingly limited reinterpretations of the prophetic marriage metaphor in Isaiah 40–55; M.E. Shields presents a new gendered reading of Jer. 3.1–4.4 together with her own response to her paper, as well as a study of body rhetoric in Ezek. 16.1-43, with another response; E. Runions considers violence and the economy of desire in the same passage of Ezekiel, while S.T. Kamionkowski comments on Israel's gender reversal there; U. Sals writes on Zech. 5.5-11; J.M. O'Brien offers a personal reading of Malachi together with her own response; and M.I. Gruber considers the violent image of the adulteress in Nahum. There are also three studies on Daniel: B.'s own contribution is her influential study of obtuse foreign rulers in the HB including Daniel, 'Who's Afraid of Feminist Criticism?' (*JSOT* 63 [1994], pp. 38-54), together with a self-response; H.J.M. van Deventer reconsiders women's wisdom in Dan. 5.10-12, and with examples from passages throughout the HB, but especially Daniel 5; E. Sampson describes the work of Julia Smith as translator. The concluding bibliography is helpful. The ongoing consideration of the voices of women in the past and the present, together with the making explicit of the issue of violence, are signs of the times.

G.J. BROOKE

BRENNER, ATHALYA and CAROLE R. FONTAINE (eds.), *The Song of Songs* (A Feminist Companion to the Bible, Second Series, 6; Sheffield: Sheffield Academic Press, 2000), pp. 211. 5 figures. £17.99/$33.95. ISBN 1-84127-052-0.

Rather than being important articles reprinted from elsewhere, the essays published here were all commissioned for the volume. Four studies consider the Song of Songs in general: J.C. Exum outlines ten things every feminist should know about the Song of Songs; A. Ostriker reads the Song of Songs as countertext; J. Bekkenkamp offers four thought-provoking models for the theological reading and appropriation of the Song of Songs; and D.V. Arbel works creatively with the diversity of voices, images and characters in the book. Three essays consider specific readings: F.C. Black analyses the similarities and differences in what Rashi, Nicholas of Lyra, Carol Myers and Athalya Brenner have to say about Song 7.1-8: Jane Barr looks at Luis de León's sixteenth-century translation and commentary; and K. Butting looks at Song 2.8-14 against a backdrop of Abraham and Sarah. Three essays, by A. Brenner, C.R. Fontaine, and M. Häusl and U. Silber, offer personalized readings of the Song of Songs and join the growing number of studies that overtly place biography and autobiography among the canon of interpretative methods. This is a very worthwhile collection that neatly expresses all the ambiguities and tensions involved in being 'beloved'.

G.J. BROOKE

BRENNER, ATHALYA and JAN WILLEM VAN HENTEN (eds.), *Bible Translation on the Threshold of the Twenty-First Century: Authority, Reception, Culture and Religion* (JSOTSup, 353; The Bible in the 21st Century, 1; London: Sheffield Academic Press, 2002), pp. x + 207. £55.00. ISBN 0-82646-029-1.

This is the first volume in a series that hopes to 'explore features and issues that are oriented to contemporary culture and the Bible's place within it' (p. 5). Its ten essays and seven responses were mostly given originally at a colloquium in Amsterdam (May 2000), and, consequently, there is a Dutch flavour to many of the contributions, though they are not at all parochial. From several of the essays it would seem that the appetite among translation theorists for 'formal equivalence', or something similar, has returned. The volume contains the last article Robert Carroll wrote: 'Between Lying and Blasphemy or On Translating a Four-Letter Word in the Hebrew Bible: Critical Reflections on Bible Translation', which treats the problems in translating the Tetragrammaton. Quotable as ever: 'To this day I remain unconvinced, where not baffled, by the tendencies of Englished Bibles to lapse into capital letters (screaming upper case letters!) at certain points in the text, as if the deity were deemed to express itself in upper case letters (cf. KJV at Rev. 17.5)' (p. 60). Aside from the editors and Carroll, contributors are S. Crisp, E. Fox,

J. Frishman, M.P. Korsak, S. Noorda, J. Punt, J. Rogerson, L.J. de Regt, L. Sanneh, C. Vander Stichele, A.J.C. Verheij, W.J.C. Weren and T. Witvliet.

P.J. WILLIAMS

BRIGGS, RICHARD S., *Words in Action: Speech Act Theory and Biblical Interpretation* (Edinburgh: T. & T. Clark, 2001), pp. xvi + 352. £25.00. ISBN 0-567-08809-X.

Readers of the *B.L.* may be disappointed that the 'biblical interpretation' of the subtitle of this Nottingham thesis is in practice NT interpretation, and that recent work on the HB using speech-act theory is not noted. But they should read on. B. considers theoretical issues in Part I before applying his results to the NT in Part II. He usefully reviews the development of the theory before considering the issue of how it may be applied to texts. Here he confronts speech-act theory with literary theory, taking Derrida and Fish as his conversation partners. The key to his account is the concept of *construal*, the act of taking X as Y, a locution as a particular illocution. Construal operates across a range of strengths, and given that it may be weak, a 'constructive' account of interpretation need not be theologically reductive, attributing all meaning to the act of interpretation. As for the contribution speech-act theory may make to the practical task of interpretation, that does not lie in reconceiving interpretation as 'speech-act criticism', but in 'investigating certain types of strongly self-involving biblical language'; which is what B. proceeds to do in Part II: the types dealt with here are the confession of faith, the forgiveness of sin and teaching. This is an important work that should not be neglected by an interpreter of any part of the Bible who contemplates appealing to speech-act theory, or indeed to postmodern literary theory.

W.J. HOUSTON

BROWN, WILLIAM P. (ed.), *Character and Scripture: Moral Formation, Community, and Biblical Interpretation* (Grand Rapids, MI: Eerdmans, 2002), pp. xx + 440. $34.00/£24.99. ISBN 0-8028-4625-4.

The central part of this collection consists of 16 studies of biblical texts arranged in the order of the Christian canon: the Decalogue, the case of King David, 1 Chronicles 29.1-25, the prose story of Job, 'the way of the righteous' in the Psalms, the pedagogy of Prov. 10.1–31.9, virtue (specifically the two cardinal virtues, prudence and temperance) in the sages, Qoheleth, the character of God in Jeremiah, Israel among the great empires, the Lord's Prayer, character ethics in Paul, Paul's preaching of suffering, martyrdom in Philippians, moral typology in 2 Peter, and the pastoral implications of apocalyptic (Revelation, with Daniel). These are introduced by three general discussions of a 'virtue' or 'character' ethics under the heading 'The Scope and Limits of Character Ethics', and the book ends with a further three general discussions described as 'Practice', covering the centrality of worship in sustaining Christian character formation, ecology, and an African-American perspective on moral education. No close relation can be discerned between the introductory and concluding sections and the exegetical studies, which themselves are extremely diverse in approach and content. Several of the writers relate the biblical material directly to modern (American) society, of which they are highly critical. Strikingly, as a result of visits to Christian communities in Alaska, the Philippines, Zimbabwe, South Africa, Egypt and Iona, Larry L. Rasmussen argues that greater attention should be paid to Canaanite and Mesopotamian religion. Symposia need a good index; the index of subjects and names is woefully inadequate.

C.S. RODD

BROYLES, CRAIG C. (ed.), *Interpreting the Old Testament: A Guide for Exegesis* (Grand Rapids, MI: Baker Academic, 2001), pp. 272. $19.99. ISBN 0-8010-2271-1.

The two longest sections of this manual are the complementary programmatic treatments of 'Principles and Steps' in interpretation by B. and 'Reading the Old Testament as Literature' by V. Phillips Long. Other chapters deal with language and text; history and sociology; traditions, intertextuality and canon; history of religions and biblical theology; ANE studies; compositional history; and theology. Each is firmly grounded in theoretical issues but the orientation is thoroughly practical, setting out systematic approaches and providing worked examples and guides to further resources. B. calls for self-examination by the interpreter of assumptions brought to the task. His own are that Scripture is divinely inspired, but clothed in human forms which require scholarly study in order to establish meaning. The reader should be open to be challenged or changed, and to that end meditation is an essential element in the exegetical process. The book challenges those who read the Bible at face value to penetrate beneath the surface and mine its richness, and seeks to provide the tools and skills to do so. There is a noticeable element of apologetic for critical study, aimed at the evangelical constituency to which the contributors belong, but the sophistication of the procedures they set out will be of benefit to all serious students. The discussion of hermeneutical issues makes the work more suitable for those wishing to advance their interpretative skills than for beginners; the section on textual criticism presupposes knowledge of Hebrew, but other chapters can be read without it.

A.K. JENKINS

BRUEGGEMANN, WALTER, *Ichabod Toward Home: The Journey of God's Glory* (Grand Rapids, MI: Eerdmans, 2002), pp. ix + 150. $15.00/£10.99. ISBN 0-8028-3930-4.

Yahweh has had a great fall. Dagon will have a great fall. Can anyone put them together again? Certainly B. is able to craft a profound message of lament and hope from the pieces. At one level this is a provocative, inventive yet inspiring reading for today's church of the obscure Ark Narrative of 1 Samuel 4–6. But as befits the 2001 Stone Lectures at Princeton, on which this book is based, this narrative is the doorway to a much bigger topic: 'What must the Church do, when it stands before the biblical text?' Here B. challenges the Church to a non-foundational reading that seeks to participate in the guerrilla theatre of biblical texts, daring to hear an alternative to our prevailing Dagon-centred culture. This is vintage B. and subject to his usual strengths and weaknesses. The book is typically inter-disciplinary (psychology, sociology, philosophy) but risks oversimplification. Historical, canonical, literary and intertextual tools are used and perhaps abused. Academia will grimace at some of the gap-filling and liberties taken to bring the text alive with an avowedly ahistorical and arational method, while the church will writhe at the attack on cherished theologies. Moreover the application is specifically American and occasionally the powerful oral rhetoric makes for an awkward written text. Yet for all, this is a reading that needs to be heard if not always agreed with. This is a book written from faith to faith. It is applied canonical scholarship and in this genre it is another B. masterpiece.

E. HARPER

BRUEGGEMANN, WALTER, *The Bible Makes Sense* (Louisville, KY: Westminster John Knox Press, revised edn, 2001), pp. ix + 102. £9.99. ISBN 0-664-22495-4.

This slim volume is a revised version with a new introduction of a work first published in 1977. The new introduction is barely two-and-a-half pages in length, and notes some recent trends in the study of the Bible. The book is designed to help Christians make sense of parts of the Bible which are often misunderstood or avoided. The twofold purpose of the title is to indicate that the Bible is understandable and that it generates meaning. B. advocates a 'covenantal-historical' perspective, and argues that the Bible 'provides hints of an alternative notion of what our humanness is, human in *history*, human in *covenant*' (p. 11). Each chapter ends with points for reflection and discussion, and suggests (and offers brief comments on) Scripture passages for meditation. This format is likely to be particularly useful in discussion groups, and can help to make insights from the academy relevant to the church.

A.H.W. CURTIS

BRUEGGEMANN, WALTER, *The Land: Place as Gift, Promise, and Challenge in Biblical Faith* (Overtures to Biblical Theology; Minneapolis, MN: Fortress Press, 2nd edn, 2002), pp. xxvii + 225. $18.00. ISBN 0-8006-3462-4.

This book was first published in 1977 and this new edition has been updated throughout in the discussion, notes and bibliography. The most significant changes in B.'s thinking are explained in the new preface in pp. xi-xxiii. He highlights five major developments in OT studies that have particular relevance; the recovery of creation as an important motif; the recognition that claims about the 'promised land' are not innocent but rather ideological assertions; the concept of 'exile' as the defining motif for Israel's self-discernment; its use as a metaphor for self-understanding in both Judaism and Western Christianity; and the environmental crisis. Developments in critical method are also discussed to highlight much that B. regards as intuitive rather than rigorous in his original interpretive methodology. Changes within the main body of the text are not significant but additions to the bibliography demonstrate the fact that the theology of land has become a topic of greater interest among current scholarship. This remains a classic text on the subject.

J.E. TOLLINGTON

DAVIES, PHILIP R. and JOHN M. HALLIGAN (eds.), *Second Temple Studies III: Studies in Politics, Class and Material Culture* (JSOTSup, 340; London: Sheffield Academic Press, 2002), pp. ix + 246. $105.00/£55.00. ISBN 0-8264-6030-5.

This is the third volume to appear as a result of the productive meetings of the SBL Sociology of the Second Temple Group (a fourth is promised). Articles range in size from 5 to 35 pages, but their weight is not dependent on the number of pages, as even the briefest articles mount challenging arguments and bring fresh perspectives. Only two essays treat the Achaemenid period: K. Hoglund argues for a recognition of a rural social construct in Persian period Judaea, rather than the urban elite model; J.W. Wright stretches back to the Neo-Babylonian period to put analysis of urban Achaemenid Judah on a firmer footing. Five essays treat aspects of 'The "Hellenistic" Period(s)': L.L. Grabbe surveys Hengel's critics; K. Hoglund identifies social developments in Seleucid Palestine moving on from his previous piece; R.A. Horsley and P. Tiller re-examine Ben Sira concerning communal conflict, while a contrasting analysis is offered by J.M. Halligan who takes in a different cross-cut of evidence; R. Doran focuses on the role of Jewish education in the Seleucid period. A final section deals with the Hasmonaeans and their times: R.A. Horsley attends to political factors accounting for the expansion of Hasmonaean rule; J. Pasto makes a new case for speaking of 'normative Judaism' in the period; L.L. Grabbe reviews the data relating to the Hasmonaean period Samaritans. The whole collection is nicely introduced by Davies whose commentary on the articles itself demonstrates the vitality of the debate, and highlights the work needing to be done. This is a provocative collection, richly detailed, clearly argued. Further volumes from the Group are eagerly awaited.

D.J. REIMER

DE LA TORRE, MIGUEL A., *Reading the Bible from the Margins* (Maryknoll, NY: Orbis Books, 2002), pp. xii + 196. $20.00. ISBN 1-57075-410-1.

The origins of this book lie in a course of introductory lectures (in a school lacking ethnic and racial diversity) on how to distinguish biblical truth from scriptural interpretation by reading the Bible through the eyes of non-Euroamericans. This is 'reading from the margins'. The intended readership is scholars, preachers and lay people at all levels with little or no awareness of institutionalized segregation and the hermeneutical power of a dominant culture. This is 'reading from the centre'. Hermeneutics of the centre go for stability and status quo. Hermeneutics on the margin begin with the need for liberation and so produce interpretations which are constantly 'on the move'. Step by step D. unpicks the way in which traditional Western hermeneutics has been used to justify racism, sexism and classism, our society's 'dirty little secrets' which prevent our dysfunctional family from getting along together (p. 152). At least three groups of people should benefit from it: those in bondage but who don't know it, those who *think* they are liberated, and those who are on the way to liberation and in need of encouragement and further insight. This is not so much a book about how those on the margin read the Bible as about how those at the centre misread it, and it will be anathema to those who believe there is only ever one meaning. With its roots in North American society and the author's choice of targets and method of handling them, readers elsewhere will be tempted to feel that 'we are not like that', but the question that remains is, 'what then *are* we like?'

A. GILMORE

DE MOOR, JOHANNES C. and HARRY F. VAN ROOY (eds.), *Past, Present, Future: The Deuteronomistic History and the Prophets* (OTS, 44; Leidene: Brill, 2000), pp. ix + 342. €125.00/$151.00. ISBN 90-04-11871-3; ISSN 0169-7226.

The 19 essays in this collection originate in the first joint meeting of the Dutch and South African Old Testament Societies in 1999. Though the policy of arranging alphabetically by author obscures any coherence, one can nevertheless see that while Dutch and South African scholarship is still by and large fairly traditional, it occasionally produces some very fine reflections on the role of ideology in the production and reading of biblical texts. U. Berges sees 'the Servants' playing a major role in the composition of both Isaiah and the Psalms in the early Persian period. W. Boshoff considers the canonical reputation of the Northern Kingdom in the light of recent South African history. P. Botha examines royal etiquette in the Deuteronomistic Historian and A. Breytenbach locates the author of the Samuel Narrative in the days of Isaiah and Hezekiah. H.J.M. van Deventer ponders what the Deuteronomist is (still) doing in Daniel, while M. Dijkstra proposes another eighth century 'royal chronology', using the Samaria ostraca. E. Eynikel considers the relation between the Eli and Ark narratives; A. van der Kooij's contribution is a study of the Hezekiah and Sennacherib story; M. Koster fulminates against suggestions that the Bible is not based on history. H. Leene argues that 'inner renewal' in the Deuteronomistic material of Jeremiah is inspired by Ezekiel. J. de Moor seeks to trace the 'oldest stratum' of Genesis 49 to the end of the second millennium. E. Noort writes on the history of Joshua from Ephraimite chief to Commander-in-chief, and E. Peels discusses the historical background and literary context of Jer. 49.34-39. L. de Regt detects a shift of person as a genre feature in Hosea, while J. Renkema presents 'Data Relevant to the Dating of the Prophecy of Obadiah'. E. Scheffler rides to the rescue of Saul from the Deuteronomists and G. Snyman argues that 'Texts are Fundamentally Facts of Power, Not of Democratic Exchange', inserting a welcome note of hermeneutical sophistication. M. Terblanche rationalizes Jeremiah's absence in Kings, and J. Walsh suggests that 2 Kings 17 may be kinder to Samaritans than is usually thought.

P.R. DAVIES

DREYTZA, MANFRED, WALTER HILLBRANDS and HARTMUT SCHMID, *Das Studium des Alten Testaments: Eine Einführung in die Methoden der Exegese* (Giessen: Brunnen Verlag; Wuppertal: R. Brockhaus Verlag, 2002), pp. 213. €14.90. ISBN 3-7655-9471-7 (Brunnen); 3-417-29471-1 (Brockhaus).

This book presents an approach to OT exegesis that is both scholarly and theological. The material is organized into six chapters. The introductory chapter includes an explanation of interpretative goals and a comprehensive overview of the history of OT interpretation. The following chapters are concerned with textual issues, literary analysis, historical questions, theological questions, and practical suggestions for preparing lessons or sermons. Each chapter is illustrated with a variety of charts and diagrams. This volume is designed both to inform and to equip the reader for the multifaceted task of exegesis. In addition to the overview of the history of exegesis, there are several excursuses that describe and analyse historical-critical concerns such as *formgeschichte*, *literarkritik* and *traditionsgeschichte*. Each excursus details the history, method and possible difficulties of the specific approach. Each is strategically placed to compliment the subject matter of the relevant chapter. A variety of analytical tools for the synchronic analysis of texts are presented. The section on literary analysis includes information regarding linguistic and structural analysis. In the chapter on theological interpretation, the reader is encouraged to view the OT both as a text unto itself and as an integral part of a larger whole, as it interrelates with the NT to form a Christian canon. The authors situate their discussion at the nexus of scholarship and theology, and engage with the OT from this perspective. This results in a handbook that successfully moves the reader from analysis to application.

E. HAYES

EBACH, JÜRGEN, *Noah: Die Geschichte eines Überlebenden* (Biblische Gestalten, 3; Leipzig: Evangelische Verlagsanstalt, 2001), pp. 249. €14.50/SwF 26.50. ISBN 3-374-01912-9.

The exact aim of the series on 'Biblical Figures', to which this volume belongs, is not made clear. The impression gained from this particular contribution to the series is that its ultimate aim is to provide a basis for sermons, devotional activity, and finding the meaning of the text for a modern Christian audience. The point is made of how full of symbols (e.g., ark, dove, olive leaf, rainbow) the story of Noah is and how it resonates for later generations. The first part of the study (*Darstellung*) is mainly a commentary on particular aspects of the text (not the whole text by any means), looking at historical and literary background, theology, and intertextual relations of the Flood story. This seems to be primarily a preparation for the second part (*Wirkung*) which is devoted to the reception history of the story, involving everything from the Internet to the *Rainbow Warrior*.

L.L. GRABBE

FANT, CLYDE E., DONALD W. MUSSER and MITCHELL G. REDDISH (eds.), *An Introduction to the Bible* (rev. edn; Nashville: Abingdon Press, 2001), pp. 472. 133 illustrations. £24.99. ISBN 0-687-08456-3.

Making repeated reference to its function as an introduction to the Bible for undergraduate students, this 'budget' price, indexed book presents a wide range of explanations, with matt black and white photographs. Part I, 'Introduction to the Study of the Bible' incorporates 'The Bible and Western Culture', 'Methods and Tools for Studying the Bible', 'The Origins and Development of the Bible' and

'The Cultural and Geographic Context of the Bible'. Part II, 'Origins and Early Development of the Jewish Tradition' includes 'Hebrew Origins and Early History', 'The Era of the Judges', 'The United Kingdom and the Yahwistic History', 'The Divided Kingdom: Israel and Judah', 'The Institution of Prophecy', 'The Pre-exilic Prophets', 'The Exile, Exilic Prophets, and Exilic Histories', 'The Restoration of Judah', 'The Psalms and Wisdom Literature', 'Judaism in the Hellenistic and Roman Eras' and 'Daniel and the Books of the Apocrypha'. Part III, 'Origins and Early Development of the Christian Tradition' surveys 'The Life and Teachings of Jesus', 'The Development of the Gospels: From Oral Traditions to Mark', 'The Further Development of the Gospels: Matthew, Luke and John', 'The Development of the Early Church: The Acts of the Apostles', 'Paul and His Cultural Environment', 'Paul and His Writings', 'The Developing Institutional Church', 'The Church in Conflict'. The book's consensus position in biblical studies provides a 'baseline' from which to evaluate other works, while its incorporation of some recent advances in critical understanding and references to ambiguities and uncertainties within biblical 'knowledge' make it valuable for undergraduate study within more conservative environments.

H.A. MCKAY

FELDER, CAIN HOPE, *Race, Racism and the Biblical Narratives* (Facets; Minneapolis, MN: Fortress Press, 2002), pp. 54. $6.00. ISBN 0-8006-3578-7.

The argument of this essay is that the Bible contains no narratives in which the original intent was to view black people in an unfavourable way, but that there are examples of *sacralization*—in which cultural and historical phenomena are recast as theological truths serving the vested interests of particular groups—and *secularization*—in which religious insights give way to the dominant ideologies of the environment. Examples of sacralization are the curse of Ham, where justification of the subjugation of the Canaanites becomes attached to the tracing of three great branches of humanity to a common ancestor; the table of nations, no objective historical account but consciously arranged to give prominence to the descendants of Shem; and the doctrine of Israel's election, which becomes progressively more radical and exclusive. (It is less clear how Num. 12.1-16 fits into the argument.) In the NT election ceases to be ethnically or racially based, but the concentration on the spread of Christianity to Asia Minor and Europe has tended to suggest that nothing good can come out of Africa. This is the prime example of secularization, Christian writers falling prey to secular ideologies. F. provides a useful indication of what African Americans see when they read the Bible.

R. TOMES

FOKKELMAN, JAN P., *Comment lire le récit biblique: Une introduction pratique* (Le livre et le rouleau, 13; Brussels: Éditions Lessius, 2001), pp. 239. €19.00. ISBN 2-87299-111-5.

This book is translated from the Dutch by the Cistercians of the abbey of Notre-Dame of Clairefontaine. F. provides a detailed and exhaustive, without being wearying, introduction to the practice of narratological and structural readings of biblical texts. He works mainly with 12 texts drawn from Genesis, Judges, Samuel and Kings, but refers to many others, providing one chapter on reading NT texts. He explicates the fundamental elements of narrative artistry, namely, the narrator, the characters, the hero(ine), time and space, perspective, values, prose and poetry in this practical guidebook for readers on how to discover (a) what a text actually 'says' and (b) to appreciate the means by which the text 'says' it. The book is written mainly for those without Hebrew or Greek, and, I believe, should be read in the order of its presentation since the level and complexity of the work provided increases as the book proceeds. F. expects his readers to read the Bible 'actively' and requests the application of 'obstinate, enthusiastic enquiry'. Finally, F. provides a list of 110 biblical stories with some pointers for their penetration and a sequence of ten questions to be put to any narrative under study in order to identify the hero, the 'quest', the helpers and opponents, the perspective of the author/narrator, time frame(s) and gaps, mistakes, deceit and self-deception, the role of dialogue, key words or repetitions, openings and closures. The English version of this book should prove valuable to any student of biblical studies, and the worked examples to tutors and Bible study leaders alike.

H.A. McKay

FOKKELMAN, J.P., *The Psalms in Form: The Hebrew Psalter in its Poetic Shape* (Tools for Biblical Studies, Series 4; Leiden: Deo Publishing, 2002), pp. 172. £29.95. ISBN 90-5854-017-0.

'This book sets out to demonstrate the crucial value of the correct division of the text.' These words, from the author's introduction (p. 10), are part of the explanation for what otherwise may seem extravagant—a volume that employs great care, and a large format (A4 pages), to clarify the structure of the psalms, namely their divisions and subdivisions. The book contains three parts: I: Introduction (pp. 9-13); II: The Hebrew Psalter in its poetic shape (pp. 15-154); III: Annotations and remarks (pp. 155-72). The volume receives backing from F.'s other publications on the psalms. The objectives of this work—to clarify the text's divisions and to indicate the connection between accurate division and well-founded interpretation—correspond broadly to objectives laid out by J. Muilenberg in his landmark presidential address to the SBL (1968) and to the objectives of the Pericope series published by Van Gorcum (Assen). As well as clarifying divisions, F. also clarifies unity; he aims 'to confront the reader with the linguistic work of art itself, in a direct visual contact that is as free from contamination as possible. Our option for a larger format has enabled us to ensure that, in most cases, each of the 148 poems occupies one page, so that the whole of the composition may be seen at a glance...' (p. 9). In the decisive process of clarifying divisions this elegant book sets a new standard.

T. BRODIE

GERTZ, JAN CHRISTIAN, KONRAD SCHMID and MARKUS WITTE (eds.), *Abschied vom Jahwisten: Die Komposition des Hexateuch in der jüngsten Diskussion* (BZAW, 315; Berlin: W. de Gruyter, 2002), pp. xi + 345. €98.00. ISBN 3-11-017121-X.

By trying to bid farewell to the Yahwist this important volume of essays hints at the directions pentateuchal criticism will take in the next generation. J.-L. Ska opens the collection with reminiscences of the many ways in which the Yahwist has been represented by scholars; the only hope for those who still believe in his existence is a leap of faith so that his plot can be described. A. de Pury considers that the undetermined and unqualified use of אלהים in most of the Pentateuch is a hallmark of P himself, not an Elohist. J. Blenkinsopp re-labels some J material in Genesis 1–11 as a postexilic lay source familiar with the Deuteronomistic History. J.C. Gertz describes the redactional history of Genesis 15 without recourse to the Yahwist, but discovers the earliest strand to be a form of patriarchal history written over against the Exodus narrative. K. Schmid proposes that the Joseph narratives were an independent pre-priestly cycle created as a critical response to Exodus to which it was connected after P to form a bridge between Genesis 12–36 and Exodus 1. E. Blum argues that Exodus 3 is the first programmatic composition of the pre-priestly D while other non-priestly elements at the end of Genesis and start of Exodus belong to a later Hexateuchal redaction. H.-C. Schmitt suggests that Exod. 34.10-28 belongs to the final deuteronomic redaction of the Pentateuch. T.B. Dozeman analyses Numbers 20–21, especially with regard to its geographical and geopolitical statements, concluding that it may represent an independent author, though not the early monarchical J historian. M. Witte arranges Numbers 22–24 into layers, all of which he assigns to post-priestly and post-deuteronomic authorship. T.C. Römer radicalizes the insights of M. Noth to show that Numbers is a Persian period link between the priestly Tetrateuch and Deuteronomy which has been separated from the Deuteronomistic History. A.G. Auld disposes of J by showing how parts of Numbers 11–12 and 22–24 are indebted to Samuel. W. Johnstone uses the reminiscences in Deuteronomy to recover a D-version of events in Exodus and Numbers, eliminating the need for J. E.A. Knauf muses on the stratigraphy of the Hexateuch and offers likely dates for the various parts which might make even the most biblicist of archaeologists blush. R.G. Kratz looks at pre- and post-priestly expansions of the Hexateuch. It is clear from these studies that the discussion has changed character, but it now appears to be going in several directions at once.

G.J. BROOKE

GILLINGHAM, SUSAN, *The Image, the Depths and the Surface: Multivalent Approaches to Biblical Study* (JSOTSup, 354; London: Sheffield Academic Press, 2002), pp. xi + 147. £55.00. ISBN 1-84127-297-3.

In this book G. offers three multivalent readings of OT passages. Her purpose is to show the limitations of the enlightenment concerns of modernist interpreters since the early nineteenth century who supposed that they could find the original historical setting of a text and, from this, one particular correct meaning. Though resisting the permissive force of postmodernist hermeneutics, G. does go as far as arguing that biblical texts are indeterminate in an objective sense. Since much of G.'s research time has been spent in interpreting the Psalms, it is not surprising that she is frustrated with an approach which is restricted to deriving meaning from known historical settings. In place of such unitary assumptions G. illustrates her approach from three texts for which she sees multiple tradents and multiple literary contexts. For Genesis 2–3 the meanings of the text rest with the wise, with prophets, with the court, and/or with more popular and familial circles, each of several different time periods, and the ever-widening literary context of the chapters, even including the NT, alters the significance of the passage radically depending upon which context forms its backdrop. For the poetic ambiguities of Psalm 23 G. considers the meanings belonging both to court officials, cultic prophets and/or even a high priest, and also to its ever-widening literary contexts, from those of its neighbouring psalms to the HB as a whole, and even within the Christian Bible as the fulfilment of prophecy. For Amos 5 and its concern with justice and righteousness she considers the prophet himself, his disciples, Josianic redactors, and/or exilic compilers, and she assesses the range of literary contexts from the role of the passage within Amos itself through to its place in the Twelve, the HB and the Christian Bible. Overall she concludes that no one meaning can be prioritized over another; a postmodern pluralist view is appropriate. But it must be said that each of G.'s range of meanings is derived from a carefully reconstructed historical scenario; it is not that any interpretation is valid, but that interpretation must be grounded in the readings of others, usually the ancients. G.'s almost exclusive focus on readings within what is known now as scriptural, for either Jews or Western Christians, offers a kind of canonical set of readings. However, overall G.'s work represents an intriguing halfway house between the naive historicist tendencies of the early modernists and the full-blown anti-historical readings of the postmodern relativists.

G.J. BROOKE

GOLKA, FRIEDEMANN W., *Joseph: biblische Gestalt und literarische Figur* (Thomas Manns Beitrag zur Bibelexegese; Stuttgart: Calwer Verlag, 2002), pp. 220. €19.90. ISBN 3-7668-3788-5.

Thomas Mann is far-famed for his quartet of biblical novels, one on Jacob, the other three on the lives of Joseph and his brothers. Following on a previous study of Mann's first volume, G. has here provided a similar assessment of Mann's contribution as (in his own way) an expositor, or at least interpreter, of the biblical narrative. Many of the individual episodes are reviewed in this light, particularly the Judah/Tamar incident (Gen. 38) and Jacob's final blessing and decease (Gen. 49), considered to be at once integral to the whole Jacob–Joseph cycle, but (more narrowly) extraneous to the story of Joseph himself. In G.'s view, Mann was far ahead of his time, in employing a form of 'canonical criticism', by concentrating his work on the final text (and distrusting conventional literary-critical speculation), and also in indulging in 'readerly response' along the way; Scripture was used to interpret Scripture. But less so (one might suggest) in invoking mythology from outside the HB, such as the largely irrelevant Tammuz-myth (still misunderstood during most of the twentieth century). G. seemingly attributes the Joseph narrative to the Persian epoch; a date lacking any objective evidence, and contradicted by Egyptian data that would point to a much earlier period for at least its origins. An interesting interplay of novelist, 'Alttestamentler' and biblical text.

K.A. KITCHEN

GREIFENHAGEN, F.V., *Egypt on the Pentateuch's Ideological Map: Constructing Biblical Israel's Identity* (JSOTSup, 361; London: Sheffield Academic Press, 2002), pp. xi + 325. £65.00. ISBN 0-8264-6211-1.

Considering the number of times Egypt is mentioned in the Pentateuch (about 375 times), an investigation of the usage of this term was called for. It has now been undertaken in this revised PhD thesis (Duke University, supervised by J.L. Crenshaw). In his introduction, G. shows how 'Egypt' has often been read from a historical and geographical perspective. The question is whether this is the only way—or even the best way—to understand the usage of the term in the Pentateuch. He takes the course of looking at usage from the rhetorical, literary and—ultimately —the ideological perspective. G. argues that the usage should be understood in the historical context of the Pentateuch's composition, which he concludes is most likely by a loyalist elite during the Persian period, perhaps during one of the Persian empire's troubles with Egypt. The generally negative view of Egypt predominates in the Pentateuch, but this is partly the result of editing: the present text tries to subordinate the earlier view that Israel somehow originated in Egypt to the view that Israel's roots were in Mesopotamia (i.e., the sojourn in Egypt was only a temporary event to be quickly skipped over). In the Persian period, with the Jewish concern over intermarriage and alien influences, Egypt would have been a symbol of 'the other'. The contrast between Israel and Egypt served one of the Pentateuch's main concerns, which is to construct Israel's identity.

L.L. GRABBE

GROSBY, STEVEN ELLIOTT, *Biblical Ideas of Nationality: Ancient and Modern* (Winona Lake, IN: Eisenbrauns, 2002), pp. x + 269. $29.50. ISBN 1-57506-065-5.

Although the fact is not reflected in the title or the 'cataloging-in-publication' data, this is a collection of reprints of ten articles by the author, extending in date from 1991 to 2001. This does not lessen the usefulness of the book, though it does mean, as often with reprint collections of this kind, that there is a considerable degree of repetition and overlap between the chapters. This reader at least would have benefited from a more continuous and coherent account of the theme. The 'ideas' of the title are, of course, modern sociological ideas applied to ancient society, including Ancient Israel. As it is, there is much for the student of the ancient world to ponder on in G.'s articles. He makes a good case for accepting the relevance of the category 'nation' to some of the collectivities encountered in anti- quity (against the sociological mainstream, represented, for example, by E. Gellner, which has argued that the concept of nationality is exclusive to modern societies). Several of the essays concern Israel and Aram, while the cases of Edom and Armenia are also used in illustrative discussion. Of particular note are the chapters on 'Religion and Nationality in Antiquity: The Worship of Yahweh and Ancient Israel' (pp. 13-51; first appeared in the *European Journal of Sociology* 1991) and 'Kinship, Territory, and the Nation in the Historiography of Ancient Israel' (pp. 52-68; *ZAW* 1993). The role of religion and monolatry in the emergence of the nation of Israel is emphasized (though with full awareness that this emergence was late rather than early). Also very interesting is a chapter on 'Borders, Territory, and Nationality in the Ancient Near East and Armenia' containing an important section on Aram (pp. 120-49; *JESHO* 1997). And another chapter is devoted specifically to Aram (pp. 150-65; *Aram* 1995). There is also material on such topics as 'The Nation of the United States and the Vision of Ancient Israel' (pp. 213-34; from *Nationality, Patriotism, and Nationalism*, ed. R. Michener, 1993). Valuable insights are to be found throughout the book, including the encouraging statement that 'many of the best minds of our civilization have been devoted to the study of the Old Testament'! (p. 14). Indexes make it possible to trace themes that recur in different chapters.

J.F. HEALEY

HAHN, JOHANNES (ed.), *Zerstörungen des Jerusalemer Tempels: Geschehen–Wahrnehmung–Bewältigung* (WUNT, 147; Tübingen: Mohr Siebeck, 2002), pp. viii + 279. €89.00. ISBN 3-16-147719-7.

The papers in this volume were first delivered at an interdisciplinary colloquium in Münster in November 2000, as part of a grand research project on 'Funktionen von Religion in antiken Gesellschaften des Vorderen Orients'. As the editor explains in his preface, since the Jerusalem Temple is the best documented temple from antiquity, in terms of its history, archaeology and functions, and in terms of reflection on its destruction, the colloquium was tasked with furnishing a paradigm for a subdivision of this project on 'Temples and Temple-destructions—the Loss of Religious Centres'. As a result the colloquium met with a clear brief, and an overarching question, which the individual contributors attempted to address. This gives a conceptual unity to the volume that is all too often missing in conference proceedings. It contains the following essays: W. Mayer, 'Die Zerstörung des Jerusalemer Tempels 587 v. Chr. im Kontext der Praxis von Heiligtumszerstörungen im antiken Vorderen Orient'; R. Albertz, 'Die Zerstörung des Jerusalemer Tempels 587 v. Chr. Historische Einordnung und religionspolitische Bedeutung'; K.-F. Pohlmann, 'Religion in der Krise—Krise einer Religion. Die Zerstörung des Jerusalemer Tempels 587 v. Chr.'; A. Cordes, T. Hansberger and E. Zenger, 'Die Verwüstung des Tempels—Krise der Religion? Beobachtungen zum Volkesklagepsalm 74 und seiner Rezeption in der Septuaginta und in Midrasch Tehillim'; H. Lichtenberger, 'Der Mythos von Unzerstörbarkeit des Tempels'; F. Siegert, '"Zerstört diesen Tempel...!" Jesus als "Tempel" in der Passionsüberlieferungen'; S. Lücking, 'Die Zerstörung des Tempels 70 n. Chr. als Krisenerfahrung des frühen Christen'; S. Panzram, 'Der Jerusalemer Tempel und das Rom der Flavier'; K. Schmid, 'Die Zerstörung Jerusalems und seines Tempels als Heilsparadox. Zur Zusammenführun von Geschichtstheologie und Anthropologie im Vierten Esrabuch'; G. Stemberger, 'Reaktionen auf Tempelzerstörung in der rabbinischen Literatur'; J. Hahn, 'Kaiser Julian und dritter Tempel? Idee, Wirklichkeit und Wirkung eines gescheiterten Projektes'. The papers are uniformly of a high standard, and in sum make a substantial contribution to an important subject.

P.S. ALEXANDER

HALIVNI, DAVID WEISS, *Revelation Restored* (Radical Traditions: Theology in a Postcritical Key; London: SCM Press, 2001), pp. xxvi + 114. £13.95. ISBN 0-33402860-4.

H. argues that recognition of the Pentateuch's inconsistencies has characterized learned Jewish commentary within the context of firm religious belief ever since Ezra established the Torah as foundation of a renewed Judaism. The similar recognition upon which modern critical scholarship is based can therefore equally well be combined with religious commitment. H. maintains that the Pentateuch as revealed by God to Moses on Sinai was perfect, but spoilt by Israel's sin. Imperfections remained in Ezra's editorial restoration of the text but this demands reverence as absolutely sacred and unalterable. The tension between such respect and the practical need for sensible exposition is illustrated by reference to rabbinic commentary down the ages. H.'s overall argument is lucid and scholarly, but this series claims to provide theological commitment informed by rational inquiry and in that context the book raises important issues. For example, scholars who read the biblical history differently from H. are not necessarily being reductionist. And if the response of the religiously persuaded mind is crucial for the proper understanding of biblical history, why should H.'s be preferred to Wellhausen's? (p. 10, cf. Peter Ochs, first Foreword, p. xvii). The relationship between a profoundly venerated, inviolable sacred text and very varied grasp of its meaning requires further investigation and elucidation. Likewise, the mediaeval notion 'that God...could not have created an imperfect instrument, subject to human corruption' (p. 7), is not so easily dismissed. And why was the revelation given to Moses and the unreceptive rather than to Ezra and the penitent?

P. ADDINALL

HARRISVILLE, ROY A. and WALTER SUNDBERG, *The Bible in Modern Culture: Baruch Spinoza to Brevard Childs* (Grand Rapids, MI: Eerdmans, 2nd edn, 2002), pp. xiii + 349. $25.00/£17.99. ISBN 0-8028-3992-4.

This second edition differs from the first (reviewed in *B.L.* 1996, p. 80) mainly in the addition of chapters on A. Schlatter, P. Ricoeur and B. Childs, together with the revision of the introductory and concluding material. These new chapters follow the pattern of the existing ones that cover interpreters from B. Spinoza to E. Käsemann. As with their predecessors, they provide admirably clear accounts of the work of the chosen scholars set in the context of what the authors call 'confessional criticism', which presents the history of historical criticism with a noticeably Lutheran flavour. The book's scope remains much narrower than the title might suggest and it would have been helpful to have had a consolidated bibliography for student reference. It continues to be useful for students in representing an informed and thought-provoking critique of historical criticism from a conservative protestant rather than postmodern standpoint.

H.S. PYPER

HEITHER, THERESIA, *Schriftauslegung: Das Buch Exodus bei den Kirchenvätern* (Neuer Stuttgarter Kommentar, Altes Testament, 33.4; Stuttgart: Katholisches Bibelwerk, 2002), pp. 221. €22.90. ISBN 3-460-07334-9.

Interpretations of the book of Exodus by 29 Church Fathers from the second to the sixth centuries CE are reviewed. Pride of place is given to Origen, with Augustine the next most frequently cited. The work is most helpfully arranged, with major pervading themes discussed first ('Egypt', 'Moses', Pharaoh', 'wilderness', 'manna', 'Law'), then the sections of the book considered in sequence. Equally helpful are the summaries of the interpretations about to be illustrated in the often-extensive citations in German translation, usually by the author herself, from the primary sources. Because no single continuous commentary on Exodus is extant among the Fathers (even Origen's is fragmentary), these comments are typically from sermons; the prevailing tone is thus homiletic and heavily Christocentric. Essentially, the Fathers follow the lead of the NT: 'these things were written for our sakes'. Their interest lies more in what they take to be the kernel of the matter, the moral, mystical, typological significance, rather than the husk, the literal, historic meaning. The OT is to NT as shadow is to reality; it foretells, prefigures, symbolizes. The copious materials supplied in Exodus for understanding the sacraments of baptism and eucharist, and the central festivals of Easter and Pentecost, and numerous motifs besides, provide the Fathers with a field-day. Processes taking place in worshippers' minds and psyches as they engage with and assimilate the significance of the text for themselves are uncovered—and therein the collection remains interesting and valid. But the Fathers' polemical tone is often jarring; H., sympathetic interpreter of them as she is, is constrained to acknowledge that their allegorical interpretation, for example, on the Tabernacle, is sometimes far-fetched ('etwas gesucht', p. 193). This volume is thus meant to be balanced by its companion-piece by D. Krochmalnik, *Schriftauslegung: Das Buch Exodus in der jüdischen Ausle-gungstradition*, vol. 33.3 in the same series (see *B.L.* 2002, p. 130).

W. JOHNSTONE

HELM, PAUL and CARL TRUEMAN (eds.), *The Trustworthiness of God: Perspectives on the Nature of Scripture* (Leicester: Apollos; Grand Rapids, MI: Eerdmans, 2002). pp. xiv + 289. £14.99. ISBN 0-85111-476.8.

In the introduction the editors explain the title and the nature of this work, the very title of which may raise eyebrows. 'Is there any Christian theologian worth his or her salt who would argue that God is inherently untrustworthy? The answer, of course, is almost certainly "No". Nevertheless there are degrees of trustworthiness, and there are forms of trustworthiness; and the purpose of this volume is to explore, from the biblical, systematic, philosophical, and historical perspectives, the nature and the implications of the trustworthiness of the God portrayed in the Bible and worshipped in the Christian Church for some two thousand years.' The book is written for Christians who believe that God has spoken, and wish to learn how this notion of a speaking, trustworthy God is reflected within the Bible and in Christian theology. The editors and contributors hope that the essays in this volume will not re-ignite the fires of past unpleasantness with regard to the issues raised. The essays are arranged in three major sections, followed by two responses. Four essays for the OT treatment of history, theology and reliability in Deuteronomy: 'A Faithful God who Does no Wrong', by J.G. Millar; 'Divine Speech and the Book of Jeremiah', by J.G. McConville; 'The Revelation of God in the Old Testament Wisdom Literature', by C.G. Bartholomew, and 'Lying Spirit Sent by God: The Case of Micaiah's Prophecy', by P.J. Williams. Essays on the themes in the NT are on Jesus and Scripture (D. Macleod), Paul's view of Scripture and the faithfulness of God (D. Williams), and God and Scripture in Hebrews (D. Peterson). Among the six essays on historical, systematic and philosophical perspectives, two are by the editors: 'The God of Unconditional Promise' (Trueman) and 'The Perfect Trust-worthiness of God' (Helm). McConville has an excellent treatment of the Book of Jeremiah, and the theme of this volume. Bartholomew also has a very good treatment of the wisdom literature and God's self-revelation. There is much on what implications the belief in the trustworthiness of God might have for the literal interpretation of Gospel and NT passages, and of fulfilment of the prophecies in Christ, God's 'Yes', his 'Amen' to them. More might have been said on the believer's experience of God's way in the Bible narratives themselves, and God's refusal, so to speak, to explain his ways (Jeremiah, Job and the Yahweh speeches); also God's expressed change of mind (as in Jer. 18.8-10) with regard to his own words of doom or welfare. There is question not so much of the truth of Scripture as of the nature of scriptural discourse. While Paul can say that all the prophecies have their YES in Christ, he well knows that God's judgments are unsearchable and his ways inscrutable. A major flaw in this work is the absence of any index.

M. MCNAMARA

HENS-PIAZZA, GINA, *The New Historicism* (Guides to Biblical Scholarship; Old Testament Series; Minneapolis, MN: Fortress Press, 2002), pp. viii + 94. $11.00. ISBN 0-8006-2989-2.

Arthur Marwick wrote long ago that the best thing to do with the word 'histori-cism' was to avoid it. H.-P.'s volume illustrates the wisdom of this advice, although that is not her intention. 'New Historicism refuses identification and explication as method' and 'provides no creed for its practitioners' since its 'overarching feature is its resistance to definition' (p. 75). Subjectivity is 'crucial to the work of New Historicists' (p. 45) and '[i]t refuses to privilege reality over text, instead under-standing that reality is constructed by texts' (p. 41). New Historicism is more 'an ethos...than anything approximating a method'. We are therefore not surprised that New Historicism is coy about illustrating itself since this might suggest some clear idea of method, 'the very notion from which New Historicists recoil'. Yet a bemused H.-P. confesses, 'to avoid illustration of what is being discussed makes the prospects for a New Historicism in biblical studies remote' (p. 55). And some might add, the remoter the better. Sometimes it seems that anything goes, at other times that the New Historicist has a privileged access to reality enabling her to correct faulty interpretation. If, for example, a subjective response to historical evidence produces a text which 'defines' historical reality why should feminist readings of biblical texts be preferred to interpretations inspired by a Prussian military mentality? The explication of scholarship in which lack of definition is a virtue and inherent confusion an achievement is a daunting task, not helped in this instance by quaintly 'crafted' phraseology and a liberal use of metaphor.

P. ADDINALL

HILLMAN, JORDAN JAY, *The Torah and Its God: A Humanist Inquiry* (Amherst, NY: Prometheus Books, 2001), pp. 581. $40.00. ISBN 1-57392-820-8.

'What remains of the Torah when we openly acknowledge that its God exists in the human mind alone?' asks H. The answer, it seems, is a great deal. H., an avowed atheist, but an atheist tenacious of his Jewish heritage, hopes by this work 'to foster an appreciation of the humanist values' underlying the Torah's creation by its human authors. The work is in form a commentary on the entire five books of the Torah, with a concise running exposition broken up by 'comments' which tackle the many cruces of the text, whether historical, literary, logical, or theological. H. is not a professional biblical scholar, but a scholar of civil law, and makes very little use of existing scholarship, though he accepts the Documentary Hypothesis and relies on R.E. Friedman for source attributions. The result is that unlike the run of professional commentators, he discusses the text rather than scholarship on the text, interrogating it with lawyerly shrewdness. The flavour may be suggested by his paraphrase of the 'Third Commandment': 'Do not claim to justify in God's name what cannot be justified in humanity's name'. The conclusion distinguishes the Torah's 'dated peculiarities', including all the worship of God, from its 'timeless concerns', which are human-directed, and of which he makes a Dodecalogue! The work may be used with profit by any reader of the Pentateuch, scholar or lay person, Jew or Gentile, theist or atheist.

W.J. HOUSTON

HOGAN, MAURICE P. (ed.), *Order and History.* I. *Israel and Revelation* (The Collected Works of Eric Voegelin, 14; Columbia, MI: University of Missouri Press, 2001), pp. ix + 606. $100.00. ISBN 0-8262-1351-0.

Voegelin's magisterial treatment of Israel's particular form of historical consciousness in the context of ANE history first appeared in 1956 as the initial part of his five-volume work on *Order and History*. It is beautifully reprinted here as one of the 34 volume set of his *Collected Works* being issued by the University of Missouri Press. The excellent introduction by H. gives a good sense of the book's continued importance. Voegelin's thesis is that the literature of the OT bears witness under the rubric of revelation to a remarkable reconfiguration of the relationship between cosmic and social order which has had a lasting effect in the political organization of the modern international order. Voegelin was not an OT specialist, but he shows a notably confident and critical grasp of the scholarship current in his day. Of course much has changed, but at a time when questions about what we mean by the historicity of the OT are as live as ever, Voegelin does offer a philosophical grounding to such debates. While this may now seem of its time, his work should remind us that the epistemological foundations of any understanding of history cannot be taken for granted and the political consequences of the biblical enterprise need to be taken fully into account.

H.S. PYPER

JANZEN, DAVID, *Witch-hunts, Purity and Social Boundaries: The Expulsion of the Foreign Women in Ezra 9–10* (JSOTSup, 350; London: Sheffield Academic Press, 2002), pp. x + 179. £55.00. ISBN 1-84127-292-2.

A number of explanations have been given for the divorcing of the 'foreign' wives in Ezra 9–10 but, according to J., none is convincing. His novel thesis (based in part on social anthropology) is that the explusion was a type of 'witchhunt', that is, the act of a social group to blame a sub-group for social dissension for which the sub-group is not responsible. This is most likely to happen in situations in which there are strong external social boundaries but weak internal boundaries. J. argues that the Jewish community in Persian Yehud set boundaries against outsiders but felt threatened because of increased trade and the presence of Persian administrative officials. The community of Yehud suffered anxiety about social integration because of these 'foreign' influences. The witch-hunt thus functioned as a ritualized act of purification for the community, since there was no obvious target for blame or resolution. In order to evaluate this interesting and innovative thesis, several points not adequately considered by J. need to be taken into account. His thesis requires the Ezra account to be historical, not just generally but also in its details. He asserts that this is the case, despite himself considering the decree of Artaxerxes (Ezra 7.12-26) inauthentic and without responding to the problems pointed out in some of my publications that he cites. J. must also assume that the Ezra account represents the view of all the community, but the details in Nehemiah suggest that the community was at least split and perhaps even that the 'anti-foreigner' view was a minority one. The anxiety that J. postulates for the people of Yehud is not convincing in my view. Yet this is a challenging book and should be read by anyone interested in Persian Yehud.

L.L. GRABBE

JOHNSON, MARSHALL D., *Making Sense of the Bible: Literary Type as an Approach to Understanding* (Grand Rapids, MI: Eerdmans, 2002), pp. ix + 161. $12.00/£8.99. ISBN 0-8028-4919-9.

This elementary introduction to the Bible is organized through the genres of the writings. The central chapters deal in turn with the wisdom literature, poetry of worship, historical narratives, prophetic literature, legal collections, apocalyptic literature, letters and the gospels, inevitably fairly sketchily in such a short work. Despite this literary approach, the basic principle which underlies the book is that '*all writings must have had a meaning for their first readers*—or at least, the author must have thought so' (pp. 2–3 [author's italics], cf. pp. 33, 38, 63, 79 for examples). Thus the 'intentional fallacy' is firmly rejected.

C.S. RODD

JUNGBAUER, HARRY, *'Ehre Vater und Mutter': Der Weg des Elterngebots in der biblischen Tradition* (WUNT, 2.146; Tübingen: Mohr Siebeck, 2002), pp. xv + 445. €69.00. ISBN 3-16-147680-8; ISSN 0340-9570.

The commandment to honour one's parents provides a major feature of the OT Decalogue and engages with a fundamental aspect of biblical ethical teaching. J.'s dissertation comprises three very extensive units, together with introductory and concluding sections noting some wider issues of method and interpretation. These three large units cover, respectively, the expression and interpretation of the commandment in the OT, in intertestamental Literature and in the NT writings. The OT section covers not only the two formulations of the Decalogue in Exod. 20.2-17 and Deut. 5.6-21, but also the prohibition on the cursing of parents in Exod. 21.12, 15-17 and echoes of the demand for respect towards parents in other writings. J. sees in the commandment a fundamental principle (*Grundnorm*) of the OT regard for the family as a social and economic unit, with primary emphasis upon the duty of economic support for ageing parents. Besides interpretations of the commandment in the LXX and Apocrypha, the section dealing with intertestamental literature covers Qumran, Philo, Josephus and early rabbinic writings. The treatment of the NT provides a major focus with special attention given to Jesus' criticism of those who fail to comply with the commandment (Mk 7.9-13), and the extension of the idea of the family to include members of the emerging Christian community. Altogether this is a fine contribution to the ethical teaching of the Bible seeing the family as the most basic social unit, and exploring the way in which the duties and obligations of family life provide a foundational ethical norm for life as a community of God.

R.E. CLEMENTS

KESSLER, RAINER and PATRICK VANDERMEERSCH (eds.), *God, Biblical Stories and Psychoanalytic Understanding* (Frankfurt am Main: Peter Lang, 2001), pp. 199. £24.00. ISBN 3-631-37641-3; 0-8204-5366-8 (USA).

This collection of 11 essays originated in an 'intensive program' on psychoanalysis and the reading of religious texts held in Groningen, Barcelona and Marburg. The reader is treated as seriously as the text, but the degree to which Freudian and post-Freudian theory is applied varies considerably between the contributions. Even those whose interpretations depend most firmly on these theories are cautious, recognizing the difference between living clients and silent texts. P. Vandermeersch discusses principles, R. Kessler describes Exod. 4.24-26 as a 'Freudian slip'. H. Raguse, J. Carlander and P.E. Jongsma-Tieleman examine from psychoanalytic perspectives Esther, the Saul-David story, and the creation of Eve respectively. J. Ribera and E. Giralt look at rabbinic treatments of the woman figure in Genesis, and E. Cortés discusses Midrash Esther Rabba. C. Thierfelder discusses the work of Ana-Maria Rizzuto and G. Luttikhuizen finds strong Aristotelian influence in the *Apocryphon of John*. E. Noort's study of vengeance in the HB and P. Vandermeersch's discussion of the ways the condemnation of homosexuality in the story of Sodom is avoided by modern readers may appeal most to OT scholars.

C.S. RODD

KORPEL, MARJO C.A. and JOSEF M. OESCH (eds.), *Studies in Scriptural Unit Division* (Pericope, 3; Assen: Van Gorcum, 2002), pp. viii + 288. €70.00. ISBN 90-232-3840-0; ISSN 1568-3443.

Until recently, scholars have generally ignored the contribution that can be provided by ancient manuscript witnesses of biblical texts in respect of layout. The present volume continues work initiated by the editors (see *B.L.* 2002, pp. 86 and 129-30). As explained in the preface, by the editors, 'The ancient scribes...have left us various methods of text division: dots, colometrical writing, many different paragraph markings, various types of spaces, blank lines all intended to enable the reader to discern the structure of the text better' (p. vii). The following texts have been examined in this way: Jeremiah 30–31 (B. Becking), Mic. 2.1-13 (J.C. de Moor), the Byzantine manuscripts of Ezra-Nehemiah (Th. Janz), Proverbs, in the light of the Septuagint (J. Cook), four major Septuagint manuscripts (W. de Bruin), Ben Sira (K.D. Jenner and W.T. van Peursen), the Greek text of Ezekiel in P[967] (J.W. Olley) and Psalms 1–14 in the Aleppo Codex (P. Sanders). The final chapter gives the findings of a workshop during the Rome Meeting of the Pericope Group in 2001, led by J.C. de Moor on unit delimitation in Mic. 4.14–5.8, with sample texts. The book includes indexes of authors and of texts. Of course, the reliability of the divisions as transmitted by the manuscripts varies, but scholars must now take account of this evidence.

W.G.E. WATSON

KUSTÁR, ZOLTÁN, *'Durch seine Wunden sind wir geheilt': Eine Untersuchung zur Metaphorik von Israels Krankheit und Heilung im Jesajabuch* (BWANT, 154; Stuttgart: W. Kohlhammer, 2002), pp. 259. €35.00/SwF 60.70. ISBN 3-17-016973-4.

This revised Halle dissertation is another in the growing number of studies which takes a particular theme as the basis for an investigation into the connections between the various parts of the book of Isaiah. Following introductory chapters on the current state of Isaiah research and the theme of chastisement and sickness elsewhere in the OT, the author devotes a chapter in turn to each occurrence of the theme in Isaiah: 1.4-8; 6.10; 30.18-26; 33.24; 36–39; 52.13–53.12; and 57.14-19. Each passage is thoroughly and carefully analysed, and indeed there are occasions when the discussion perhaps goes rather further than the main topic warrants. K.'s primary interest, however, is in what the relationship between these passages can tell us about the redaction-history and growth of the Isaianic corpus. On this he has many perceptive and interesting suggestions to advance. Although he seeks to relate his conclusions to other more broadly based studies it is difficult to escape the impression that sometimes he is building rather a lot on a narrow foundation. Nevertheless, because of the care with which he works his arguments will demand the most respectful attention in future.

H.G.M. WILLIAMSON

LAMP, IDA and THOMAS MEURER, *Bibel* (Basiswissen: Gütersloher Taschenbücher, 673; Gütersloh: Gütersloher Verlagshaus, 2002), pp. 95. €6.90/SwF 12.80. ISBN 3-579-00673-8.

This little book is unashamedly Christian in approach, but nevertheless it makes some incisive comments about how the OT and the Bible as a whole might best be approached by the intelligent reader. It is good to see the popular presentation of feminist, psychological and intertextual approaches and a clear statement on the way in which fundamentalism is a cul-de-sac. The Christian perspective may result in some confusion for those who consider the OT: in itself it is presented as Law, Prophets and Writings, but overall in the same chapter it is understood as having a prophetic tendency, something which really only becomes possible in the Christian canonical order. The authors don't beat about the bush and hit their readers hard, forcing them to think. English-speaking churchgoers need more of these kind of popular books about the Bible to help make the insights of scholars less threatening.

G.J. BROOKE

LEE, NANCY C., *The Singers of Lamentations: Cities Under Siege, from Ur to Jerusalem, to Sarajevo* (BIS, 60; Leiden: Brill, 2002), pp. xiv + 231. Plates. €60.00/ $70.00. ISBN 90-04-12312-1; ISSN 0928-0731.

Using oral-poetic and socio-rhetorical methods, L. analyses Jer. 4.3-31; 8.18–9.2; 10.17-25 and the book of Lamentations in an attempt to understand how two distinctive poetic voices interact within these passages. One is the prophet, whom L. identifies with the historical Jeremiah, and the other is the city's female poet, whom she thinks may have been a female cultic singer. She concludes there is not a single literary 'author'; instead, a later editor has presented the two lead poetic singers in dialogue. She focuses on the individual modifications of formulaic language found in the two voices she identifies as personal responses to the context of the destruction of Jerusalem. She compares her findings with modern laments written in the immediate aftermath of the wars in Croatia and Serbia. L. concludes that Jeremiah's laments helped the community process grief after the devastation of Jerusalem. They incorporate disagreeing voices in explanation of what had happened. Lamentations moves away from the belief in retributive justice, holding there can be individual innocence in spite of corporate guilt. The volume is a PhD thesis written at Union Theological Seminary in Virginia. Its focus on oral compositional techniques and the dialogical format provide useful insights and the

comparisons with modern laments will interest some. Comparison with Mesopotamian city laments, however, will yield different explanations for the timing of the
composition of such a lament, its use of dialogue, its methods of composition, and
its function within ancient Israel.

D. EDELMAN

LEVITT KOHN, RISA, *A New Heart and a New Soul: Ezekiel, the Exile and the
Torah* (JSOTSup, 358; London: Sheffield Academic Press, 2002), pp. xii + 148.
£45.00. ISBN 0-8264-6057-7.

This short monograph is a revised version of a doctoral dissertation completed in
1997 within the University of California, San Diego. The volume explores the
presence of Priestly and Deuteronomistic language and concepts in the book of
Ezekiel. Study of 97 terms leads to the conclusion that Ezekiel appropriates Priestly
terminology but also feels comfortable situating it in new contexts. Analysis of 21
terms common to Ezekiel and the Deuteronomist leads to the conclusion that there
is considerable evidence of Deuteronomistic influence on Ezekiel. Ezekiel appears
to fuse P and D material, creating a synthesis all his own and yet similar to that
effected by the redactor of the Torah. It is thus argued that Ezekiel in fact anti-
cipates the production of the Torah in its final form. This is a bold thesis, whose
value does not depend upon its being acceptable to all. It will stimulate healthy
debate. The author underestimates the need to defend documentary analysis of the
Pentateuch in the present scholarly climate. Her picture of Ezekiel as synthesizer
and reconciler stands somewhat at odds with the evidence that he was an intense
and distinctive figure, influenced of course by various traditions but far from being
a 'lowest common denominator' man. Again, in arguing that the exclusivity proposed by both P and D proved inadequate in the exilic situation, the author perhaps
overstates the extent to which Ezekiel offers a unified national theology. Nonetheless, this monograph is to be welcomed as a valuable addition to the critical
literature on Ezekiel.

P.M. JOYCE

LIM, JOHNSON T.K., *A Strategy for Reading Biblical Texts* (Studies in Biblical
Literature, 29; New York: Peter Lang, 2002), pp. xvii + 152. £31.00. ISBN 0-8204-
5028-6; ISSN 1089-0645.

L. introduces his readers to the full range of non-devotional ways of interpreting
the Bible from the historical-critical method, through author-orientated, text-
orientated and reader-orientated approaches to deconstructive, final form and postmodern reading methods. Avowedly written from a confessional stance, L.
nonetheless paints an even-handed portrait of the methods surveyed, listing for each
its strengths and weaknesses as a means of widening and/or deepening readers'
capacity to generate meaning(s) from the texts. No biblical exegetical method is
privileged over the others. Throughout, L. provides his readers with a plethora of
relevant quotations from a wide range of authors, encouraging the readers to interact with the argument he makes. L.'s 'attitude of reading' demands that the reader

read: synchronically, the text (rather than events 'behind' the text), in the source language (preferably), responsibly (in terms of genre and sense), receptively (without too much either scepticism or credulity), respectfully, regularly, reflectively, raptly, resourcefully and religiously a list that many tutors would endorse. The book provides a thorough introduction to biblical hermeneutics for those who wish to understand all the terms involved, and without excluding those with a confessional perspective, although the proofreading leaves something to be desired.

H.A. McKAY

LYONS, WILLIAM JOHN, *Canon and Exegesis: Canonical Praxis and the Sodom Narrative* (JSOTSup, 352; London: Sheffield Academic Press, 2002), pp. x + 317. £60.00. ISBN 1-84127-295-7.

L. has given us an excellent work on the canon and exegesis, built mainly around the contribution of B. Childs. His introduction opens with a citation from J. Barr's *The Concept of Biblical Theology* (1999) on Childs' canonical approach: 'Though I have come to disagree with almost everything in his proposals about the subject, I realise how very much I owe to him, in that his thinking has been the catalyst for much that has become my own'. L. goes on to refer to the split personality, the fate that P.R. Davies has suggested should await ecclesiastical users of the biblical text in the academy. L. has a very systematic and thorough treatment of most questions involved with regard to biblical theology: the history of the subject, definition, history from Irenaeus to the Post-Reformation period; from Gabler to Wrede; early twentieth century; to the contribution of B. Childs, with a section on the historical development of the biblical theology of Childs and its canonical approach to the biblical text. He notes Childs' interest in building a bridge from the biblical text to the theological reality. Lyons gives an outline of the canonical approach of Childs, with its various elements, among them the *sensus literalis*, and the meaning this has for Childs ('the plain sense witnessed to by the community of faith') and other scholars. This is followed by another chapter on the hermeneutics of the canonical approach reconsidered, in dialogue with modern writers on hermeneutics, such as P.R. Noble, S.E. Fish, A.C. Thiselton. Here we have discussion of the proper locus for biblical interpretation: the Christian Church, the 'community of faith' as 'interpretative community'. In summary L. says that it seems clear that Childs' canonical approach can be understood hermeneutically in such a way as to leave it essentially unchanged. Three chapters on the canonical exegesis of Genesis 18–19 follow, ending with a conclusion; a select bibliography of Childs' works, a general bibliography and indexes of citations and of authors. This work should prove invaluable in the ongoing debate on the theological/Christian use or interpretation of the Bible, a discussion which, in the opinion of this reviewer, will need to further refine the meaning in this context of such terms as church/Church, community of faith, interpretative community—indeed (and possibly more importantly) of 'interpretation' itself, whether it means an understanding of the texts in theological or spiritual continuity with the thrust of the original writers or canon rather than just identifying the original/literal meaning. Such study may lead to greater understanding between exegetes within the community of faith and those in the 'academy'—reducing the risk or need of schizophrenia!

M. MCNAMARA

MATHEWSON, STEVEN D., *The Art of Preaching Old Testament Narrative* (Grand Rapids, MI: Baker Academic, 2002), pp. 279. $16.99. ISBN 1-84227-138-5.

This lively and enthusiastic volume is divided into three parts. The first ('From Text to Concept') is a good summary of recent biblical scholarship on the nature of narrative. The next section discusses how a narrative can be preached to a congregation ('From Concept to Sermon'). The final part consists of five fine sample sermons, including one by the author. An appendix introduces text linguistics as a method for analysing the plot. The influence of Haddon Robinson is particularly evident (he writes the foreword), for example in M.'s stress on the big idea as a way to bridge the gap between past and present. The approach throughout is positive, the main concern being to engage with contemporary culture rather than critical scholarship. This is a wise, creative and well-written guide that is warmly commended to preachers and anyone concerned with interpreting and communicating the OT for today.

A.K. JENKINS

MCCONVILLE, J. GORDON, *Exploring the Old Testament*. IV. *The Prophets* (London: SPCK, 2002), pp. xxxii + 272. £16.99. ISBN 0-281-05432-0.

This volume is one of a series of six textbooks covering the OT and NT. As the title suggests, it takes an exploratory approach, encouraging direct engagement with the text and inviting readers to engage in further reflection at lesser or greater depth by means of panels inserted into the main text. These are subdivided into 'Think About' Panels, 'Digging Deeper' Panels and (less inspiringly!) 'Other' Panels providing background information. It is made clear that the textbook is primarily envisaged as being used by 'students undertaking introductory courses on the Bible in broadly Christian contexts' (p. xiii). Occasionally this feature shows itself very clearly; for example, there is a 'Think About' panel headed 'Should Christians Tithe?' (p. 264), and the panel on 'Election' relates the concept to modern church life (p. 168). The book treats the prophetic section of the Christian canon, so Lamentations and Daniel are included, and the discussions of the various prophetic books in relation to the wider canon envisage the canon as OT and NT. After a general introduction, each book is dealt with according to the following pattern: date and destination; critical interpretation (involving a brief section-by-section commentary); structure and outline; theological themes; rhetorical intention; 'X' in the canon; further reading. The book packs in plenty of useful information and there are plenty of suggestions for further reading. This is a very welcome, user-friendly textbook for use in class, discussion group, or individual study.

A.H.W. CURTIS

MIES, FRANÇOISE (ed.), *Bible et sciences: Déchiffrer l'univers* (Le livre et le rouleau, 15; Namur: Presses Universitaires de Namur; Brussels: Éditions Lessius, 2002), pp. 200. €20.00. ISBN 2-87037-362-7 (Namur); 2-87299-114-X (Éditions Lessius).

This book is the product of one of a series of conferences held at the University of Namur on aspects of the relationship between biblical studies and the modern world. In the first essay, 'La science dans la bible: méthode et resultants', J. Trublet argues that, although the HB contains little scientific fact, the Wisdom literature does contain an embryonic discourse on method in its interest in observation and classification of phenomena. J. Vermeylen's essay 'Les répresentations du cosmos dans la bible hébraïque' then discusses the tension in the prophetic literature between the claim that social and celestial orders mirror each other and the reality of the disorder of the human world. F. Euvé then traces 'L'imaginaire biblique des scientifiques', finding in Einstein a representative of a cosmic spirituality which, if not to be equated with the biblical, reminds the theologian of a neglected cosmic dimension in the wisdom tradition. In 'Teilhard et la bible', D. Lambert reflects on the insight that while Teilhard demythologizes the creation accounts of Genesis he conversely seeks to read Pauline passages about the cosmic Christ in material terms. In the final essay, '"Le soleil s'arrête à Gabaon": interpretations de la Bible et avancée des sciences', P.-M. Bogaert finds a rapprochement between the seemingly contradictory biblical and modern scientific cosmologies which underlie the account of the sun standing still in Josh. 10.12-15 in the fact that both serve to displace humankind from the centre of the physical or spiritual universe. This is an intriguing collection which valiantly tries to find some middle position while remaining responsible both to exegetical and scientific method, with inevitably modest success at best but some fruitful insights.

H.S. PYPER

MOWINCKEL, SIGMUND, *The Spirit and the World: Prophecy and Tradition in Ancient Israel* (ed. K.C. Hanson; Fortress Classics in Biblical Studies; Minneapolis, MN: Fortress Press, 2002), pp. xiv + 174. $16.00. ISBN 0-8006-3487-X.

Three studies by M. relating to Israelite prophecy are republished here. As a sample of his work as it developed they are best read in the reverse order. 'The Prophets and the Temple Cult' is a translation of the first chapter of *Psalmenstudien* 3 (1922), in which M. argued that prophets had a prominent place in the cult and were responsible for composing and reciting from memory the oracular passages in the psalms. 'The Spirit and the Word in the Prophets' is an article from 1934, making the case that the reforming prophets distrusted ecstatic experience and relied on the word which came to them, which might or might not confirm their own prior convictions. The most substantial of the three studies reproduces *Prophecy and Tradition* (1946), an apologia for traditio-historical criticism in general and of the prophets in particular. It is a careful account of the methods employed by H. Gunkel, H. Gressmann and M. himself, and a defence of them against I. Engnell, who was maintaining that it was futile to try and go behind the tradition in its present form, and the older literary critics, who thought solely in terms of the use and revision of written sources. It has to be said that the case for oral transmission seems rather vague. Much of the debate is carried on in the notes, which should not be neglected. K.C. Hanson has translated the German study, tidied up M.'s English, supplemented the notes with references to later literature, supplied a bibliography and written a short account of M.'s distinguished career.

R. TOMES

MURPHY, ROLAND E., *The Tree of Life: An Exploration of Biblical Wisdom Literature* (Grand Rapids, MI: Eerdmans, 3rd edn, 2002), pp. xiv + 286. $24.00/£17.99 ISBN 0 8028 3965 7.

The second edition was reviewed in *B.L.* 1998, although the original does not seem to have been covered. This third edition brings this useful introduction up to date with comments on articles and commentaries to 2001. Note that the index covers only the original 1990 edition.

P. BALLANTINE

NICHOLSON, SARAH, *Three Faces of Saul: An Intertextual Approach to Biblical Tragedy* (JSOTSup, 339; London: Sheffield Academic Press, 2002), pp. 276. £55.00. ISBN 1-84127-248-5.

Biblical Saul, Lamertine's *Saül* and the *Mayor of Casterbridge*—read them together and you have this fascinating intertextual doctoral thesis. After a brief summary of the rise of post-structuralism and the nature of intertextual studies from a postmodern perspective, N. turns to her three texts. Saul as tragedy is not a new concept and N. draws heavily on others' work. Her contribution is a more detailed study of the mechanics of tragedy in Saul, with passing reference to Greek tragedy and a more focused questioning of Yahweh's role in creating tragedy. In this she demonstrates a coherent tragic reading, even if she seems too intent on aligning method and message. N. then turns to comparing and contrasting biblical Saul with Lamartine's *Saül* and the *Mayor of Casterbridge*. By inter-reading these three faces of Saul, N. argues that we not only better understand the later works but also gain a clearer picture of the tragic nature of biblical Saul. In good postmodern style N. concludes by revealing that her aims involve more than new insights into a biblical text. Her political goals include challenging current notions of and introducing ethics into hermeneutical results. Her success in these is more implicit than obvious, becoming lost behind the detailed comparisons, and her postmodern assumptions will be open to question by some. However, her main intertextual work is excellent and illuminating. She makes a strong case for a tragic reading and issues a challenge to traditional understandings of Yahweh that needs engagement.

E. HARPER

NITSCHE, STEFAN ARK, *König David: Sein Leben-seine Zeit-seine Welt* (Gütersloh: Chr. Kaiser Verlag, 2002), pp. 319. Maps and illustrations. €25.70/ SFr42.90. ISBN 3-579-05191-1.

The writing of biographies of David seems to be a boom industry at the moment. N.'s contribution to the genre is not simply a retelling of the story, but uses the figure of David to lead the reader in a searching but unthreatening way through the problems and techniques of studying the development over time of this culturally significant figure. The book is aimed at intelligent readers with a minimal background in the history of the ANE but who can be expected to have an interest in Florentine art of the Renaissance or contemporary Hasidism in Jerusalem. So, for instance, there is little discussion over the reliability or translation of the Hebrew text, but literary questions as to why and how the present text of Samuel took shape are raised, the implications of various modern hypotheses for the reader's understanding are explored and well-chosen archaeological illustrations are provided. N. sums up his position by saying that David *was* a historical figure and *is now* a myth, but, above all, that he is the 'personified Gestalt of an epoch of upheaval' (p. 280) and therefore becomes a central figure round which the communities of the Bible can accumulate their reactions to radical change. There is much useful illustrative material collected here and those seeking a text which could act as an examplar of the exploration of the *Wirkungsgeschichte* of a biblical character will find this suggestive.

H.S. PYPER

NOËL, DAMIEN, *En tiempo de los reyes de Israel y de Judá* (Cuadernos bíblicos, 109; Estella: Editorial Verbo Divino, 2002), pp. 66. €7.81. ISBN 84-8169-465-7.

This brief introduction to the history of the Israelite monarchies from Saul to the Babylonian Exile will be a useful resource for Spanish-speaking beginners in Biblical Studies. N. shows awareness of recent historical scepticism about the early monarchy, but is content for the most part to summarize the account as it stands in Samuel–Kings, and to offer interpretative commentary, setting events in their wider ANE context. From time to time the alternative evidence of Chronicles is brought to bear, and all the pre-exilic prophets are examined as 'witnesses to the period'. Readers of the *B.L.* may find some interest in N.'s appended essay 'Teaching the History of Israel in a Faculty of Theology', in which he defends the importance of historical study alongside more exegetical and theological concerns.

A. MEIN

OCKER, CHRISTOPHER, *Biblical Poetics before Humanism and Reformation* (Cambridge: Cambridge University Press, 2002), pp. xvi + 265. 1 plate. £40.00/ $60.00. ISBN 0-521-81046-9.

O. explores a world likely to be unfamiliar to many biblical scholars today. He discerns in the late mediaeval period a hermeneutical shift from natural signification to verbal signification as the key to a text's meanings. This was evidenced by new interest in the literal sense, whether historical or figurative, which prepared the way for the application of the newly rediscovered discipline of rhetoric to written texts.

Rhetoric in turn provided a means of handling metaphor and imagery without resort to allegorical interpretation. O. traces in the works of a range of late mediaeval commentators an integration of the literal and spiritual senses of the four-fold mediaeval scheme, and an erosion of the grip of logic which sought to interpret texts in relation to timeless theological truths. This is an impressive work of original scholarship, with extensive citation and translation of hitherto unpublished Latin manuscript texts of scholars such as Johannes Klenkok, Henry of Langenstein (oddly absent from the bibliography), John Wycliffe and Nicholas of Lyra. It will not, however, make easy reading for those unfamiliar with the concepts of med-iaeval philosophy, including, for example, accounts of authorship in terms of the Aristotelian 'efficient cause' of an object of which God was 'the material cause'. As well as opening up a rich vein of hitherto little known material for the study of the use of the Bible in the church, it is important for showing that changes that revol-utionized biblical scholarship in the sixteenth century did not arise in a vacuum.

A.K. JENKINS

O'KANE, MARTIN (ed.), *Borders, Boundaries and the Bible* (JSOTSup, 313; London: Sheffield Academic Press, 2002), pp. xii + 358. 40 figures. £65.00. ISBN 1-84127-148-9.

This is a conference collection of above-average quality and interest, and not only because you get two conferences (held in 1999 and 2000 by the Bible and Arts Programme Newman College/Catholic Biblical Association) for the price—or at least in the volume of—one. The collection includes contributions by well-known names such as R. Carroll (published posthumously, without revision), M. Douglas and M. Stocker, as well as several names unknown to me, perhaps because they don't usually write on the Bible, or perhaps because they go to Catholic conferences that many of us Protestants and Post-Protestants(?) should probably start going along to (I speak for myself). Highlights for me were 'John Hull's Open Letter from Blind Disciple to a Sighted Saviour', G. Oritz's essay on '(Holy) family values' in film, and the detailed reception history work in M. O'Kane's essay on the flight from Egypt and E. Kessler's work on early artistic representations of the Akedah. Though some contributions (e.g. M. Douglas's and S. Prickett's) take a different tack, the main emphasis of the volume is on tracking permutations of the biblical in art, film, music, politics, national identity-myth and opera.

Y. SHERWOOD

PERSON, RAYMOND F., JR., *The Deuteronomic School: History, Social Setting, and Literature* (Studies in Biblical Literature, 2; Atlanta, GA: SBL, 2002), pp. x + 175. $29.95 ISBN 1-58983-024-5.

Anyone familiar with the author's previous monographs on *Second Zechariah and the Deuteronomic School* (1993; see *B.L.* 1994, p. 70) and *The Kings–Isaiah and Kings–Jeremiah Recensions* (1997; oddly not noted in *B.L.*) will have keen expectations of a fresh treatment of the Deuteronomic school, and these are not disappointed. P. is rightly persuaded that text-critical evidence is amply to hand to control redactional arguments about the development of Joshua–Kings. The MT generally presents a later and expanded version of these books than that attested in LXX; and the MT additions are sufficiently Deuteronomic in language and style to prove that the school which produced them was still in operation in the postexilic period. This, he argues, requires a fresh understanding of its social setting: 'the Deuteronomic school has its roots in the scribal institutions of the exiled Jerusalem bureaucracy'. The scribes had been among the returnees under Zerubbabel, but had been disappointed when he did not become king; and their demise may have followed their loss of favour after the mission of Ezra. It is far from clear to me that all the passages whose postexilic date he correctly advocates are sensibly called 'Deuteronomic' (1 Sam. 16–18, for example); but the defence of that proposition may require another monograph.

A.G. AULD

PETERSEN, DAVID L. *The Prophetic Literature: An Introduction* (Louisville, KY: Westminster John Knox Press, 2002), pp. xii + 260. $29.95. ISBN 0-664-25453-5.

As the subtitle makes clear, this volume is intended as an introduction. It seeks to deal with 'the salient features of prophetic literature' (p. xi) rather than to offer a history of prophecy or of the prophetic literature. The Introduction sets the scene by dealing with issues of definition and origins (including the terminology employed in the HB, the historical and social setting of the prophets, and problems such as 'true' and 'false' prophecy). After a brief look at prophetic literature in the ANE, P. considers literary perspectives within the HB under the two basic sub-headings of 'prose accounts' and 'poetic speech', and then the growth of the prophetic literature. The final part of the Introduction deals with theological and ethical issues. There follow four major chapters on the Latter Prophets as envisaged in the HB (Isaiah, Jeremiah, Ezekiel and the book of the Twelve), and finally a chapter on prophetic literature and prophetic traditions 'outside Prophetic Books'. Each chapter is provided with a select bibliography. The book of Daniel is not dealt with in detail (there are just two references in the index), a decision which is entirely justifiable but which perhaps merits an explanation (in a work designed to be an Introduction) particularly for the elucidation of those who come to the study of the prophets from the perspective of the Christian canon. This is a thorough, readable introduction which is likely to prove very useful as a textbook for students.

A.H.W. CURTIS

POSTMA, FERENC, KLAAS SPRONK and EEP TALSTRA (eds.), *The New Things: Eschatology in Old Testament Prophecy, Festschrift for Henk Leene* (Amsterdamse Cahiers voor Exegese van de Bijbel en zijn Tradities, Supplement 3; Maastricht: Shaker Publishing, 2002), pp. x + 296. n.p. ISBN 90-423-0190-2.

This collection honours the Professor of Old Testament at the Free University of Amsterdam. Because of Leene's interests, many of the essays relate to the book of Isaiah. The collection contains the following studies (mostly in English): the understanding of eschatology in Mic. 4.1-5 (B. Becking), the new heaven and earth in

Isa. 65.17 and 66.22 (U. Berges, in German), interfacing the story of Assyria and the image of Israel's future in Isaiah 10–11 (W.A.M. Beuken), Second Isaiah and Paul's eschatology in the letter to the Galatians (M.C. de Boer), Eschaton (a poem in Dutch and English by H.J. Bosman), David in the eschatology of the prophets (K.A. Deurloo), from history to eschatology in Second Isaiah (M. Dijkstra), fertility and infertility in Isaiah 24–27 (B. Doyle), 'Deutero-Isaiah' and 'eschatology' (H.-J. Hermisson, in German), eschatologizing in the Greek translation of Joshua (C.G. den Hertog, in German), prophetic eschatology in Deuteronomy (C. Houtman, in German), the worship of Yahweh on the holy mountain in light of the idea of return (K.D. Jenner), Isaianic terminology as understood in Ben Sira and the LXX of Isaiah (A. van der Kooij), threshing and yoking in Hos. 10.11 (G. Kwakkel), text-critical, literary-critical and linguistic observations regarding Ezek. 36.16-38 (M.N. van der Meer), Isa. 52.8 in light of verbal valency patterns (R. Oosting), the increased dramatization of the prophet in the MT edition of Jeremiah compared to the LXX (L.J. de Regt), ruler expectations and ruler oracles in Isaiah (K. Schmid, in German), (dis)continuity between present and future in Isa. 26.7-21 (J. Snoek), remarks on the painting of Samson by Lovis Corinth (K. Spronk), Second Isaiah and Qohelet in dialogue (E. Talstra), unrealized eschatology and a poem from Ibn Ezra (N.A. van Uchelen), the imperative forms of *hophal* verbs (A.J.C. Verheij), the first and second creation in 1 Corinthians and in Pseudo-Justin's 'De Resurrectione' (J.S. Vos, in German), Isa. 2.2 within the framework of the book of Isaiah (A.L.H.M. van Wieringen), Isa. 41.14-20 and the drama theories of K. Baltzer and H. Leene and Isa. 41.14-20 (A. van der Woude). A bibliography of the honoree is included.

L.L. GRABBE

REIS, PAMELA TAMARKIN, *Reading the Lines: A Fresh Look at the Hebrew Bible* (Peabody, MA: Hendrickson, 2002), pp. x + 227. £17.95. ISBN 1-56563-696-1.

These 11 essays in sophisticated close reading of the narratives of the HB have all been previously published, but make a good and coherent collection which should draw scholars' attention to the work of R. The essays discuss: Genesis 1–3; Gen. 4.8; the patriarchal wife/sister stories; Hagar; Genesis 37; Exod. 4.24-26; Jephthah's daughter; 1 Samuel 21–22; 1 Samuel 28; 2 Samuel 13; 1 Kings 13. R. is not religiously observant or theologically conservative, but she holds strongly to the integrity and coherence of the biblical text, partly for temperamental reasons (self-confessed sass and 'attitude') and partly for literary reasons. She is delightfully difficult to pigeon-hole. Her style is entertainingly anecdotal, relating the circumstances that gave rise to her readings (one essay begins: 'When I was a child I decided to be a courtesan when I grew up'!). She dismisses documentary analysis of pentateuchal narratives as intellectually banal, in apparent complete innocence as to the nineteenth-century historical and developmental concerns which motivated it. She puts her feminism to imaginative rather than ideological purposes. Despite her professed non-religiosity she often draws out significant moral and theological dimensions in the text (has her biblical study unwittingly drawn her deeper into her

Jewish heritage?). R.'s readings are always thought-provoking, and should engage and inspire many an undergraduate. I was by no means always persuaded, and once or twice astonished by her blind spots. But R. is definitely one of the more worthwhile of current close readers of biblical Hebrew narrative.

R.W.L. MOBERLY

ROWLAND, CHRISTOPHER and JOHN BARTON (eds.), *Apocalyptic in History and Tradition* (JSPSup, 43; London: Sheffield Academic Press, 2002), pp. xvi + 332. n.p. ISBN 0-82646-208-1.

The papers from the Oxford Millennium Conference are for the most part analyses of literature. The volume as a whole makes for fascinating reading, but five contributions will be of special interest to readers of the *B.L.* No volume on apocalyptic would be complete without an essay by J.J. Collins; he argues that in all its diversity 'the main political impact of the apocalyptic literature lies not in any program it may imply for the future but in its rejection and condemnation of the present order' (pp. 40-41). B. Becking pays attention to Amos 5, Zephaniah, Micah 4 and Daniel, and denies that there are explicit expectations of the end of time in the HB. D.J. Bryan observes subtly on the basis of the *Assumption of Moses*, the *Psalms of Solomon*, and the writings of Philo that the themes of exile and return are used in a wide variety of reinterpreted and recontextualized ways; NT scholars should beware of thinking of assuming only a single pattern. D. Valeta explores the viability of a satirical reading of Daniel to show how the tales and the visions belong together as variations on the theme of cutting kings and empires down to size. Y. Sherwood looks at a range of literature to provide a psychological reading of Eccl. 12.1-8; humans cannot maintain a sense of impending cataclysm for very long. C.H.T. Fletcher-Louis looks at the temple as microcosm in early Jewish literature to appreciate better what is said in Mark 13. P.A. de S. Nogueira envisions the transfiguration narrative in apocalyptic terms. C. Rowland surveys with astuteness the place of the book of Revelation in Christian theology and life. Other studies are by H. Mayr-Harting on apocalyptic book illustration in the early middle ages, B. Wilson on millennialism in the nineteenth and twentieth centuries, J. Jarick on 6000 AM, D.J. Chalcraft on Shakespeare's Sonnet 102, C. Garbowski on Tolkein's eschatology, and L.J. Kreitzer on the abomination of desolation and J. Conrad. The whole is introduced by P.S. Fiddes' thoughts on millennium and utopia and dedicated to the memory of Carol Smith, who among many other things, was a much-loved member of SOTS.

G.J. BROOKE

SANDY, D. BRENT, *Plowshares and Pruning Hooks: Rethinking the Language of Biblical Prophecy and Apocalyptic* (Leicester: Inter-Varsity Press; Downers Grove, IL: InterVarsity Press, 2002), pp. 263. 26 figures. £12.99. ISBN 0-85111-277-3 (UK); 0-8308-2653-X (US).

The intended audience for this book seems to be conservative Christians who have not been educated in even the most obvious ways of reading the Bible intelligently. With a light touch which conceals much deeper scholarly expertise, S. introduces and discusses the topic of metaphorical language in prophecy and apocalyptic. He draws many telling modern analogies to illustrate the problems and pitfalls of a literalistic reading of such material. Although he clearly has primarily in his sights all those who use prophecy to predict current events, his discussion moves more widely than consideration of that topic alone. He includes the NT in his analysis, though it is the OT literature which dominates. While his position will still be too conservative for some, it would be difficult to fault him for the general direction in which he is trying to draw his readers. There will be little here for scholars, of course, and sadly those who could most benefit from this book are the least likely to read it, but for the many who want to take the Bible seriously but have no reliable guide S. will seem to come as a breath of fresh air.

H.G.M. WILLIAMSON

SCHLATTER, ADOLF, *Die Bibel verstehen: Aufsätze zur biblischen Hermeneutik* (ed. W. Neuer; Gießen: Brunnen Verlag, 2002), pp. 203. €14.95. ISBN 3-7655-1281-8.

The 150th anniversary of the birth of Adolf Schlatter (1852–1938) has provoked a revival of interest in his work within German biblical scholarship. He was primarily a NT scholar, but he saw the whole Bible as the word of God worked out in the church; Jesus is taken to be the fulfiller of the OT. The present collection consists of an extended introduction by Neuer, and then 13 pieces by S., whose original publication dates from 1881–1928. Most are short occasional pieces aimed at a general readership; the most substantial essay explores the relation between NT theology and dogmatics.

R.J. COGGINS

SHARON, DIANE M., *Patterns of Destiny: Narrative Structures of Foundation and Doom in the Hebrew Bible* (Winona Lake, IN: Eisenbrauns, 2002), pp. xii + 244. $29.50. ISBN 1-57506-052-3.

S.'s revised doctoral dissertation from the Jewish Theological Seminary of America seeks to use Vladimir Propp's methodology for analysing the structure of Russian fairy tales as a way of uncovering significant structures embedded in narrative episodes in the HB. Propp argued that each genre of tale consisted of a limited number of narrative events termed 'constants' or 'functions' that had a specific order of juxtaposition, although the way in which these constants were expressed might vary from tale to tale within the genre. Using this approach, S. identifies a genre that she terms a 'Pattern of Destiny', which consists of the constants 'eating and drinking' and an 'oracle'. According to her analysis, such patterns occur at foundational moments throughout the history of the Israelite people, and serve either to establish important social and religious institutions or to account for their downfall. S. also argues for the presence of the same pattern in a variety of ANE literatures. The analysis is certainly suggestive, but unsatisfying. First, there is as much discussion of what S. regards as exceptions to her pattern as there is of examples of the pattern. Second, the analysis of the patterns of destiny is rather superficial, based on broad descriptive paraphrases of the text under discussion, sometimes without even verse references. Third, many of the examples appear rather forced—it seems that any eating or drinking, or any suggestion of it, combined with any oracle, constitute a Pattern of Destiny, whether or not the eating and drinking and the oracle have any intrinsic narrative.

D. ROOKE

SICKER, MARTIN, *Reading Genesis Politically: An Introduction to Mosaic Political Philosophy* (Westport, CN: Praeger, 2002), pp. xviii + 153. £48.95. ISBN 0-275-97493-6.

S. is a former teacher of political science and a student of rabbinic exegesis. He considers that the Pentateuch as a whole 'consists of essentially political teachings'. This is not implausible, but here he treats only of Genesis 1–11, and the meaning of 'political' is stretched to breaking point; a better term for the aspect of the text which is brought out, as S. more or less concedes, would be moral, or relational. Although he asserts that the chapters are myth, his commentary presents them in realistic fashion. His method is to elaborate the text with prolonged speculation on the characters' motives and inner reflections, often guided by one or another rabbinic exegete, and often with a rationalistic slant: for example in Gen. 3.1-7 the serpent did not 'really' speak; what 'really' happened is that the woman reasoned from the serpent's presence on the tree unharmed that the fruit could not be harmful—an interpretation derived from Abravanel. No doubt this work will be dismissed by most critical scholars, and indeed it offers them little; yet how much less do their own works depend on speculation?

W.J. HOUSTON

SOLVANG, ELNA K., *A Woman's Place Is in the House: Royal Women of Judah and their Involvement in the House of David* (JSOTSup, 349; London: Sheffield Academic Press, 2003), pp. xiii + 196. £50.00. ISBN 0-8264-6213-8.

This Princeton dissertation seeks to go beyond the 'male/public/autonomous and female/domestic/subordinate categories' and to identify functional areas in which royal men and women both participate on behalf of the monarch. After a clearly expressed overview in the Introduction, S. devotes a chapter to looking at royal women in a variety of areas and periods in the ANE, including Ugarit, Mari, Egypt, the Hittites, and the Assyrians, and a further chapter to 'women's space' in the royal palaces (including so-called 'harems'). The second part of the book has a chapter on general matters (e.g., the queen mother and the fact that Judahite king lists are unique in including the mother's name) and then three studies on specific women (Michal, Bathsheba, Athaliah). S. finds that the women pictured in the OT literature are involved in the same functions as the royal women known from the texts of other ANE societies. To speak of women's relative lack of power, status, and value in this society is to overly simplify the social dynamics that existed; on the contrary, it is important to give proper attention to the relationships and expectations that link men and women together as partners (or competitors) in the on-going social process. The royal women of Judah are in fact portrayed in the narratives as essential actors in and representatives of the Judahite monarch. This is a commendably nuanced work, a pleasant change from those studies (unfortunately, still appearing) that seem not able to advance beyond the 'patriarchal society' stage of analysis. It should be noted that S.'s basic thesis receives additional support from the royal household of Achaemenid Persia, as argued in P. Briant's *From Cyrus to Alexander: A History of the Persian Empire* (reviewed on p. 32 above).

L.L. GRABBE

SOULEN, RICHARD N. and R. KENDALL SOULEN, *Handbook of Biblical Criticism* (Louisville, KY: Westminster John Knox Press, 3rd edn, 2001), pp. xiii + 234. £12.99. ISBN 0-664-22314-1.

More of a short dictionary than a handbook, this volume contains succinct entries on a number of topics relating to biblical interpretation. It covers all the major terms in biblical criticism including much German terminology. There are also entries for each of the English Bible versions and for some of the key figures in biblical criticism (although the selection seems somewhat arbitrary). To the historical-critical subjects of the earlier editions have been added many literary-critical and postmodern topics. The explanations are balanced, concise but technically fairly sophisticated. There are helpful diagrams where necessary, including a useful foldout map relating types of biblical criticism to the worlds behind, of and in front of the text. For substantial entries, references to recent literature enable readers to take study further. Unlike similar dictionaries it is the work of only two authors, which gives it an overall unity; it is also smaller and more affordable, with the inevitable consequences that some topics are missing. The two-column format is readily accessible, although there is the occasional error in cross-referencing (e.g., although 'Deconstruction' refers to 'Reading', 'Reading' contains no reader-response definition). Overall a very useful and inexpensive reference volume for those reading or studying hermeneutics.

E. HARPER

STIEBERT, JOHANNA, *The Construction of Shame in the Hebrew Bible: The Prophetic Contribution* (JSOTSup, 346; London: Sheffield Academic Press, 2002), pp. x + 196. £50.00. ISBN 1-84127-268-X.

For the past 20 years or so, discussion of shame in the HB has been dominated by conclusions drawn from anthropological studies of Mediterranean societies where its opposite is seen as honour. In challenging this approach, S. first draws attention to such general considerations as the difficulty of moving from text to social reality, the role of ideology in the texts we have and the complications of knowing what or who God represents in socio-anthropological terms. She further observes, however, that whereas most of the recent studies have focused on narrative material, the vocabulary of shame is more frequently attested in the prophets. She therefore devotes a chapter to each of Isaiah, Jeremiah and Ezekiel, and has little difficulty in pointing out the inadequacies of the anthropological model. In Isaiah, for instance, honour is God's exclusive preserve and it is not at all a quality for humans to aim towards. There are contexts where shame is closely related to guilt, and there are both the objective and the subjective aspects of shame to be considered as well. S.'s discussion is a little leisurely (her introduction and survey of previous study comprise over half the whole) and it would have been good to see rather more detailed textual analysis of key passages, but on the whole her point is well made and well taken.

H.G.M. WILLIAMSON

STONE, KEN (ed.), *Queer Commentary and the Hebrew Bible* (Cleveland, OH: Pilgrim Press, 2001), pp. 250. $28.00. ISBN 0-8298-1447-7.

This is the American co-publication of the volume originally published by Sheffield Academic Press as JSOTSup, 334, and reviewed in *B.L.* 2002, pp. 144-45.

G.J. BROOKE

STUART, DOUGLAS, *Old Testament Exegesis: A Handbook for Students and Pastors* (Louisville, KY: Westminster John Knox Press, 3rd edn, 2001), pp. xx + 179. £12.99. ISBN 0-664-22315-X.

The first edition of this book, which has been widely used and translated, was reviewed in *B.L.* 1981, p. 80. The basic structure (guide for full exegesis; short guide for sermon exegesis; aids and resources) remains the same, while the text has been revised and the catalogue of resources has been updated, with some indication of what is available online. The exegesis envisaged is demanding: the student compares the versions, translates the text, researches the historical context, looks for patterns, analyses the text's relation to the rest of Scripture, identifies the theological issues—and only then investigates what others have said about the passage. Even the pastor is expected to spend five hours a week on research for a sermon. The author admits to biases of his own: he has not emphasized techniques which give meagre results theologically and homiletically, and conservative scholarship is strongly represented in the aids and resources. Some of the examples of exegesis he offers seem designed to show that critical conclusions are often wrong. However, the *B.L.* gets honourable mention for its mini-reviews, the advice on application in sermons is generally sound, and there is an amusing list of frequent hermeneutical errors. Unfortunately the transcription of Hebrew contains too many mistakes.

R. TOMES

THELLE, RANNFRID I., *Ask God: Divine Consultation in the Literature of the Hebrew Bible* (Beiträge zur biblischen Exegese und Theologie, 30; Frankfurt am Main: Peter Lang, 2002), pp. 284. €42.50/£30.00/$47.95. ISBN 3-631-37161-6; 0-8204-4825-7 (US); ISSN 0170-8716.

This thesis covers occasions when men consult deities for guidance. *Consultation* is a good word to use in the title as this embraces much more than prophetic oracles and includes both laymen and priests. In the Introduction main tendencies in past research are covered with recent developments, and then the scope of the present study is outlined. The book is organized not under persons consulting the deity (i.e. prophets, priests, and so on) but under the verbs used for consultation, that is, *šā'al, dāraš, hitpallēl, 'ātar* and *ḥālāh*. English translations of the passages are given, revealing a regular pattern: a situation of distress leads to a religious expert consulting the deity; then a divine response, favourable or otherwise, is given. The most common situation is one of war, but other contexts include directions for travel (particularly in war), illness and threat of divine punishment. There are four appendixes covering the categories of meaning of the verbs studied. The study is painstaking in detail, but seems somewhat negative in its conclusion that no parti-cular *Gattung* is followed, even though all accounts of divine consultation follow the same pattern. This is largely because this pattern reflects the natural way to go about a divine consultation. Dichotomy between divination and prophecy is ruled out, and T. reaches the very common-sense conclusion that ordinary readers would reach anyway. It seems that scholars have tried to fabricate differences in approaching the deity when the words used are only the natural ones with no particular significance.

J.G. SNAITH

TITA, HUBERT, *Gelübde als Bekenntnis: Eine Studie zu den Gelübden im Alten Testament* (OBO, 181; Fribourg: University Press; Göttingen: Vandenhoeck & Ruprecht, 2001), pp. xv + 251. SwFr 78.00. ISBN 3-7278-1353-9 (University Press); 3-525-53995-9 (Vandenhoeck & Ruprecht).

Originally a doctoral dissertation done at the University of Freiburg (A. Schenker, supervisor), this is a study of vow in the HB. T. begins with a provisional definition of vow as a 'promise to a deity'. After a look at some recent studies, he surveys the vows in narrative passages, the psalms, a postexilic prophetic text (Isa. 19.21), and wisdom literature. The results of this systematic study give rise to the surprising observation that an essential feature of vows is confession, of which the *tôdâ* (thanksgiving) offering is a celebration. This leads him to argue that vow has frequently been too narrowly defined in much OT study as a conditional request to God in a time of emergency, with a gift promised if the prayer is answered—a bargain or agreement with God in which an offering is promised when God fulfils his part. On the contrary, T. urges that in biblical vows the offering is only an element in the confession, and praise and honouring of God is the goal and not just the means to the end. The vow can also be a cultic confession which takes an unconditional form of thanking and praising Yahweh. It is thus a part of public worship and not just private piety. T. concludes with some biblical theological perspectives on a theology of monastic vows.

L.L. GRABBE

UPKONG, JUSTIN, *et al.*, *Reading the Bible in the Global Village: Cape Town* (Global Perspectives on Biblical Scholarship, 3; Atlanta, GA: SBL, 2002), pp. 221. $24.95. ISBN 1-58983-025-3.

This volume of papers comes from the meeting of the 2000 SBL International Meeting in Cape Town. U.'s paper sets methodological boundaries for a contextual biblical hermeneutics in which there is a self-conscious involvement of the people of a particular culture in the reading process. The focus is on the reading site of Africa and on the experience of ordinary people as the foundation both for hermeneutic and for exegesis. This sets the tone for a contrast between the Academy, with its links to Western cultural interpretative modes, and the meanings drawn from texts by audiences in African and other decolonized settings. The volume insists on the need for an Ethics of Reading within a globalized world, which properly emphasizes the local as against what are held to be universally acceptable readings. However, it is not easy to attain that goal, since it proves difficult to avoid creating new meta-narratives. The papers of M.W. Dube, G.O. West and A. Masaga variously attempt to produce valid practical examples of African, liberationist interpretations of biblical texts, each contributor seeking for an authenticity, only to be challenged by the next respondent. N.K. Gottwald and J. Punt point to the variety of concepts of freedom to be found in the OT and in Paul's Letters. T.S. Maluleke explores the importance of the Christian Bible to African religion today, suggesting that it might be less central than generally supposed. In these ways the papers deconstruct each other and offer the reader, as V.L. Wimbush states, a decentring and destabilizing of discourse which opens up fresh interpretative possibilities.

M.E. MILLS

VAN FLETERN, FREDERICK and JOSEPH C. SCHNAUBELT (eds.), *Augustine: Biblical Exegete* (Augustine Historical Institute Series, 5; New York: Peter Lang, 2001), pp. xvii + 397. £44.00/$69.95. ISBN 0-8204-2292-4.

The principal concern of the 18 essays included in this volume is hermeneutical in character, a point emphasized by the opening paper (van Fleteren), which seeks to present an overview of Augustine's approach to textual interpretation as part of a wider presentation of ancient and modern thinking on the subject. Seven essays touch on OT topics: V.J. Bourke deals with Augustine on the Psalms; M. Cameron examines his use of Song of Songs in anti-Donatist polemic; R.J. O'Connell analyses his use of Sir. 10.9-14; T. Renna investigates his treatment of Zion and Jerusalem in the Psalter; and K.B. Steinhauser traces the part played by exegesis of Job in the Pelagian controversy. The two remaining essays, though concerned with OT topics, deal mainly with writers other than Augustine: J.P. Burns writes on creation and the fall in the writings of Ambrose, while J.F. Kelly deals with Bede's use of Augustine's exegetical work on Genesis. The opening paper abounds in typographical errors (including a misquotation of Vulgate 1 Cor. 10.11 on p. 7); but the remaining essays are well presented and offer significant insights into Augustine's hermeneutical theory.

C.T.R. HAYWARD

VANHOOMISSEN, GUY, *En commençant par Moïse: De l'Égypte à la Terre promise* (Collection écritures, 7; Brussels: Lumen Vitae, 2002), pp. 254. €25.00 ISBN 2-87324-167-5.

This volume is an introduction to the story of Moses in the books of Exodus–Deuteronomy, aimed at a popular or novice audience, and derived from courses taught at the Center Lumen Vitae. Chapters 1–3 deal with methodological theories about the formation of the texts, the historicity of traditions, and the conditions of believable reading. These chapters provide a balanced overview of the current status of debate in the field. Chapter 2 argues that the Bible is not a history book in the modern sense but contains some historical information and that archaeology gives the cultural context in which the texts were produced. Chapter 3 presents arguments against a fundamentalistic approach to the text, citing the Catholic Dei Verbum that says that the word of God is expressed in the limitations of human language. Chapters 4–8 pursue a literary, theological and historical analysis of the texts that is intended to be a guide for a first reading that leads to the text itself, which is to be read and reread. The volume is well conceived and well executed and would make an excellent textbook for students.

D. EDELMAN

WATTS, JAMES W. (ed.), *Persia and Torah: The Theory of Imperial Authorization of the Pentateuch* (SBL Symposium Series, 17; Atlanta: SBL, 2001), pp. xi + 228. $39.95. ISBN 1-58983-015-6.

P. Frei's revival of a theory about the influence of the Persian Empire on the promulgation of Jewish law in the time of Ezra was discussed in 2000 at the SBL meeting in Nashville. The papers presented are published here, preceded by the editor's translation of a 1995 article by Frei ('Die persische Reichsautorisation: Ein Überblick', *ZABR* 1, 1-35) which summarized his views. J. Blenkinsopp accepts that the Persian authorities may have initiated the consolidation of Jewish law, but suggests that there is no evidence as to how this might have influenced the content of the Pentateuch. L. Fried argues that Ezra's commission was to appoint Persian judges who would have enacted Persian, rather than Pentateuchal or Jewish, law. L.L. Grabbe questions the emphasis on the role of Ezra; 'he was not the sole pos-sessor of this new Pentateuch, assuming that he had the whole Pentateuch' (p. 112) and the suggestion that the Persian king would be directly concerned to authorize such a law is unlikely. G. Knoppers suggests that it is important to recognize the extent to which the Persian authorities allowed local leaders 'to be active players in shaping policies within their communities' (p. 134). D.B. Redford argues that if Darius was interested in Egyptian laws it was not with a view to authorization or codification; it involved the translation into Aramaic of those Egyptian regulations which related to wealth-production with a view to controlling that wealth. J.-L. Ska believes there is no need to posit Persian intervention to account for the emergence of the Pentateuch, and defends the view that the Pentateuch contained 'the "official and national archives/library" of the Second Temple community' (p. 170). The editor (at the end of his brief introduction) suggests that the Persians may have designated the Pentateuch as the official law of the Jerusalem temple community simply as a token favour, with little or no attention to the law's form or content. The volume makes a useful contribution to the discussion of the possible extent of Persian influence on a formative period of Judaism.

A.H.W. CURTIS

WHEDBEE, J. WILLIAM, *The Bible and the Comic Vision* (Minneapolis, MN: Fortress Press, 2002), pp. xii + 315. $16.00. ISBN 0-8006-3486-1.

This is a welcome reprint of a volume originally published by Cambridge University Press in 1988 and favourably reviewed in *B.L.* 1999, pp. 121-22.

E.W. DAVIES

WILLIS, TIMOTHY M., *The Elders of the City: A Study in the Elders-Laws in Deuteronomy* (SBLMS, 55; Atlanta, GA: SBL, 2001), pp. xiii + 353. $45.00. ISBN 1-58983-013-X.

A Harvard PhD thesis revised for publication after a decade, this monograph examines the five laws in Deuteronomy that specifically mention elders—19.1-13; 21.1-6; 21.18-21; 22.13-21 and 25.5-10—to understand the role they played in local ancient communities. W. follows traditional American scholarship in assuming that the core of Deuteronomy is pre-exilic and that redactions took place in the later pre-exilic or exilic periods. He sees his contribution to lie in his use of comparative ethnographic evidence and his conclusions, which reverse the findings of recent studies. He argues that the Deuteronomistic redactions of the pre-Deuteronomic laws expanded an already existing concern for the community outward by tying the welfare of each community to that of the nation at large. He sees this expanded perspective to be the natural consequence of cult centralization under Josiah. The laws reflect a concern for the reconciliation of a social rift motivated either by moral integrity of the community or the socio-economic solidarity of the community. If one accepts his proposed redactional history of each law, the underlying ideologies he identifies would be more consistent with a date of redaction in post-exilic Yehud, after the rebuilding of the temple in Jerusalem than with his suggested date under Hezekiah or Josiah, when adherence to the laws would define membership in the 'true' Israel that consisted of those associated with the golah community. The biblical bibliography has been updated through the revisions concluded in 1998, with one entry from 1999. This volume belongs in university research libraries.

D. EDELMAN

WOLFF, HANS WALTER, *Anthropologie des Alten Testaments* (Gütersloh: Chr. Kaiser Verlag, 7th edn, 2002), pp. 368. €39.95. ISBN 3-579-05091-5.

This is the seventh edition of a book outlining the basic perceptions of human nature that was first published in 1973 (cf. *B.L.* 1974, p. 76). An English translation was published in 1974 (cf. *B.L.* 1975, p. 88). Apart from some corrections only minor changes have been introduced.

R.E. CLEMENTS

7. LAW, RELIGION AND THEOLOGY

AVEMARIE, FRIEDRICH and HERMANN LICHTENBERGER (eds.), *Auferstehung—Resurrection: The Fourth Durham-Tübingen Research Symposium, Resurrection, Transfiguration and Exaltation in Old Testament, Ancient Judaism and Early Christianity (Tübingen, September 1999)* (WUNT, 135; Tübingen: Mohr Siebeck, 2002), pp. xii + 401. €99.00. ISBN 3-16-147534-8.

The papers of the 1999 Durham-Tübingen symposium comprise 11 contributions on mythological representations of the victory over death in ancient Judaism and Christianity. The first section of the volume includes articles by B. Janowski on Psalm 88 (and Psalms 16 and 73), A. Chester on Ezekiel 37, Daniel 12, 1 Corinthians 15 and related texts, and H. Lichtenberger on the almost total lack of evidence for the hope of a resurrection in the Qumran texts. In a section 'Resurrection in the NT', A.M. Schwemer presents a close reading of Lk. 24.13-35, M. Hengel discusses the phrase 'and that he was buried' in 1 Cor. 15.4 in the light of ideas about otherworldly journeys and about a bodily resurrection in antiquity, O. Hofius analyses the hymn in Col. 1.15-20, and G.S. Oegema studies the reception history of Rev. 20.4-6 in the writings of Irenaeus of Lyons, Hippolytus of Rome, Origen, Tertullian, Victorinus of Pettau and Augustine. A third section is devoted to the story of the transfiguration of Jesus in the gospels of Mark and Matthew (S.C. Barton, C.H.T. Fletcher-Louis), and a fourth section to the story of the ascension of Jesus in Luke's work (J.D.G. Dunn, A.W. Zwiep). An appendix contains an exchange between P. Stuhlmacher (on justification in Paul) and J. Dunn (on 'conditionality' in Paul's soteriology). The contributions in German and English are of unequal length (12–65 pages); most of them offer useful traditio-historical surveys of the sources. Some authors engage with hermeneutical issues or express more or less distinctly ecclesial concerns.

C. BULTMANN

BOERSEMA, JAN J., *The Torah and the Stoics on Humankind and Nature: A Contribution to the Debate on Sustainability and Quality* (Leiden: Brill, 2001), pp. ix + 322. €64.00/$75.00. ISBN 90-04-11886-1.

The author is Reader in environmental science and philosophy in the University of Leiden, and his discussions and bibliography show that he is equally well read in both his own subject and OT studies. The book is in three parts. The first chapter discusses the current environmental situation. In the long central section (Chapters 2 and 3, pp. 47-188) he considers the two creation stories in Genesis and the dietary laws in Leviticus 11 and Deuteronomy 14. Chapter 4 (parts of which had been previously published in 1994) looks more sketchily at Greek attitudes to nature from the pre-Socratics to Plutarch and Porphyry (the title of the book is slightly misleading). In the final chapter B. argues that Christian cosmologies have been more strongly influenced by Greek ideas than by the Bible, and calls for fresh thinking on environmental concerns. This is a study well worth consideration by biblical specialists, both for the detailed exegesis of the biblical passages with many interesting ideas and for the many references to studies by Dutch scholars unavailable to those who do not read the language, even if questions may be raised about the narrow scope of the biblical material and a failure to recognize that the Bible of early Christianity was the LXX not the MT.

C.S. RODD

CERESKO, ANTHONY R., *Prophets and Proverbs: More Studies in Old Testament Poetry and Biblical Religion* (Quezon City: Claretian Publications, 2002), pp. xiv + 160. PhP 199. ISBN 971-501-929-3.

This modest set of republished essays deals with passages from Genesis, 2 Samuel, Isaiah, Amos, Proverbs, Ben Sira and the book of Wisdom as well as other topics. Of these essays, which to some extent are brief talks coloured by the author's own experiences in India, perhaps the best are those on Janus parallelism in the refrain in Amos 1.3 (and parallel passages) and on irony in 2 Sam. 5.6-10. Indexes of authors quoted and references to biblical books are provided. As intended, C.'s work is therefore now available to a wider audience.

W.G.E. WATSON

CHACKO, M.M., *Liberation and the Service of God: A Theological Evaluation of Exodus 1:1–15:21* (Delhi: Indian Society for Promoting Christian Knowledge, 2002), pp. xxvi + 290. $12.00/£9.00. ISBN 81-7214-648-5.

This doctoral dissertation by an Indian scholar, completed apparently around 1990, makes a contribution to the theological study of the Exodus that remains useful. It includes an annotated translation of Exod. 1.1–15.21 and five chapters dealing with major themes of the Exodus story. The extensive notes to the translation are both explanatory and text-critical and would be a useful companion for an intermediate level student reading the Hebrew text. The dissertation proper examines, on the basis of the 'final form of the text' (but with plentiful reference to mainstream critical scholarship), five topics: the nature of the charismatic leadership as exemplified by Moses, the incomparability of Yahweh ('the central motif'), cultic features (which include the significance of the name of Yahweh for worship), epic history and remembrance, and liberation. The most important feature of C.'s study is his refusal to limit the theological content of Exodus to a single theme. His argument, in the final chapter, is directed specifically against a narrowly 'liberation theology' hermeneutic, stressing that the repeated appeal to Pharaoh is to 'Let my people go, *so that they may serve me'*. But a similar argument could be (and is in passing) mounted against a purely 'salvation history' approach to Exodus.

G.I. DAVIES

COSGROVE, CHARLES H., *Appealing to Scripture in Moral Debate: Five Hermeneutical Rules* (Grand Rapids, MI: Eerdmans, 2002), pp. viii + 224. $22.00/£15.99. ISBN 0-8028-4942-3.

This examination of the hermeneutical assumptions made in appealing to the Bible as an authority on moral issues brings some much needed clarity into a confused area. Five assumptions, described as rules, are selected for detailed exposition and assessment: the rule of purpose (the principles underlying biblical moral rules are what can be applied to modern issues), the rule of analogy (between the biblical situation and the current moral problem), the rule of countercultural witness (the claims of oppressed minorities have greater weight than the dominant ideology), the rule of the non-scientific scope of Scripture (all empirical matters are outside the moral and theological scope of the Bible), and the rule of moral-theological adjudication (conflicting interpretations should be tested against the highest morality that we know). These are not seen as mutually exclusive approaches, although biblical ethicists often favour one over the rest. The study is notable for the wide range of general ethical and legal learning displayed, the many examples from both testaments that are offered to explicate the application of the rules, and the discussion of weaknesses in each of the methods as well as their positive value. Although C. usefully points out the difference between the reasons for holding ethical views and the arguments which are offered to defend them, some will find it difficult to avoid feeling that the effect of applying these hermeneutical rules is to make the Bible say what we want it to say.

C.S. RODD

DAY, JOHN, *Yahweh and the Gods and Goddesses of Canaan* (JSOTSup, 265; London: Sheffield Academic Press, 2002 [2000]), pp. 282. £19.99 (paper). ISBN 0-8264-6830-6.

This study appeared only two years ago (*B.L.* 2002, p. 159), but it is now appearing in a welcome paperback edition.

L.L. GRABBE

DUMBRELL, W.J., *The Faith of Israel: A Theological Survey of the Old Testament* (Grand Rapids, MI: Baker Academic, 2nd edn, 2002), pp. 352. $25.99. ISBN 0-8010-2532-X.

This book is not a synthetic theology of the OT, but a brief commentary on individual sections of each book (treated in the order of the HB). The author's stance is conservative and his style didactic rather than dialogical. Questions of history and dating are discussed briefly, with the very conservative option (e.g. an early dating of Daniel, a Solomonic connection to Ecclesiastes) usually left open since the focus is the final canonical text. There are occasional references to the NT, and the underlying theology builds on the author's earlier studies in tracing a line from creation to covenant to new covenant. The bibliography has been only lightly updated from the 1988 first edition (reviewed in *B.L.* 1989, p. 104), and lacks reference to many significant recent monographs and commentaries. As in many introductions there is little innovative or distinctive, but it would be a useful introductory survey for those from a conservative background wanting to discover more about the structure and content of the OT.

P. JENSON

FABRY, HEINZ-JOSEF and KLAUS SCHOLTISSEK, *Der Messias: Perspektiven des Alten und Neuen Testaments* (Die Neue Echter Bibel, Themen, 5; Würzburg: Echter Verlag, 2002), pp. 124. €14.40/SwF 25.50. ISBN 3-429-02171-5.

The OT section of this volume is written by H.-J. Fabry. His first chapter discusses matters of definition concerning messiah and messianism, on the right place of eschatology and apocalytpic in the discussion, and on messianic expectation as a problem in Jewish–Christian dialogue. He then presents short chapters on the various items of terminology, on kings, high priests and prophets as 'anointed', on the roots of messianic expectation in the OT, on messianic expectation in early Judaism and on the writings from Qumran. Fabry concludes that the designation 'anointed' is variously used to qualify historical persons so that no one office becomes predominant, that the prophetic promises of deliverance were formulated entirely without any reference to a messiah of any sort, that messianism only began to emerge in the third and second centuries BCE, that the term 'messiah' was first used in a technical eschatological way only in the first century BCE, that the Qumran evidence reveals a number of disparities, that the NT shows how the priestly and prophetic roles could be subsumed within kingly messianism, and that the NT usages show obvious continuities and discontinuities with earlier Jewish usages. The brevity of the presentation in many places prevents Fabry from demonstrating the veracity of his conclusions; the book reads as a set of assertions. As a result, though many will agree, others will only too readily disagree.

G.J. BROOKE

FITZGERALD, ALOYSIUS, FSC, *The Lord of the East Wind* (CBQMS, 34; Washington, DC: Catholic Biblical Association of America, 2002), pp. vi + 234. $12.00. ISBN 0-915170-33-7.

The author's investigation starts with the hypothesis that Dalman's approach to a theophany text like Nah. 1.2-8 is the right one. In his *Arbeit und Sitte in Palästina* I (Gutersloh: Evangelischer Verlag, 1928), p. 108, Dalman reckoned that Nahum's description of the angry God is to be understood in terms of the east wind, the sirocco from the desert. So F.'s starting-point is the metereology of the Syro-Palestinian litoral. The first chapter deals with the nature of the Palestinian sirocco. In the following chapters the author isolates vocabulary and motifs in OT texts in which he believes the sirocco is described and the emphasis is to use nature as experienced in modern Palestine for the interpretation of texts like Psalms 96–97, Isaiah 34–35, Joel, Habakkuk 3, and other shorter ones. This reviewer was not convinced by the metereological explanation but found the discussions of the texts both interesting and provocative. The view that the book of Joel is organized around the shifting metereological conditions of the seasons of the year is worth examining, especially since F. brings in the development into eschatological imagery. The chapter on 'Vocabulary and Motif Studies' is particularly useful, and the brief discussion of the 'Day of the Lord' is a reminder that a new monograph on this theme would be very welcome.

K.J. CATHCART

GERSTENBERGER, ERHARD S., *Theologies in the Old Testament* (trans. John Bowden; Minneapolis, MN: Fortress Press; Edinburgh: T. & T. Clark, 2002), pp. x + 358. $30.00. ISBN 0-8006-3465-9 (Fortress); 0-5670-8812-X (T. & T. Clark).

The German original of this important work was reviewed in *B.L.* 2002, p. 161. Author, publisher and especially John Bowden as translator are to be commended for its rapid appearance in English.

P.S. JOHNSTON

GOLDSTEIN, JONATHAN, *Peoples of an Almighty God: Competing Religions in the Ancient World* (Anchor Bible Reference Library; New York: Doubleday, 2002), pp. xiv + 575. $36.95. ISBN 0-385-42347-0.

Known, no doubt, to many *B.L.* readers for his *magna opera* on the books of Maccabees in the AB commentary series, G. here presents another *magnum opus*, this time on the question of henotheistic religions in the ancient world. The book offers a comparison of Jewish, Babylonian and some Persian religious responses to political events during the period c. 733–142 BCE, responses which display a number of corresponding features. The correspondences are especially marked between the Jewish and Babylonian literatures, and G. argues that this is because both literatures reflect the mindset of those who believe that their god is superior to all other gods and is therefore controlling history. G. sets out to prove his point by giving detailed accounts of the political events that would have affected each ethno-religious group in each period, and by analysing both their political and their literary responses to those events. As a mine of detailed information, the work is impressive; as a sustained presentation of an argument, it is less so. The extremely detailed discussion of political events not infrequently feels gratuitous and detached from the discussion of religious elements, and on occasion it is difficult to see quite where the argument is going. In this respect, the title does not aid the reader; it generates expectations of a presentation of the points of conflict between various religious systems, whereas the book discusses religions' mutual influence upon each other and their responses to outside events rather than their mutual hostility.

D. ROOKE

HAFEMANN, SCOTT J. (ed.), *Biblical Theology: Retrospect and Prospect* (Leicester: Apollos; Downers Grove, IL: InterVarsity Press, 2002), pp. 300. £16.99. ISBN 0-85111-279-X (UK); 0-8308-2684-X (US).

This worthy collection arises from the Wheaton Theology Conference in 2000. The volume covers the OT (Part 1), NT (Part 2), the Unity of the Bible (subtitled 'The Challenge of Biblical Theology'; Part 3), and finally sets out some Prospects (Part 4). The authors write from a broadly evangelical perspective with an inclusive range of conversation partners. Of greatest interest to readers of the *B.L.* are the articles in Parts 1 and 3. In the OT section, Genesis looms large, providing over-arching themes and categories stretching into the rest of the OT (W.J. Dumbrell, S.G. Dempster) and even into the NT (B.G. Toews). A perspective from the Psalms is offered by G.H. Wilson. Problems dogging identification of the proper 'canon' for biblical theology appear *seriatim*, and are especially tackled in articles by J.H. Sailhamer and R. Schultz. M.J. Wells's reflections on 'figural interpretation' fit better in Part 3 with the articles by C.R. Seitz and N. Perrin which explore issues in relating OT and NT in a pan-biblical theology. (The offerings of S.E. Fowl and D.P. Fuller belong in Part 2.) There is much food for thought in these pages. Recurring most often are struggles with canon (*b. Bat.* 14b looming especially large), and theological unity, the latter less of a concern beyond the bounds of evangelical scholarship. Perhaps this aspect explains the surprising (to this reviewer) lack of impact of Walter Brueggemann's writings. While the absence of an author index makes it difficult to check this impression, his privileging of diversity would not be helpful to those rather seeking unity.

D.J. REIMER

HUMPHREYS, W. LEE, *The Character of God in the Book of Genesis: A Narrative Appraisal* (Louisville, KY: Westminster John Knox Press, 2001), pp. x + 284. $29.95. ISBN 0-664-22360-5.

Using the insights of literary theory and narrative modes of characterization, H. presents a reading of Genesis from the perspective of God as a focal (literary) character in the extended narrative that is the book of Genesis. An initial chapter, relying in part on the work of R. Alter, explores the means by which narrators shape the characters in the stories they tell. He also draws attention to the formative role of readers in making use of what narrators offer in the construing of characters. H. then examines the Genesis material in seven chapters, looking at the character of God as it emerges in the respective stories of the First Humans (1–4), the First Human Community (5–9), Abraham (12–17), Abraham and Sarah (18–24), Isaac and Rebecca (25–27), Jacob and Leah and Rachel (28–36) and Joseph and his family (37–41). A final ninth chapter draws together some perspectives on the means of characterization employed to depict the character of God in the several segments of the Genesis narrative, and the type of character this God is. At an early stage in his work H. reminds his readers that the character of God that he is in pursuit of is a 'figure made of words', the God of the text. As such this character is male, since 'many of his actions and attributes are conventionally masculine in the gender conventions or codes of the cultural world out of which the text emerged' (p. 4). In this study H. insists that 'this God does not exist prior to the text and its creation, and he does not exist beyond it, except as readers of the text continue to remember and ponder him' (p. 6). H.'s final conclusion is that this 'God, as read across the narrative that is Genesis, is a complex and at points conflictual character' (p. 255), one who 'receives recognition of the sovereignty he first demonstrated in creation, but only as he is created in turn by his creations in images that serve their own designs for their own lives' (p. 256). This character God gives a coherence and structure to the extended narrative of Genesis, the author claims, that is often otherwise experienced as episodic. His focus on a sequential reading process rather than on historical background or theological categories will provide a fresh approach that should complement rather than replace other more conventional analyses of Genesis material.

C. McCarthy

JOHNSTON, PHILIP S., *Shades of Sheol: Death and Afterlife in the Old Testament* (Leicester: Apollos; Downers Grove, IL: InterVarsity Press, 2002), pp. 288. £14.99. ISBN 0-85111-266-8.

This paperback is a thorough and carefully argued study of Sheol in the OT. It is also very well documented, with over 800 items cited in the bibliography, and it should certainly be read by all who are interested in evaluating the state of research on what the OT has to say about death and the underworld. Among J.'s conclusions he argues that the term Sheol is especially used in contexts of judgment, that references to psalmists having been in Sheol are to be interpreted metaphorically, that *'ereṣ* is not a term for the underworld, and that though the waters are sometimes mentioned in connection with the underworld they are not simply to be equated with it. He concludes that though veneration of the dead may have occurred in ancient Israel, it was of marginal importance. The last two chapters discuss the emergence of more positive views of the afterlife in ancient Israel, and here, among other things, he holds that any foreign influence on the development of Israel's belief in resurrection was minimal. In view of the fact that our evidence for the topics treated in this book is often uncertain and fragmentary, it is sometimes possible to take a different standpoint from that adopted by J., but it has to be stated that he always argues his positions carefully.

J. Day

KEEL, OTHMAR and SILVIA SCHROER, *Schöpfung: Biblische Theologien im Kontext altorientalischer Religionen* (Göttingen: Vandenhoeck & Ruprecht, 2002), pp. 302. 169 figures. €32.00. ISBN 3-525-53500-7.

The authors assert the central significance of creation for biblical theology, too often obscured by emphasis on soteriology. They present a thoroughgoing and very useful survey of the biblical literature and related ANE texts. Genesis 1–3, fundamental to the book's theme, receive much helpful exegesis but comment is sometimes questionable. The claim that *creatio ex nihilo* is not found in the HB seems inconsistent with understanding *bārā'* as 'ein hochtheologisches Schöpfungsverb' expressing creation without reference to any material out of which God creates (pp. 174-75). We are told that Genesis 2 describes the formation of an 'Erdling' and that God does not want 'Menschen' to be alone (pp. 142-45, 147); but these assertions are incorrect; as are 'Die Erschaffung der Menschen in zweierlei Spezies, als männlich und weiblich, ist ein zentralen Thema' (p. 142) and reference to woman as 'das Meisterwerk des Schöpfergottes' (p. 148). Contrary to Keel and Schroer (p. 152), *'ādām* is *'îš* from the start as is plain from 2.23; and 3.16 assumes the essentially child-bearing nature of woman. The implied suggestion that Gen. 1.1–2.4a might have been written by women (*Autorinnen*, p. 173) is far-fetched, especially for a 'Priesterschrift' and 'priesterschriftliche Schöpfungsbericht'. An overassertive feminism distracts attention from the basic and well-supported thesis of the book that a created world is fundamentally other than an evolved one. The far-reaching implications in terms of epistemology and ecology demand much further exploration. What, for example, is that knowledge, fitting for gods but catastrophic for men?

P. ADDINALL

KEEL, OTHMAR and ERICH ZENGER (eds.), *Gottesstadt und Gottesgarten: Zu Geschichte und Theologie des Jerusalemer Tempels* (Quaestiones Disputatae, 191; Freiburg: Herder, 2002), pp. 288. 48 plates. €24.90. ISBN 3-451-02191-9.

These eight papers were read at the August 2002 annual meeting of German-language Catholic OT scholars. As the title suggests, they focus on the theological significance of the Jerusalem temple. The first and shortest essay, that of O. Keel, interprets the oracular sayings in Josh. 10.12-13 and 1 Kgs 8.12-13, the latter emended following the expansive LXX version, as indicating that the pre-Israelite Jerusalem cult was directed to the sun deity *Šmš*, with whom Yahweh came to be associated as co-occupant of the temple. B. Janowski discusses aspects of the symbolic and cosmological system within which the temple was understood, using the categories of horizontality (centre/periphery) and verticality (sky/underworld). With the help of relevant psalms (46, 48, 93) and Isaiah's vision (Isa. 6.1-7), he concludes that the basic concept is Zion as the locus of Yahweh's cosmic rule. U. Berges concentrates on the intimate link between temple theology and creation, with special reference to passages in Isaiah, especially the last two chapters, which speak of new heavens and new earth and the miraculous transformation of Zion into a paradisal garden. Some of the other essays explore beyond the confines of current consensus positions. According to C. Frevel, Lamentations was not written to bewail the destruction of the temple but to develop ways of overcoming the crisis of the loss of religious meaning. For M. Konkel, the 'law of the temple' in Ezekiel 40–48 is not a utopian construct from the exilic period but a critique of Second Temple cult practice. D. Böhler urges a reading of Ezra–Nehemiah not as a historical source book but as promoting collective identity in the early Maccabean period on the basis of Temple, Torah and City. There is also an essay from E. Zenger on temple piety which makes a useful distinction between psalms aimed to promote and enrich everyday religious living (e.g., Psalm 26) and those written for those too distant to participate in temple worship directly (e.g., Psalms 63 and 84). A final essay by S. Schroer suggests that a study of the religious and cosmological significance of Greek sanctuaries would help to clarify the religious and social function of the Jerusalem temple. Each essay has its own bibliography, there are numerous illustrations (photographs and line drawings) but no index.

J. BLENKINSOPP

KLEIN, JOEL T., *Through the Name of God: A New Road to the Origin of Judaism and Christianity* (Contributions to the Study of Religion, 64; Westport, CN: Greenwood Press, 2001), pp. xxvi + 271. £56.95. ISBN 0-313-31656-2.

The author describes this book as 'the accomplishment of' his 'lifetime': he says in the Preface that he 'has lived with the theme in mind for a half-century'. The book lacks clear direction, resembling rather an assembly of ideas collected through a lifetime put down without much order. In early chapters the emphasis is on Egypt with some reference to the work of David Rohl. Later ramblings cover the tetragrammaton, the ark, Job and continue right into the NT period. In the course of this come many strange ideas: for example, following Ikhnaton's sun worship the burning bush (*s^eneh*) seen by Moses is claimed to be the sun, not a bush at all! The English word, *sun*, is claimed to be derived from it. The *h* in Abraham's name represents Yahweh's name added to the original Abram as a sign of his faithfulness, as also in Aaron/Aharon. *Adonai Elohim* is claimed to be a 'hyphenated name', though biblical Hebrew knows no hyphen. The origin of later Judaism is found wholly in Egypt: 'the originally Egyptian priestly caste created a belief system that survived and became the foundation of Judaism and Christianity'. Hebrew transliteration is inaccurate and grammar unreliable. The sources of festival rituals are all seen to point to Egyptian sources. I am not competent to assess his knowledge of Egyptology, but if it is no better than his Hebrew we can place little credence in what he says. Not a very helpful book, and very expensive.

J.G. SNAITH

KRATZ, REINHARD G. (ed.), *Religion und Religionskontakte im Zeitalter der Achämeniden* (Veröffentlichungen der Wissenschaftlichen Gesellschaft für Theologie, 22; Gütersloh: Chr. Kaiser Verlag, 2002), pp. 312. 18 figures. €49.94/SwF 84.00. ISBN 3-579-05350-7.

This important collection of essays deriving from annual symposiums held in Göttingen between 1996 and 2000 deals with the whole of the ANE in the Persian period. After an opening chapter on what is known about the existence and date of Zarathustra (Heidemarie Koch prefers a sixth-century date amid the many uncertainties), there are essays dealing with the culture, languages and religion of Babylon under the Persians, a section on Egypt, one on Judah, with a final contribution by K. Koch on the kingdom of Commagene. Readers of the *B.L.* will be most interested in the essays on Elephantine by I. Kottsieper and E.A. Knauf and on Judah by A. Lemaire, E. Blum (who argues that the process of the authorization of the Law under Ezra partly explains what Blum takes to be the irreconcilable differences between episodes in the Pentateuch) and T. Willi who examines various aspects of the terms Law and Scripture (*Schrift*). The general picture that emerges is of a far-from-monolithic empire that allowed indigenous cultures to flourish, albeit within certain limits. There are excellent bibliographies following each essay and useful indexes.

J.W. ROGERSON

LANG, BERNHARD, *The Hebrew God: Portrait of an Ancient Deity* (New Haven, CT; London: Yale University Press, 2002), pp. x + 246. £25.00. ISBN 0-300-09025-0.

L. applies Dumézil's tripartite division of Indo-European culture and religion to Hebrew religion. He reconfigures the original categories slightly and expands the final one into three sub-categories. The priest/sovereign gods become the Lord of Wisdom, the warriors/war deities become the Lord of War, and the food producers/ divine providers of wealth become the Lord of Life, which is then subdivided into the Lord of the Animals, Lord of the Individual, and Lord of the Harvest. In the Hexateuch, the Sinai legislation relates to the Lord of Wisdom, the exodus and conquest to the Lord of War, and the promise of land and descendants to the patriarchs to the Lord of Life. Dumézil was not convinced that his categories consciously shaped the ancient Israelite approach to reality and L. has only been partially successful in demonstrating this point. He has focused on religion rather than culture and so has left the reader to presume that the scheme applies to both because one mirrored the other. The volume is intended primarily for a popular audience and so has minimal footnotes. There is, however, a number of intriguing assertions made throughout the work that warrant serious scholarly attention. Three examples are: (1) Shaddai is the old name of the Lord of the Animals; (2) Yahweh was an Edomite god adopted from Israel's 'twin' Esua/the Edomites; and (3) the monarchic-era belief in royal heavenly ascent was eliminated in the Persian-era temple and replaced by the permanent revelation of the divine will in a sacred book. The book deserves a place in university libraries and in personal collections of those with a strong interest in the development of Judaeo–Christian monotheism.

D. EDELMAN

LANGE, ARMIN, *Vom prophetischen Wort zur prophetischen Tradition: Studien zur Traditions- und Redaktionsgeschichte innerprophetischer Konflikte in der Hebräischen Bibel* (FAT, 34: Tübingen: Mohr Siebeck, 2002), pp. xi + 371. €74.00. ISBN 3-16-147732-4; ISSN 0940-4155.

In this very thoroughly documented *Habilitationsschrift*, L. looks again at the topic of true and false prophecy. He finds that some previous studies were more or less correct for part of the time (e.g., S. Mowinckel for the pre-exilic period and J. Crenshaw for the early exilic period), but that none was right all of the time. His approach is strictly diachronic, tracing the focus of dispute from early innerprophetic conflict through to a time in the postexilic period when prophecy as such was rejected and attention moved towards the exegesis of what had by then become authoritative texts. One of the key turning points in this development comes with the Deuteronomic redaction of Jeremiah, which L. dates just after the period of the restoration of the Second Temple and in which he finds an element of polemic against the prophecies of Haggai and Zechariah, and its culmination is found in Zech. 13.2-6. In order to sustain his method, L. has inevitably to make some fine distinctions in terms of separating between, for instance, the words of the historical Jeremiah and the work of the later redactor, and he admits that the progression he traces was not always as neat as a brief summary might suggest. In addition, there is an element of chickens and eggs about the relationship between the end of prophecy and the development of authoritative texts, and it is not clear to me that his solution based on Zechariah 13 is fully grounded in the text rather than in the desire for a tidy solution. While others will thus not have difficulty in finding areas to question if they are so minded, they will surely agree that L. has made a detailed and learned case for his preferred solution.

H.G.M. WILLIAMSON

MIGGLEBRINK, RALF, *Der zornige Gott: Die Bedeutung einer anstössigen biblischen Tradition* (Darmstadt: Wissenschaftliche Buchgesellschaft, 2002), pp. 168, €14.90. ISBN 3-534-15582-3.

The concept of divine anger figures prominently in the OT, and from this has heavily influenced the language and imagery through which God is portrayed generally in Christian literature and liturgy. M.'s valuable study reviews the Deuteronomic and prophetic writings and the manner in which portrayals of divine anger are employed to express approval, or disapproval, of human actions and to relate this to events, supremely those of national defeat and collapse. The connections with concepts of justice, power and divine uniqueness are noted. The development of ideas of divine anger in the wisdom writings encounters difficulties by attempting to reconcile them with individual experience and ideas of punitive retribution. Resolution for such problems was sought in developing images of an ultimate eschatological divine intervention, which became a prominent feature of the NT writings. The second part of the study traces the way in which imagery of divine anger has been developed in the central lines of Christian doctrinal development, particularly in regard to ideas of atonement and the necessity of human reparations to placate an angry God. The third, and shortest, part considers the difficulties and dangers that modern readers feel in respect of this prominent feature of the biblical portrait of god, suggesting an irrascible and all-powerful tyrant. M. suggests several more positive lines of interpretation, besides noting the danger of promoting a negative and hostile world-view.

R.E. CLEMENTS

PHILLIPS, ANTHONY, *Essays on Biblical Law* (JSOTSup, 344; London: Sheffield Academic Press, 2002), pp. xvi + 295. £70.00. ISBN 0-8264-6147-6.

P. is best known for his 1970 book, *Ancient Israel's Criminal Law: A New Approach to the Decalogue*. Following that book, he wrote a series of articles amplifying the thesis of the book and replying to criticisms. These and some other essays included here were published over the period from 1966 to 1998. It is welcome to have these essays all under one cover; however, it would have been even more useful if P. had provided some guidance to them. A survey of how the debate has developed over the past three decades since his book appeared, how the essays relate to that debate, and how they relate to each other would have made the book much more useful and also gained additional readers.

L.L. GRABBE

RENAUD, BERNARD, *Nouvelle ou éternelle Alliance? Le message des prophètes* (LD, 189; Paris: Les Éditions du Cerf, 2002), pp. 378. €38.00. ISBN 2-204-06931-0; ISSN 0750-1919.

Only one passage (Jer. 31.31-32) speaks of a 'new covenant', but the terms 'eternal covenant' and 'covenant of peace' occur quite a few times in the Latter Prophets. R. investigates the relationship between these different terms. Much of his study takes the form of a detailed exegesis of the relevant passages in Jeremiah, Ezekiel, and Second and Third Isaiah. There is also a separate chapter on the Servant Songs. He concludes that the 'covenant of peace' is basically equivalent to the 'eternal covenant', though the former term sometimes includes connotations of security. The 'new covenant' implies a significant breach with the Sinai covenant which made Israel a nation. It is new in that a radical 'anthropological renewal' is envisaged, the writing of Yahweh's laws on the heart. The terms 'eternal covenant' and 'covenant of peace' are found in passages all to be dated to the exile or post-exilic period and, according to R., a reaction to the 'new covenant' of Jeremiah. Whereas the 'new covenant' emphasized a rupture, 'eternal covenant' emphasizes the continuity of the original covenant. Some final brief thoughts take the implications of this study into the NT.

L.L. GRABBE

REVENTLOW, HENNING GRAF and YAIR HOFFMAN (eds.), *Creation in Jewish and Christian Tradition* (JSOTSup, 319; London: Sheffield Academic Press, 2002), pp. xiii + 356. £55.00. ISBN 1-84127-162-4.

These essays, the outcome of a joint symposium between the Department of Bible at Tel Aviv University and the Faculty of Theology at the University of the Ruhr, Bochum, cover only very selected aspects of their theme. They are grouped somewhat loosely into three sections: I. The Bible: F.H. Polak, 'Poetic Style and Parallelism in the Creation Account (Genesis 1.1–2.3)'; Y. Hoffman, 'The First Creation Story: Canonical and Diachronic Aspects'; W. Thiele, 'God as Creator and Lord of Nature in the Deuteronomistic Literature'; M. Polliack, 'Deutero-Isaiah's Typological Use of Jacob in the Portrayal of Israel's National Renewal'; G. Nebe, 'Creation in Paul's Theology'; E. Toenges, '"See I Am Making All Things New": New Creation in the Book of Revelation'; and H.G. Reventlow, 'Creation as a Topic of Biblical Theology'. II. Religious History and Early Judaism: H.-P. Hasenfratz, 'Patterns of Creation in Ancient Egypt'; I. Gruenwald, 'The Creation of the World and the Shaping of Ethos and Religion in Ancient Israel'; E.L. Green-stein, 'God's Golem: The Creation of the Human in Genesis 2'; and B. Nitzan, 'The Idea of Creation and its Implications in Qumran Literature'. III. Systematic Theology: C. Link, 'Providence: An Unsolved Problem of the Doctrine of Creation'; W. Gräb, 'Creation or Nature? About Dialogue between Theology and Natural Sciences'; and E. Geldbach, 'The Concept of Creation in the Conciliar Process of Justice, Peace and the Integrity of Creation'. The lack of any serious discussion, except in passing, of Jewish tradition in the Talmudic era (e.g., the *Ma'aseh Bere'shit* tradition) and in the Middle Ages (in philosophy and Qabbalah) is keenly felt, and the balance of the collection unwittingly reinforces the stereotype that only Christians are interested in theology, when (as Reventlow's paper incidentally shows) there is a highly impressive strand of theological reflection about creation in contemporary Jewish thought. That said, many of the essays are fine in their own right, the first two being particularly 'meaty' and thoroughly argued. The volume is well edited, with an excellent classified bibliography and indexes.

P.S. ALEXANDER

SAMUELSON, NORBERT M., *Revelation and the God of Israel* (Cambridge: Cambridge University Press, 2002), pp. x + 259. £45.00/$60.00. ISBN 0-521-81202-X.

This is the second of a planned trilogy in Jewish religious philosophy. The first, Judaism and the Doctrine of Creation, was noted in *B.L.* 1995, p. 119. Samuelson understands revelation as 'a relationship between God and the people of Israel out of which arises a form of content-information (i.e. communication) called "Torah"' (p. 221). He first discusses the meaning of 'God', and then asks whether the God of revelation is believable. His conclusion is that it is not reasonable to believe that God speaks words to people. Revelation must be understood as 'a pure experience that inspires human response' (p. 237). This is an important study in the philosophy of religion, but biblical specialists may regret that the final chapter, 'Are the Hebrew Scriptures revealed?' is so short, especially as it faces up to the consequences of critical scholarship.

C.S. RODD

SCHÖPFLIN, KARIN, *Theologie als Biographie im Ezechielbuch: Ein Beitrag zur Konzeption alttestamentlicher Prophetie* (Forschungen zum Alten Testament, 36; Tübingen: Mohr Siebeck, 2002), pp. ix + 392. €84.00. ISBN 3-16-147869-X; ISSN 0940-4155.

This volume is a slightly revised version of a *Habilitationsschrift* submitted in Göttingen in 2001. It asks how far the book of Ezekiel is an authentic auto-biography of the Prophet that may be read for its historical value. The author argues that the external form of autobiography amounts in fact to a fiction. Autobiography serves here as a literary device furthering the overall theological purpose of the book, at the heart of which is the revelation of the divine word. The figure of Ezekiel is employed as a mouthpiece for God and at the same time also as a sign. Within Ezekiel, the evidence of chs. 1–7, 12–14, 21, 24 and 33 is subjected to particular scrutiny. Close attention is also paid to key formulae employed more generally in the book. Some attempt is made to set the study within the context of OT prophecy as a whole. It is refreshing to find the autobiographical format of the book read without the naïve credulity that is so common. However, there may be more of the historical Ezekiel to be known: the mix of historical reality and literary artifice may be subtler than S. allows.

P.M. JOYCE

SMITH, MARK S., *The Early History of God: Yahweh and Other Deities in Ancient Israel* (The Biblical Resource Series; Grand Rapids, MI: Eerdmans, 2nd edn, 2002), pp. xlvi + 243. $25.00/£17.99. ISBN 0-8028-3972-X.

This is a second, enlarged edition of the work which was first reviewed in *B.L.* 1992, p. 112. Since its first appearance in 1990, a significant amount of material has come to light, both epigraphic and iconographic; and there has been a renewed interest in the origins of biblical monotheism. In the substantial (37-page) preface to this second edition, Smith reviews the literature on these matters with characteristic seriousness, taking into account criticisms of his earlier work. In addition, in the body of the work, he has integrated further up-to-date observations especially noticeable in his chapters on Asherah and Yahweh's solar character. This is a timely and welcome volume.

R.B. SALTERS

SMITH, WILLIAM ROBERTSON, *Religion of the Semites* (with a new introduction by Robert A. Segal; New Brunswick, NJ and London: Transaction Publishers, 2002), pp. xlix + 507. £33.50. ISBN 0-7658-0936-2.

This volume contains a reprint of the second edition of S.'s classic work, *Lectures on the Religion of the Semites* (First series, The Fundamental Institutions; London: A. & C. Black, 1894). It also contains a new introduction by R.A. Segal, a scholar best known previously for his contributions to the interpretation of myth and the sociology of religion. The first edition of this work appeared in 1889, while the posthumous third edition of 1927 was simply a reprint of the second edition, with a new introduction and additional notes by S.A. Cook. It is to be noted that the title of S.'s book has been somewhat changed in this reprint. This is not the first time, however, that S.'s work has been reprinted: earlier reprints were undertaken by Meridian Books in 1956, Ktav in 1969 and Routledge/Thoemmes Press in 1997. These various reprints testify to the continuing interest in S.'s work over the years. Although in many ways its theses are dated, it is still worth reading because of the seminal nature of S.'s researches and the unrivalled knowledge he possessed of Semitic religion, such as was available at the time, as well as of the relevant biblical and classical texts. (What remains of the second and third series of *Lectures on the Religion of the Semites* was edited by the current reviewer and published in 1995; see *B.L.* 1997, p. 120).

J. DAY

SMITH-CHRISTOPHER, DANIEL L., *A Biblical Theology of Exile* (Overtures to Biblical Theology; Minneapolis, MN: Augsburg Fortress, 2002), pp. xiv + 209. $20.00. ISBN 0-8006-3224-9.

'Exile' here signifies the situation of those under alien rule and lacking political power, whether in or out of their own land, and in S.-C.'s first chapter it is made a paradigm of the newly powerless state of the Christian Church as it emerges from Christendom. A substantial historical essay then convincingly demonstrates the historical reality of the exile (in a narrower sense) and emphasizes the destruction, disruption and loss of life which accompanied it. Five exegetical chapters then follow on rather loosely connected themes: the trauma of destruction and humiliation in Ezekiel and Lamentations; the function of historical shame in the penitential prayers of Ezra, Daniel and others; the conversion of the oppressor in Deutero-Isaiah and Jonah; purity and the ban on mixed marriage as a means of maintaining minority identity; and a comparison of the Daniel stories and various wisdom texts as 'trickster' ways of survival for a people in a subordinate position. The lessons are drawn in a brief theological conclusion that calls on Christians to accept 'exile' as a vocation. There is much here which is provocative and illuminating; however, some of the exegesis is unconvincing, and, more important, a deliberate selectivity has screened out all those aspects of reflection on exile which look towards political restoration. In Deutero-Isaiah, Ezekiel and Daniel these are intimately connected with themes that S.-C. has chosen. If he is to convince us of his theological contentions, he will have to wrestle with these aspects also.

W.J. HOUSTON

VANHOOZER, K.J., *First Theology: God, Scripture and Hermeneutics* (Downers Grove, IL: InterVarsity Press; Leicester: Apollos, 2002), pp. 384. $25.00. ISBN 0-8308-3681-5.

This is a collection of 12 essays that were originally published in various journals and collections between 1993 and 2001. Some have been left basically unchanged while others have been substantially revised. A brief preface overviews the content and traces some key themes. Flowing through these essays is a central affirmation (inspired by speech-act theory) that the Scriptures represent God's communicative action. This is worked out in relation to a wide variety of debates in the fields of philosophy, theology and hermeneutics. Along the way are significant discussions of reader response, understanding, genre, meaning, love, grace, revelation, covenant, canon, providence, body piercing (!), mission and virtue. There is relatively little discussion of the Bible in depth, but V. regularly addresses the larger issues of interpretation that are increasingly to the fore. V. is incisive in his criticism of modernist and postmodernist hermeneutics. He approaches the Bible in a way that is unapologetically orthodox and conservative, yet by no means fundamentalist or naive. He also writes with a sophistication and elegance that is both demanding and rewarding. This volume confirms V.'s stance as one of the most perceptive thinkers in the field, and a worthy conversation partner of those who would take a very different view of the Bible.

P. JENSON

VANONI, GOTTFRIED and BERNHARD HEININGER, *Das Reich Gottes: Perspektiven des Alten und Neuen Testaments* (Die Neue Echter Bibel, Themen, 4; Würzburg: Echter Verlag, 2002), pp. 136. €14.40/SwF 25.50. ISBN 3-429-02170-7.

The purpose of this series on 'Themes/Topics' is to show where the tension and the unity between the two parts of Holy Scripture (i.e., OT and NT) lie. It is a Catholic, ecumenical series on the central topics of biblical theology. This study on the kingdom of God has a section each on the OT and NT. For the OT, Vanoni looks at the terminology (mainly *mlk* and *mšl*) and then surveys first the HB, followed by the Greek Bible. He notes that 'kingdom of God' is not a major theme of the OT, though the kingship of Yahweh is found widely from an early time. His main concern, however, is not to find the theme of 'kingdom of God' in the OT but to address the question of what is meant by the 'God (of Israel) as king'. The future kingdom of God becomes a major theme in postbiblical Jewish literature (treated in the NT section). A 'Dialogue' section, in which the two authors interact on the topic, concludes the book.

L.L. GRABBE

8. THE LIFE AND THOUGHT OF THE
SURROUNDING PEOPLES

ABUSCH, TZVI, *Mesopotamian Witchcraft: Toward a History and Understanding of Babylonian Witchcraft Beliefs and Literature* (Ancient Magic and Divination, 5; Leiden: Brill/Styx, 2002), pp. xvi + 314. €75.00/$87.00. ISBN 90-04-12387-3; ISSN 1566-7952.

The present *opera minora* are articles that have already been published or are now in press and will soon be published, all concerned with witchcraft in Mesopotamia. Most of the discussions are based upon the text of the Akkadian incantation series *Maqlû* and related texts in the Babylonian medical corpus. The second part of this book deals with the structure of *Maqlû*, but the problem is that many of the magico-medical texts are not available in modern critical editions, and otherwise comments are based upon a rather outdated edition of *Maqlû*, dating from 1937. Furthermore, the articles themselves are conceptually theoretical in the analysis of Mesopotamian witchcraft, and to a certain extent controversial, such as the positive view of the witch as healer (Chapter 4), or in the demonization of the witch within Mesopotamian magic (Chapter 1). Of general interest is the discussion of being bewitched through devouring bewitched food or drink (Chapter 4). Nevertheless, there is a wide range of relevant material presented here, with a subject index for guidance, and the volume will prove useful for specialists and non-specialists wishing to consult a particular view of Mesopotamian witchcraft.

M.J. GELLER

ABUSCH, TZVI (ed.), *Riches Hidden in Secret Places: Ancient Near Eastern Studies in Memory of Thorkild Jacobsen* (Winona Lake, IN: Eisenbrauns, 2002), pp. xxvii + 333. 1 plate; 8 figures. $45.00. ISBN 1-57506-061-2.

Thorkild Jacobsen (1904–93) was a leading expert on Mesopotamia. Having studied in his native Denmark, he continued his career in Chicago and Harvard. This volume's editorial appreciation indicates that his special interests were (1) Mesopotamia's history and institutions during the third and early second millennia; (2) Sumerian language and literature; and (3) Mesopotamian religion. The volume's other contributions deal with: Jacobsen's bibliography (prepared by T. Abusch and J. Huehnergard); the socio-religious framework of the Babylonian witchcraft ceremony *Maqlû* (Abusch); punning and reversal of patterns in the Atrahasis Epic

(B. Alster); the Sumerians in their landscape (J. Black); the oldest attestation of the scribes' awareness of the existence in Sumerian of binary verbal stems (M. Civil); Gilgamesh, Enkidu and Mesopotamian homosexuality (J.S. Cooper); the Hymn to Inanna (M.J. Geller); wisdom, nature and piety in some biblical psalms (S.A. Geller); the gradual stages of Old Babylonian marriages (S. Greengus); a model court case in Mesopotamia (W.W. Hallo); the name Ningirsu, 'Lady of Girsu' (W. Heipel); the Akkadian verbs *izummum*, 'to stand', and *itūlum*, 'to lie down' (J. Huehnergard); the 'Oppression of Uruk' episode in the Gilgamesh Epic (J. Klein); a rare exorcist fragment (W.G. Lambert); a Mari letter correcting a scribe's misleading report (J.M. Sasson); three Sumerian texts dealing with the 'Beginning' (Å.W. Sjöberg); archaic city seals and early Babylonian unity (P. Steinkeller); the identity of King Lugalbanda (H.L.J. Vanstiphout); and the Codex Urnamma (C. Wilcke). The high quality of the contributions makes this volume a fitting tribute to Thorkild Jacobsen.

T. BRODIE

ARNOLD, BILL T. and BRYAN E. BEYER (eds.), *Readings from the Ancient Near East: Primary Sources for Old Testament Study* (Grand Rapids, MI: Baker Academic, 2002), pp. 240. 1 map, 19 figures. $21.99. ISBN 0-8010-2292-4.

This is a useful and affordable collection in English translation of 'the ancient Near Eastern texts that most closely parallel or complement the biblical text' (p. 9). It can function well as a textbook for an undergraduate survey course on the OT world, and can also be of use to other interested readers unwilling to purchase a major collection like W.W. Hallo and K.L. Younger's *The Context of Scripture*. There are 90 texts anthologized here, mostly relating to the Pentateuch and historical books (wisdom and prophecy are not so well served in this collection). In their brief introductory pieces to the documents, the editors are at pains to stress the uniqueness of the biblical material, and in their choice of translations they show a preference for certain disputed interpretations: they put forward the allegedly 'probable' presence of Jehoram and Ahaziah in the Tel Dan inscription, and the Kuntillet Ajrud blessings appear here as 'I bless you by yhwh...and by Asherata'. Nevertheless, in other respects the evangelical agenda of the Encountering Biblical Studies series, within which this volume is placed, does not intrude too noticeably —the texts are largely allowed to speak for themselves, despite the inevitable compromises that excerpted collections must make. For an anthology geared towards biblical students, however, the indexing leaves something to be desired: many biblical characters appearing in the notes do not appear in the index (e.g., only one of the references to Abraham is indexed, none of the references to Moses), nor is there an index of scriptural references.

J. JARICK

ASIRVATHAM, SULOCHANA R., CORINNE ONDINE PACHE and JOHN WATROUS (eds.), *Between Magic and Religion: Interdisciplinary Studies in Ancient Mediter-*

ranean Religion and Society (Lanham, MD: Rowman & Littlefield Publishers, Inc., 2001), pp. xxix + 212. 21 figures. $27.95. ISBN 0-8476-9969-2.

Focusing primarily on Graeco-Roman culture and religion, this collection of essays endeavours to apply a wide range of interdisciplinary methodologies to the fluid terms 'magic' and 'religion'. The objective is to rethink radically the use of these two terms and their traditional application in classical scholarship (e.g., 'religion' as the practice of the *polis* and 'magic' as outside the *polis*) with the intent to understand the two terms in a broader and deeper way. Three distinct sections divide the essays. In Part I, 'Ancient Religion, Self and Other', four essays deal with issues of definition and self-identity of groups (those inside and outside), in particular, how ethnic, cultural and political perceptions shape religious beliefs and practices. Religious and national identities tended to be inseparable, but C. Ondine Pache and Z. Várhelyi examine the syncretistic religious practices of the Athenians and the Hellenized communities of Asia Minor. P. Jones and K. Blair-Dixon recognize the strong and enduring influence of Roman myths and definitions upon a community. In Part II, 'Man, Hero or God?', three chapters focus on the link between literature and cult. Both Greeks and Romans practised hero cults, ancestor worship and even deified living human beings. S. Cole, S.R. Asirvatham and E. Bradshaw Aitken investigate the strategies used by such authors as Horace, Virgil, Plutarch and Philostratus to create and promote the religious identities and divine status surrounding emperors (Augustus), great leaders (Alexander), and legendary heros (Achilles). In Part III, 'Religious Iconography in Late Antiquity', M.M. Fulghum, A. Walker and A. Luyster reconsider the established scholarly classification of amulets, marriage rings and iconography as 'magical' or 'religious' artefacts. Overall, the essays succeed in challenging traditional applications of these two terms. However, readers should be more than casually familiar with Graeco-Roman history and the 'magic-religion' debate in order to appreciate fully the conclusions of the authors.

J.M. SHEPHERD

BAKER, HEATHER D. (ed.), *The Prosopography of the Neo-Assyrian Empire, Vol. 2, Part 1: H–K* (Helsinki: The Neo-Assyrian Text Corpus Project, University of Helsinki, 2000), pp. ix + 425-646. $50.00. ISBN 951-45-9045-7.

BAKER, HEATHER D. (ed.), *The Prosopography of the Neo-Assyrian Empire, Vol. 2, Part 2: L–N* (Helsinki: The Neo-Assyrian Text Corpus Project, University of Helsinki, 2001), pp. ix + 947-975 + 32. $60.00. ISBN 951-45-9055-4.

The first volume of this work appeared in two parts in 1998 and 1999, on which see *B.L.* 2000, p. 166. This second volume has kept up the pace and with it the first half is now completed. It continues the excellence of the first volume not only with a listing of occurrences of the names, but also with authoritative statements on the etymologies (not every OT scholar knows that *Joash–Iū'āsu* most likely means 'Yahwe has given') and concise but full and reliable summaries on the people and the events in which they participated, with bibliography for each item. The five-

and-a-half pages devoted to Merodach-baldan–Marduk-apla-iddina is the best available source for beginning a study on this man. With so comprehensive a work its lacks are significant. In the first volume no vizier of Esarhaddon named Aḥiqar appears, from which one may doubt if the figure of later Near Eastern literature was historical, since the reign of Esarhaddon is well documented. Hebraists with no Akkadian will have some problems since the names are arranged in their Akkadian forms.

W.G. LAMBERT

BOSSE-GRIFFITHS, KATE, *Amarna Studies and Other Selected Papers* (ed. J. Gwyn Griffiths; OBO, 182; Fribourg: University Press; Göttingen: Vandenhoeck & Ruprecht, 2001), pp. 244. SwFr 74.00. ISBN 3-7278-1360-1 (University Press); 3-525-53997-5 (Vandenhoeck & Ruprecht).

Part I of the reprinted papers in this collection concerns Amarna and Part II is more miscellaneous. The article of most direct interest for readers of the *B.L.* is 'The Fruit of the Mandrake in Egypt and Israel' (pp. 82-95, with an addendum, p. 96), though curiously there is no reference to the occurrence in Song 7.14. Even so, there are discussions of many items, such as wigs, beads and amulets, that provide some insight into daily life in Egypt. The book, which is enlivened by many photographs and drawings, closes with a bibliography of the author's publications and there are indexes.

W.G.E. WATSON

CHAVALAS, MARK W. and K. LAWSON YOUNGER, JR. (eds.), *Mesopotamia and the Bible: Comparative Explorations* (Grand Rapids, MI: Baker Academic, 2002), pp. 395. $29.99. ISBN 0-8010-2420-X.

Most of the contributions to this volume originated as papers read at a meeting of the Near East Archeological Society in Philadelphia in 1995. They do not add up to a comprehensive survey of the field but deal with certain aspects of the relationship of Mesopotamia (more strictly Syro-Mesopotamia) and the Bible. Two papers are concerned with method: the history of the sometimes tense relationship between Assyriology and biblical studies (M.W. Chavalas), and the principles which should govern comparison between, say, temple building accounts in the Bible and in Sumer (R.E. Averbeck). There is an interesting account of how Sargon II was proved to be a real king and how Pul and Tiglath-pileser became identified (S.W. Holloway) and a review of recent work on Sargon (K.L. Younger). In recent years the major discoveries have been made in Syria and Northern Mesopotamia (M. Chavalas; V.H. Matthews), at Emar (D.E. Fleming) as well as at Ebla; the documents from Nuzi and Mari continue to repay study (D.C. Deuel; V.H. Matthews), but knowledge of both the Old Babylonian and the Neo-Babylonian Periods remains disappointing (R.A. Veenker; B.T. Arnold). The origin of the Aramean states is still mysterious (W. Schiedewind). The articles on Alalakh (R.S. Hess), Ugarit (W.T. Pitard) and the Diaspora in Babylon (E. Yamauchi) are largely summaries of what is already familiar. The bibliographies at the end of each article will be found useful.

R. TOMES

COHEN, SUSAN L., *Canaanites, Chronologies, and Connections: The Relationship of Middle Bronze Age IIA Canaan to Middle Kingdom Egypt* (Harvard Museum Publications Studies in the Archaeology and History of the Levant, 3; Winona Lake IN: Eisenbrauns, 2002), pp. ix + 168. 27 figures. $39.95. ISBN 1-57506-908-3.

As shown by the summary of previous research (Chapter 1), the date of the period in question is much debated. Furthermore, Middle Bronze Age IIA 'has been classified variously as both urban and nonurban, and as either extremely short...or lasting as long as two centuries. Its culture has been considered by some as isolated from the rest of the ancient Near Eastern world and by others as part of a larger international empire controlled by Egypt' (p. 137). To resolve these inconsistencies, C. re-examines evidence from Egypt (Chapter 3), including documents such as the Tale of Sinuhe and the Execration Texts, the finds from 133 MB IIA sites in Canaan and their distribution (Chapter 4). This evidence is then evaluated (Chapter 5) on the basis of the theoretical considerations set out in Chapter 2. The conclusions (pp. 136-39) relate to chronology (MB IIA overlaps with the XIII Dynasty, as shown by the table on p. 131) and to the contacts between Canaan and Egypt. A bibliography and an index are provided. This is a work of assured scholarship.

W.G.E. WATSON

DIETRICH, M. and O. LORETZ (eds.), *Ugarit-Forschungen. Internationales Jahrbuch für die Altertumskunde Syrien-Palästinas.* Band 33. *2001* (Münster: Ugarit-Verlag, 2002), pp. vii + 777. $122.00. ISBN 3-934628-11-7.

A small number of articles in this volume are of concern for biblical scholars. They are as follows. O. Loretz examines the Ugaritic radical *'tq,* and considers its relation with *'tq* in Ps. 6.8; the same author mentions Hebrew *bāmôt* in the context of Ugaritic *bmt* and the 'Baal au foudre' stela; he also considers a possible 'Amorite-Canaanite' Vorlage to Genesis 1–2, with Egyptian links; N. Na'aman examines Solomon's district list of 1 Kgs 4.7-19 in the light of Assyrian provincial organization; Y. Sadka discusses Hebrew *hinnēh*; and O. Tammuz writes on 'Canaan, a land without limits'.

N. WYATT

GORDON, CYRUS H. and GARY A. RENDSBURG (eds.), *Eblaitica: Essays on the Ebla Archives and Eblaite Language, Vol. 4* (Center for Ebla Research at New York University; Winona Lake, IN: Eisenbrauns, 2002), pp. xvi + 269. $39.50. ISBN 1-57506-060-4.

The third volume of this series (*B.L.* 1994, p. 122) appeared a decade before this one due to the death of a major benefactor and then the death of its chief promoter and editor. This is to be the final one and has been delayed. Gordon himself contributes a two-page article on 'Gnostic Light on Genesis 1 and 2 via Maśśa'' claiming to have an Ugaritic parallel to Yahweh-Elohim and an Ebla example (there are in fact more) of the place named in Proverbs 30–31. One hopes this will not detract from Gordon's memory as a very serious Ugaritic scholar. The largest contribution by far is the second part of M.A. Astour's 'History of Ebla', the two comprising

238 pages, though the final section was not finished in time to be included here. It is a staggering achievement in gathering and presenting data, but the conclusions may not meet with general approval. The author is neither a cuneiformist nor an archaeologist. *Inter alia* he discusses at length the recently published Hurrian text with Hittite translation which deals with Ebla. A. Archi on Ebla prepositions is concise but comprehensive, and his article on a religious confraternity is also good. G.A. Rendsburg's 'Eblaite and Some North West Semitic Lexical Links' offers little of OT relevance and is often speculative. R.R. Stieglitz writes on divine pairs at Ebla and on 'The Deified Kings of Ebla', the latter relevant to study of the early ancestral lists in Genesis. A. Wolters deals with the metrological nouns *prs*, which occur everywhere in the ANE except in biblical Hebrew.

W.G. LAMBERT

HALLO, WILLIAM W. and K. LAWSON YOUNGER, JR (eds.), *The Context of Scripture*. III. *Archival Documents from the Biblical World* (Leiden: Brill, 2002), pp. liv + 406. €111.00/$129.00. ISBN 90-04-10620-0.

This is the third and final volume in this prestigious Brill publication, intended to update and supersede Pritchard's *ANET* (1950–69). For the earlier parts see *B.L.* 1998, pp. 168-69 (vol. 1) and *B.L.* 2001, pp. 25-26 (vol. 2). As previously, the volume is divided into sections dealing with each cultural-linguistic zone, Egyptian (pp. 3-40), Hittite (pp. 43-72), West Semitic, vernaculars (pp. 75-230), Akkadian—including West Semitic documents in Akkadian (pp. 233-90), and Sumerian (pp. 293-318). The West Semitic section in particular has benefited from enormous advances in research in the last half-century, as is indicated by its bulk. The dispute between a man and his Ba and the Akkadian Anzu story appear as two addenda (pp. 321-35). This very diverse material is framed within an extensive introductory section (pp. xxi-liv), containing a number of perceptive and balanced short essays on issues of context and comparability; and two indices, scriptural and general topical, covering all three volumes. Of the essays, Younger's is perhaps the most important in its cogent argument for the essential nature of collections such as this, as basic research materials that should be familiar to all biblical scholars in a generation all too often seduced by the more extreme ahistorical and navel-gazing tendencies of postmodernism.

N. WYATT

HANSEN, WILLIAM, *Ariadne's Thread: A Guide to International Tales Found in Classical Literature* (Myth and Poetics; Ithaca, NY: Cornell University Press, 2002), pp. xvii + 548. $45.00. ISBN 0-8014-3670-2.

HB scholars interested in the folkloristic aspects of the wisdom tradition will find H.'s guide an interesting parallel study to some which have been undertaken in their own field. Since the primary focus is classical literature in Greek and Latin, this volume is not immediately relevant in detail to biblical studies. However, H.'s introduction is useful and thought-provoking: his suggestion that the Greek material has examples of folk tales adapted in the form of legend or history will echo with those familiar with, for example, J. Van Seters' treatment of the wife-sister stories in Genesis. The Judgement of Solomon and Potiphar's Wife are the only two obviously biblical tales which make an appearance, but other hints may be found. A parallel volume on the theme of 'International Tales in Biblical and Related Literature' would be interesting, if there are any takers!

A.G. HUNTER

HAUL, MICHAEL, *Das Etana-Epos: Ein Mythos von der Himmelfahrt des Königs von Kiš* (Göttingen Arbeitshefte zur altorientalischen Literatur, 1; Göttingen: Seminar für Keilschriftforschung, 2000), pp. xii + 259. 16 plates. €22.00. ISBN 3-00-008706-0.

The Etana Epic is a Babylonian text combining a story of conflict between a snake and an eagle, and a legend about an early king of Kish who lacked a son and heir, sought to find the 'plant of birth', tried to reach heaven on the back of an eagle, failed the first time, but apparently succeeded the second time. Unfortunately the text is poorly preserved at this point and the end of the story is lost. The last critical edition was that of J.V. Kinnier Wilson, *The Legend of Etana: A New Edition* (reviewed in *B.L.* 1986, pp. 104-105) which offered idiosyncratic interpretations and reconstruction of the end of the text. This new edition by Haul is more down to earth, but thorough and reliable. While addressed to cuneiform scholars, the introductory discussions and translation are fully available to Hebraists.

W.G. LAMBERT

HEEßEL, NILS P., *Pazuzu: Archäologische und philologische Studien zu einem altorientalischen Dämon* (Ancient Magic and Divination, 4; Leiden: Brill/Styx, 2002), pp. viii + 253. 164 plates and 1 map. €99.00/$115.00. ISBN 90-04-12386-5; ISSN 1566-7952.

Pazuzu was a Babylono-Assyrian demon which appears first only in the first millennium BC and disappears during the Hellenistic age. Amulets consist of winged statuettes or heads, some with inscription, or are plaques with reliefs and sometimes related to cuneiform text. The texts also appear on clay cuneiform tablets. Though from a human standpoint he was evil, he was cultivated because he could be used against other evil demons. This book meticulously collects all the examples of amulets with full details, giving photographs or drawings, and edits all the texts with translations and notes, with introductory chapters. It is generally reliable. Though Pazuzu seems not to be named in the OT, he was probably known at least to some Israelites since a fibula with his head was excavated at Megiddo.

W.G. LAMBERT

HEINZ, MARLIES, *Altsyrien und Libanon: Geschichte, Wirtschaft und Kultur vom Neolithikum bis Nebukadnezar* (Darmstadt: Wissenschaftliche Buchgesellschaft, 2002), pp. xi + 286. 5 maps. €34.90. ISBN 3-534-13280-7.

This is an attempt at reconstructing the history of the region of Syria and Lebanon from 10,000 BCE to the end of the Persian period and the arrival of

Alexander the Great, taking into account the latest results from archaeological excavations. The focus is on economics and politics and the structure of society. After an introduction on the Fertile Crescent, chapters are devoted to each of the periods (Neolithic, Chalcolithic and so on), some with subtitles indicating the trend of a particular period (e.g. 'Trade, Cities and Nomads') and Chapter 8 deals with de-urbanization. The evidence from the various sites is set out with the help of tables and each chapter has its own bibliography. There are references to these works within the text as well as a few footnotes. In addition, there are several excursuses (e.g. on art and communication, p. 86) though these are not listed in the contents, and helpful summaries are provided throughout. This evidence-based survey is clearly written and well laid out.

W.G.E. WATSON

HORNUNG, ERIK, *The Secret Lore of Egypt: Its Impact on the West* (trans. D. Lorton; Ithaca, NY: Cornell University Press, 2001), pp. ix + 229. £19.95. ISBN 0-8014-3847-0.

This is a translation of *Das esoterische Aegypten* (Beck, 1999). H. illustrates his theme with a mass of briefly detailed examples from ancient times to modern in which Hermetism figures largely. There is little of direct relevance to OT study but H.'s volume is a vivid reminder that popular religion in ancient Palestine was probably much more influenced by Egypt than concentration on OT's main religious teaching would suggest; although, as H. makes clear, influence could be a two-way process. H. refers to 'the negative attitude towards Egypt that characterizes the Old Testament' (p. 45) and he celebrates Hermetism as offering hope, 'a body of knowledge independent of the Bible and the Quran' (p. 191), and the kind of humane tolerance and freedom from rigid dogma which provide 'an antidote to the fundamentalism that must be overcome if we desire to live in peace' (p. 145). This is well said. But H. also provides striking examples of superstitious nonsense and pseudo-philosophy looking back to a real or supposed Egypt for their inspiration, and to which we might also feel the need of an antidote whose claims to revelation are based on something more solid than the shifting sands of overheated imagination. For those whose interest in the Bible is part of a more general interest in religious belief this is a stimulating book.

P. ADDINALL

HÜBNER, ULRICH and ERNST AXEL KNAUF (eds.), *Kein Land für sich allein: Studien zum Kulturkontakt in Kanaan, Israel/Palästina und Ebirnâri für Manfred Weippert zum 65. Geburtstag* (OBO, 186; Freiburg: Universitätsverlag; Göttingen: Vandenhoeck & Ruprecht, 2002), pp. viii + 331. 10 figures; 3 maps. SwF 98.00. ISBN 3-7278-1402-0 (Universitätsverlag); 3-525-53043-9 (Vandenhoeck & Ruprecht); ISSN 1015-1850.

This fine, thought-provoking collection of studies is a fitting tribute to Manfred Weippert. The majority of studies consider pre-exilic matters: M. Nissinen writes on the prophets and the divine council, Z.A. Kafafi provides new light on Egyptian governors' residences in Jordan and Palestine, U. Hübner considers Jerusalem and the Jebusites, A. Lemaire reconsiders the tradition about the Queen of Sheba, C.S. Ehrlich supports the identification of Tell eṣ-Ṣāfī with Gath, H.M. Niemann reassesses the Philistines, insisting on adjustments to the biblical pictures of them, C. Uehlinger takes a fresh look at the relief of Tiglathpileser III, S. Timm asks whether an Assyrian temple is attested in Samaria, F.M. Fales reads about Central Syria in the letters received by Sargon II, B. Becking considers West Semitic evidence in texts found at Tell Šēḫ Ḥamad as support for the exile from the Northern Kingdom, L. Massmann re-evaluates the politics of Sennacherib in Judah, and E.A. Knauf enquires about who destroyed Beersheba II. The remaining studies are mostly engaged with postexilic matters: A. Berlejung considers what happens to temples and their cultic activity after the wars are over, F. Israel looks at the term Amorite in Ezek. 16.3, 45 for linguistic evidence on the development of Hebrew, P.-E. Dion concludes that the religion of the Elephantine papyri attempts to imitate that of Judah before the exile, B. Halpern suggests that Job's astronomies reflect concerns close to 500 BCE, K. van der Toorn discusses revelation as a scholarly epistemological construct in Second Temple Judaism, H.-P. Mathys puts into the current debate T. Boman's views from the 1950s on the OT as a hellenistic book, and J.M. Sasson argues that a clear understanding that cooking meat in milk was forbidden belongs only to the time of the LXX. All the articles come with comprehensive bibliographies; and one is also provided listing the works of Weippert himself.

G.J. BROOKE

LECOQ, PIERRE, *Les inscriptions de la Perse achéménide Traduit du vieux perse, de l'élamite, du babylonien et de l'araméen, présente et annoté* (Paris: Gallimard, 1997), pp. 330. 16 plates. FF 160. ISBN 2-07-073090-5.

Biblical scholars often need to use information from fields over which they have no first-hand control. Few OT scholars master Old Persian or Elamite. It is then tempting to copy things from previous OT scholars who were in fact amateurs in these matters. For scholars working on Hebrew writings of or referring to the Persian period this book is to be highly recommended. It is written by an expert but specifically as a work of *haute vulgarisation*. Not only does it for the first time offer in one book translations of all the royal inscriptions from all their languages, with notes, but it also gives 13 introductory chapters covering such things as languages of the empire, the palace of Susa, religion of the Achaemenids and institutions of the Achaemenids. There is a map with the satrapies marked, a genealogical table of the dynasty, details of the calendar, and so on.

W.G. LAMBERT

LEICK, GWENDOLYN, *The Babylonians: An Introduction* (London and New York: Routledge, 2003), pp. vi + 182. £12.99. ISBN 0-415-25315-2.

This is an attractively written work, drawing mainly on publications of the past three decades, weaving together evidence from material remains and texts in four main chapters: 'History', 'Society and Economy', 'Religion' and 'Material Culture', the last covering furniture, clothes, personal appearance and hygiene, cuisine, health, sexuality and death. The first chapter, 'Setting the Scene', deals with topography, then, interestingly, 'Babylonian geographical and cosmic notions' (including ancient maps and plans) and, rather inadequately, 'writing'. Most statements are supported by reference to standard and first-hand publications, revealing a wide range of knowledge. Unaccountably, there is no discussion of the use and designs of the quintessentially Babylonian artefact, the cylinder seal and there are a few slips (e.g. Akkadian is not a West Semitic language; Shu-Sin was not the last Ur III king). While not on the scale of H.W.F. Saggs' *The Greatness that was Babylon* (1962) and with only 12 illustrations, it will serve its purpose, revealing the richness of information available about Babylonia.

A.R. MILLARD

MORAN, WILLIAM L., *The Most Magic Word: Essays on Babylonian and Biblical Literature* (CBQMS, 35; Washington, DC: Catholic Biblical Association of America, 2002), pp. x + 212. $11.50. ISBN 0-915170-34-5.

There is much in this posthumously published collections of articles which will be of interest to biblical scholars. The articles discuss aspects of major themes from Assyriology which are relevant to biblical studies, for example, Gilgamesh, the flood and Akkadian prophecy. For example, after sexual congress with a prostitute, Gilgamesh's companion, Enkidu, was no longer able to live in the wild and converse with animals. This motif was proposed as the basis for Ovid's views on the civilizing effect of *voluptas* on early man. The Akkadian flood story of Atrahasis is explained against the background of the creation of man as a compromise between arguing gods. When younger gods refused to work to support more senior gods, man was created to do this work instead, thus providing man's *raison d'être*, but when man made too much noise, Enlil decided to bring first plagues and then a flood, to destroy mankind. The gods soon went hungry, however, as the flood progressed, since man was needed to support the gods, to maintain the balance. The biblical flood story rejects such a notion of balance, and the biblical command to man to 'be fruitful and multiply' is a conscious adaptation of the Mesopotamian story.

M.J. GELLER

PARDEE, DENNIS, *Ritual and Cult at Ugarit* (Writings from the Ancient World, 10; Atlanta, GA: SBL, 2002), pp. xiii + 299. $29.95. ISBN 1-58983-026-1.

The difficulties of translating Ugaritic prose and poetry are legendary, but this collection of cultic texts—mostly dealing with sacrifices, divination and incantations—is a sober and useful treatment. Particularly valuable is a concluding section giving parallels and differences between Ugaritic cultic texts and biblical passages dealing with sacrifices and the cult. Some differences between Ugarit and the Bible are obvious, such as polytheism versus monotheism, although Ugaritic is less polytheistic and the Bible less monotheistic than they might seem. More interesting is the fact that most sacrificial animals in Ugaritic sacrifices correspond to the same animals in biblical sacrifice, with a few exceptions (such as a reference to sacrifice of a donkey). Furthermore, the cultic month at Ugarit appears to be divided into four divisions, which are lunar divisions which may approximate but cannot correspond to the week, which is a solar division of time. The presence of so-called 'scientific' texts in Ugarit's curriculum which relate to Mesopotamian divination (such as lunar omens and dream omens) might explain why similar texts also appear in later Jewish sources, for example, Qumran and the Talmud, indicating an ancient scribal tradition in the West which survived much later in Palestinian curriculum. This book is to be highly recommended.

M.J. GELLER

ROTH, SILKE, *Gebieterin aller Länder: Die Rolle der königlichen Frauen in der fiktiven und realen Ausse politik des ägyptischen Neuen Reiches* (OBO, 185; Freiburg: Universitätsverlag; Göttingen: Vandenhoeck & Ruprecht, 2002), pp. xii + 168. €46.00. ISBN 3-7278-1395-4 (Universitätsverlag); 3-525-53042-0 (Vandenhoeck & Ruprecht); ISSN 1015-1850.

This book surveys the international role of queens of Egypt (particularly in the New Kingdom period, c. 1550–1070 BC), in two aspects. These are from the Egyptian ideological viewpoint (misleadingly termed 'fictive'), and from the angle of actual political practice in real life in those times. In relation to the Egyptian ideals and ideology, the author reviews the formal titularies borne by Egypt's queens. Not very surprisingly, these come to include nominal claims to wide (and local world) dominion, the 'lady of lands' of the book's title. But this, after all, is because such queens were consorts to kings who were termed 'conqueror of all lands', or 'Lord to the limit(s)', so their queens received a matching macho style. By contrast, queens in Egypt came late to the practice of international politics. The first clear case is that of Queen Tiyi at her husband's death, when Akhenaten was new to the job. Later, Ramesses II included his queen-mother Tuya and leading spouse Nefertari in the exchanging of congratulatory cuneiform 'telegrams' on the occasion of the great Hittite treaty, c. 1259 BC. R. also considers foreign princesses entering Egypt to receive queenly status, and Egypt's ambivalent attitude towards sending her princesses abroad (despite biblical scholars' misunderstanding of Amenophis III's opposition to such a practice). The book is a useful conspectus of the whole topic for its theme and period.

K.A. KITCHEN

SCHRAMM, WOLFGANG, *Bann, Bann! Eine sumerisch-akkadische Beschwörungsserie* (Göttingen Arbeitshefte zur altorientalischen Literatur, 2; Göttingen: Seminar für Keilschriftforschung, 2001), pp. vi + 119. 27 plates. €24.00. ISBN 3-00-008707-9.

Demons and incantations to ward off their attacks do not belong to the world of orthodox Yahwism, but the OT does have occasional allusions to them and the poetic books may carry over elements of incantation language. But there are not many reliable sources for relevant information on this subject. Existing translations are often out of date and are not adequately explained. This volume edits two long and fully preserved Sumero-Babylonian incantations which form a short series. They are lucidly introduced and the editions and translations are up to date, meticulous and reliable. While much of the commentary is for cuneiformists, the introduction and translations suit the needs of OT scholars.

W.G. LAMBERT

SINGER, ITAMAR, *Hittite Prayers* (Writings from the Ancient World, 11; Atlanta, GA: SBL, 2002), pp. xv + 141. $24.95. ISBN 1-58983-032-6.

The topic may seem a little esoteric, but this collection of 24 Hittite prayers in translation gives a profound insight into Hittite religious culture which could be of enormous value in the consideration of similar topics in other ANE traditions, including that of the HB. The translator has chosen a synchronic and subject-oriented rather than a diachronic approach in order to show how prayer functioned in the context of Hittite ritual (which is always in the background even if not explicit). Subjects covered include prayers concerning plagues and enemies and a king's prayers for his sick wife and about his scheming stepmother. For the Hittites human troubles arose from accusations brought forward by one of the gods in the divine assembly and led to emotional laments by the individual concerned. They conceived of prayer as forensic pleading before this assembly of the gods: the word for 'prayer' is juridical. Individual gods (especially sun-deities) were invoked and praised as part of a procedure aimed at persuading the god to support the supplicant. The plea often takes the form of self-justification (e.g. the foolishness of youth in a plea to minimize the seriousness of an offence). The outcome of the prayers is not known, so there is no element of thanksgiving as such within the texts. It seems to have been Hittite practice to thank the gods by promising better cultic practice in future and good works on the gods' behalf (for example the offering of cult-objects). Without making explicit comparisons S.'s 18-page introduction repeatedly touches on points which are bound to be of interest in relation to Israelite prayers. He notes, for example, that there is no neat separation of hymns and prayers: they both form part of the approach to the gods for help. Most Hittite prayers are uttered by the king (sometimes called 'priest') or his representative and the king has total responsibility for what goes on in his kingdom, including the sins of his predecessors. The assembly of the gods is central, since the plea ultimately has to be judged by it.

J.F. HEALEY

SMITH, MARK S., *Untold Stories: The Bible and Ugaritic Studies in the Twentieth Century* (Peabody, MA: Hendrickson, 2001), pp. xix + 252. 9 plates. $29.95. ISBN 1-56563-575-2.

The purpose of this book is to fill a gap in Ugaritic studies by offering an 'intellectual history' of the discipline from its beginning in 1928 to 1999. As its subtitle indicates, the emphasis is on the relationships between the two disciplines and is reflected in the issues that are brought to the fore, for example, the enthronement festival, myth and ritual, the asherah, the emergence of monotheism, without forgetting the questions of syntax and philology. The book is organized around four chapters, chronicling what the author perceives as four phases in Ugaritic studies—'Beginning: 1928 to 1945'; 'Synthesis and Comparisons: 1945 to 1970'; 'New Texts in Comparative Method: 1970 to 1985'; and 'Resurgence in Tools and Methods: 1985 to 1999'. Each chapter provides a section with a list of the major tools of the period, with advances in language, and so on, some of the questions and debates raised by scholars, and accounts of the main scholars involved in each periods. If there is much material to delight, *Untold Stories* is in many ways a rather 'chatty' book for which this reviewer suggests 'Who's Who in Ugaritic Studies' (with a focus on North Atlantic scholars) as a more appropriate title. It is a book which is better viewed as a resource rather than an assessment of the major scholarly debates (which in fairness it does not pretend to be) and could be conceived as a companion to the *Handbook of Ugaritic Studies* (1999). There is one index of modern authors, and no general bibliography, although there are abundant footnotes and the beginning of each chapter (Texts and Tools) provides the reader with a list of the major publications.

A. JEFFERS

TÖRÖK, LÁSZLÓ, *The Image of the Ordered World in Ancient Nubian Art: The Construction of the Kushite Mind (800 BC–300 AD)* (Probleme der Ägyptologie, 18; Leiden: Brill, 2002), pp. xix + 525. 30 figures. €132.00/$154.00. ISBN 90-04-12306-7; ISSN 0169-9601.

Using as its sources the decorated temples, formal inscriptions and archaeological sites, this very substantial volume seeks to present an overall view of the development of official and royal religious beliefs of the kingdoms of Nubia (Kush, Napata, Meroe) from the eighth century BC to the third century AD. Earlier, the Egyptians had left temples and texts throughout much of Nubia; these and Nubian intervention in Egypt in the eighth/seventh centuries BC led to the Nubians making full use of Egyptian religious conventions, as in planning and decorating temples. They did not do so slavishly, but adapted these models to their own beliefs and forms of expression. The writer divides his work into four large chapters: (1) the meaningful settings of temples in settlements; (2) and (3) an exposition of the forms, functions and decorative programmes of the major temples; and (4) illustration of the state's uses of literacy and official texts, a topic of interest for OT studies. The wholly misleading term 'royal novel' should be replaced by a better term, 'royal acts' or *res gestae*. This is a valuable survey of the official manifestations of a civilization not otherwise easily accessible.

K.A. KITCHEN

TROPPER, JOSEF, *Ugaritisch: Kurzgefasste Grammatik mit Übungstexten und Glossar* (Elementa Linguarum Orientis, 1; Münster: Ugarit-Verlag, 2002), pp. xii + 168. €100.21. ISBN 3-934628-12-5.

A new series, Elementa Linguarum Orientalium, edited by R.G. Lehmann and T., will offer teaching material for languages, texts and scripts of the ANE. The first of these teaching aids makes T.'s monumental *Ugaritische Grammatik* (*B.L.* 2002, p. 196) available for students in condensed and very much cheaper form, supplemented by nine exercise texts (six accompanied by the cuneiform text) and a glossary. The nine chapters (introduction, script, phonology, the pronoun, the noun, numerals, the verb, particles and syntax) correspond to the chapters in the reference grammar, for ease of consultation, and the bibliography is brief but to the point. Where necessary, explanatory footnotes are provided. It is to be hoped that students will take advantage of this work to study Ugaritic, and for those less fluent in reading German, an English language version is in preparation.

W.G.E. WATSON

TUBB, JONATHAN N., *Peoples of the Past: Canaanites* (London: British Museum Press, 2002), pp. 160. 18 colour and 106 black and white illustrations. £17.99. ISBN 0-7141-2766-3 (paper).

The book presents a brief history of Syria-Palestine from the Neolithic to the Roman periods. It relies heavily on artefactual remains, making extensive use of material from Tell es-Saidiyeh, where the author has dug for over a decade. The volume is easy to read and could be used with undergraduates. Although footnotes are limited, there is a suggested reading list for each chapter at the end. It has a good introductory chapter explaining dating issues and the excavation process succinctly. T.'s use of the term 'Canaanite' is problematic. While employed essentially as a geographical designation, he distinguishes Iron Age political groups within the territory, like the Philistines, Israelites and Phoenicians, from other unspecified Canaanites of the time; yet all are still Canaanites in a wider sense. In spite of the wider rubric, undue emphasis is placed on Israel, with discussions creeping into the Early Bronze and Middle Bronze sections, even though Israel only arose as an entity in the Late Bronze period. There is an excellent discussion of the Sea Peoples and of the history of the Jordan Valley. More attention to religious practice within each period would have been welcome, however. The book is well illustrated and is definitely worth adding to personal and university libraries.

D. EDELMAN

WYATT, NICOLAS, *Religious Texts from Ugarit* (The Biblical Seminar, 53; London: Sheffield Academic Press, 2002), pp. 502. £29.99. ISBN 0-8264-6048-8.

The second edition of this 'landmark' translation (*B.L.* 1999, pp. 155-56) includes minor corrections, four changes of translation and additional bibliography. Also, the subtitle of the first edition ('The Words of Ilimilku and his Colleagues') has been dropped. It should be mentioned that W. always takes care to acknowledge suggestions made to him by other scholars and he would have included my recent proposal that the difficult word *uzr* may mean '(on a) table-cloth' rather than 'enrobed' (p. 251, n. 6). The translations are set out in the sequence of the one volume edition of the Ugaritic texts (KTU) with marginal references to columns and lines, making this excellent version easy to consult.

W.G.E. WATSON

YON, MARGUERITE and DANIEL ARNAUD, *Études Ougaritiques I. Travaux 1985–1995* (Ras Shamra-Ougarit, 14; Paris: Édition Recherche sur les Civilisations, 2001), pp. 422. €63.00. ISBN 2-86538-284-2.

This long-overdue volume brings together the important discoveries of the seasons of excavation at Ras Shamra down to 1994, together with some studies of older periods, which have suffered comparative neglect. The book falls into two parts. The first contains essays on early work at Minet al Beida from 1929 to 1935, chapters on houses excavated in three zones of Ras Shamra in the 1936, 1966 and 1979–90 seasons, a catalogue of the palace ivories and their inscriptions from the 1955 season, and a Phoenician inscription found in 1963. The second part contains the *editiones principes* in most instances of the long-awaited archive from the 'house of Urtenu' on the southern side of the tell, from the 1986, 1988 and 1992 seasons. Nos. 1 to 28 are in Akkadian, 29 and 30 in Sumerian and 31a, b in Hittite. Nos. 32 to 53 are in Ugaritic. The texts of most intrinsic interest are a number of letters (§§1-19, 20-21?, 49-51), sacrificial lists (§§22a, b), a fragmentary fable of the hyena and the fox (§29), a divinatory text (§30), an incantation (§52), and a 'mythico-magical' text (§53), which probably contained the signature of Ilimilku in the colophon (l. 40).

N. WYATT

9. APOCRYPHA AND POSTBIBLICAL STUDIES

BAIRD, J. ARTHUR, *Holy Word: The Paradigm of New Testament Formation* (JSNTSup, 224; Classics in Biblical and Theological Studies Supplement Series, 1; London: Trinity Academic Press, 2002), pp. 268. £55.00. ISBN 1-8264-6025-9.

When J. Arthur Baird died in 1995 after approximately 40 years as NT Professor at Wooster College, Ohio, he left a manuscript which, as the title page of this volume indicates has now been 'selected and edited by Craig A. Evans and Stanley E. Porter with the assistance of Scott N. Dolff'. The editing is light; by and large B.'s text has been maintained. The editors are also restrained in their designation of the new series in which this book appears. They refer to it not as 'Classics...' but as 'Current Issues in Biblical Theology'. B. critiques scepticism about Jesus' historicity. He believes Jesus' followers had a profound respect for his words ('the Holy Word') and that that respect lasted for centuries. As the preface indicates (p. 12), 'the crucial insight that guides these pages is that in understanding the process of New Testament formation and canonization, theology precedes historical process ... The Holy Word about God and his Kingdom comes first'. In practice B.'s historical thesis concerning Jesus follows much of Birger Gerhardsson's *Memory and Manuscript: Oral Tradition and Written Transmission in Rabbinic Judaism and Early Christianity* (Lund, 1961). Despite B.'s insistence that methodologically theology precedes history, the problems scholars have found in Gerhardsson's work would seem to be present also in his own volume.

T. BRODIE

BALTRUSCH, ERNST, *Die Juden und das Römische Reich: Geschichte einer konfliktreichen Beziehung* (Darmstadt: Wissenschaftliche Buchgesellschaft, 2002), pp. 223. €24.90. ISBN 3-534-15585-8.

B., Professor of Ancient History at the Free University of Berlin, seeks to explain how the relationship between Jews and the Roman Empire reached its nadir in three major and catastrophic revolts. He rejects explanations that trace the causes of the first revolt only to 6 CE, and equally rejects recent studies of diaspora Judaism based on the evidence of archaeology, which have emphasized various models of successful integration. He argues for a fundamental incompatability between the political implications of Jewish monotheism and the hellenistic, and later Roman, understandings of empire. His account begins with Hezekiah in the eighth century BCE, traces the earlier relations of Judaea with the great eastern empires, pays close attention to the various documents from the Persian and Seleucid, and later from the Roman periods in Josephus and the Maccabean literature, but also sets against that Rome's changing relations with outsiders and sense of her own values as she expanded her influence from the second century BCE. He concludes with Gabinius's organization of Judaea in 57 BCE, by which time conflict was inevitable, the only surprise being its delay until 67 CE. The argument is thorough and consistent, but its strength is also its weakness—the exclusion of anything but the political, the focus on 'diplomatic' texts in literary sources, the limited attention to the variety and distinctive character of diaspora life, and a cut-off point before the establishment of the 'empire' of the title.

J. LIEU

BOCKMUEHL, MARCUS, *Jewish Law in Gentile Churches: Halakah and the Beginning of Christian Public Ethics* (Edinburgh: T. & T. Clark, 2000), pp. xvi + 314. £24.95. ISBN 0-567-08734-4.

B. draws together a number of his essays published or presented elsewhere to probe the question of the role of Jewish law in the creation of public ethics in the early Gentile Churches. The argument develops in three phases. First, B. reaffirms the view that Jesus did not intend to abrogate the Torah. Rather, he can be seen as a first century halakhist—radical, to be sure, but one whose 'ethical teachings can be shown to be conversant with contemporary legal Jewish debate and readily accommodated on the spectrum of "mainstream" first-century Jewish opinion'. Secondly, B. argues that the early Church (cf. Acts 15 and Pauline letters) developed a non-proselytizing, that is, non-Judaizing, mission to the Gentiles. Gentile believers in the Jewish Messiah would be under obligation only to those laws which the Torah itself applied to them—laws which were already part of a long interpretative tradition within Judaism of universal ethics. Finally, he explores how the Gentile churches themselves took this Jewish universal ethics and developed it in the Graeco-Roman setting. This is a refreshing and important study. The author's knowledge of the Jewish sources and his sensitivity to the deeper issues that they raise is exemplary. His discussion of the role that the definitions of the borders of the Land of Israel may have played in the dispute at Antioch between Paul and Peter shows a concreteness of thinking often lacking in NT scholarship on Judaism. However, one is left wondering whether he has done more than find a nuanced way of restating the old view that Gentile Christianity simply took over the ethical principles of the Torah and ignored the rest. The Torah's ethical principles are easily universalized (that is of the nature of ethical norms). But the Rabbis and other full-Torah parties would have denied that the Torah was only ethics. The question for them would remain: How can Gentile Christians (especially those living within the Land) be regarded as *full* members of *Kelal Yisra'el* if they reject the bulk of the Torah? It is hard to see any answer to this question that does not involve a concept of abrogation.

P.S. ALEXANDER

BRIN, GERSHON, *The Concept of Time in the Bible and the Dead Sea Scrolls* (STDJ, 39; Leiden: Brill, 2001), pp. xiv + 394. €103.00/$120.00. ISBN 90-04-12314 8; ISSN 0169-9962.

This study is primarily in the form of a catalogue of virtually all temporal terminology in the HB (including Ben Sira and Wisdom) and the Dead Sea scrolls, examining every nuance of meaning with regard to the flow and experience of time, and larger issues such as historical consciousness and eschatology. The latter concept is perhaps too readily read into biblical passages where a futuristic historical account seems quite adequate, though things have changed vastly in the Qumran literature. Some terms reappear in successive chapters, examined from different angles. The argumentation is perceptive and meticulous, and some old problems, such as the time of the beginning of the day in Hebrew thought, given a useful airing (Chapter 11). Two themes conspicuous by their absence are the calendar as a particular form of managing time in a complex society (and creating important cosmological and therefore sacred structures), and in particular the clash of calendars (merely hinted at in remarks on pp. 241-42, for example) which probably explains some of the Qumran–Jerusalem tensions during the community's life; and the language of orientation, which roots temporal and spatial vocabulary in very archaic layers of human experience (on which see Wyatt, in *Ugarit, Religion and Culture*, pp. 351-80 [reviewed in *B.L.* 1997, pp. 133-34]).

N. WYATT

BROOKE, GEORGE J., and PHILIP R. DAVIES (eds.), *Copper Scroll Studies* (JSPSup, 40; London: Sheffield Academic Press, 2002), pp. xvi + 344. £95.00. ISBN 0-8264-6055-0.

This wide-ranging collection, covering most aspects of the Copper Scroll (3Q15, abbreviated CS below), arises out of the International Symposium on the Copper Scroll held in Manchester in 1996. Part I on Opening, Restoring and Reading the Copper Scroll has the following essays: conservation and restoration of the CS (R. Bertholon, N. Lacoudre, J. Vasquez), John Allegro and the CS (Davies), the CS and the career of Henry Wright Baker (W. Johnson), the potential of photographic and computer imaging technology for the CS (M.J. Lundberg, B. Zuckerman), and some results of a new examination of the CS (É. Puech). In Part II on Archaeological and Linguistic Studies are aqueducts in the CS (H. Eshel), the linguistic affiliation of the CS (J.F. Elwolde), the meaning of דמע in the CS and ancient Jewish literature (A. Lange), whether the treasure is fact or fiction and the abbreviations כב and ככרין (J.K. Lefkovits), the CS and language issues (J. Lübbe), כלי דמע (S.J. Pfann), and the architectural vocabulary of the CS and the Temple Scroll (L.H. Schiffman). The final section, Interpreting the Copper Scroll, includes the process of writing the CS (M. Bar-Ilan), *inclusio* and symbolic geography in the CS (R. Fidler), further reflections on the CS (S. Goranson), new light on the CS and 4QMMT (I. Knohl), 40 years of discussion on the origin of the CS (P. Muchowski), novel approaches to the CS (B.L. Segal), whether the CS was Herod's bank account (B. Thiering), some palaeographical observations concerning the number of engravers (L. Tov), David

J. Wilmot and the CS (M.O. Wise), and palaeography and literary structure as guides to reading (A. Wolters). An introduction (Brooke) provides a useful orientation to the essays.

L.L. GRABBE

CAMPBELL, JONATHAN G., *Deciphering the Dead Sea Scrolls* (Oxford: Blackwell Publishers, 2nd edn, 2002), pp. xv + 224. 4 maps, 6 plates. £12.99. ISBN 0-631-22993-0.

It is evidence of both the accessibility of this introduction to the Dead Sea Scrolls, and the added perspective offered by the completion of publication of the manuscripts from Qumran, that a second edition is already made available. The first edition, strangely, did not make it into the *B.L.* Chapters have been reconfigured and renamed, but this book continues to be a sane and balanced introduction to the history, contents and significance of the scrolls. The scrolls themselves are covered in the early chapters: 'What are the Dead Sea Scrolls?' rehearses the basics of discoveries and contents in a straightforward manner; 'The Dead Sea Scrolls and the Bible' relates the manuscripts to current editions of the Bible; and in two chapters the identity of the Covenanters is argued to be Essenes. The significance of these matters for the present are discussed in two further chapters: in 'The Dead Sea Scrolls and Judaism' Campbell argues that Conservative and Reformed positions today will be more comfortable with the historical questions raised by the scrolls— and the Reformed more than the Conservative; yet, the modern Orthodox position is probably closest to late Second Temple period Jewish belief. In 'Christianity Reconsidered', the scrolls are seen to have fostered improved relations between Jews and Christians as Christians rediscover their Jewish roots. At the same time, the conservative Christian approach to Scripture is rendered less sustainable by the evidence of the creative and pluralist approach to the biblical text at Qumran. The final chapter puts 'Controversy and Conspiracy' in perspective. This new edition continues to be one of the most useful introductions to the Dead Sea Scrolls available.

D.D. SWANSON

CARSON, D.A., PETER T. O'BRIEN and MARK A. SEIFRID (eds.), *Justification and Variegated Nomism*. I. *The Complexities of Second Temple Judaism* (Grand Rapids: Baker Academic, 2001), pp. xiv + 619. $44.99. ISBN 0-8010-2272-X.

The European edition of this volume, published by Mohr Siebeck, was reviewed in *B.L.* 2002, pp. 204-205.

S.G.D. ADNAMS

CHANCEY, MARK A., *The Myth of a Gentile Galilee* (SNTSMS, 118; Cambridge: Cambridge University Press, 2002), pp. xv + 229. 3 maps. £45.00/$60.00. ISBN 0-521-81487-1.

This 1999 Duke University doctoral dissertation addresses the assumption, common in NT and 'historical Jesus' scholarship, of a strong Gentile presence in Galilee at the turn of the eras, arguing that the evidence for this is lacking. His argument is based on a close reading of the literary sources and on a detailed analysis of the archaeological evidence, rigorously including only material from the late Hellenistic and early Roman periods. After surveying scholarly images of Galilee, a study of the sources for the history from the depopulation of the Assyrian conquest to the first century CE argues for a major influx of population in the Hasmonaean period establishing the Jewish majority in the area. C. then takes each of the main settlements, reviewing the (often limited) literary and the archaeological testimony, before demonstrating that the evidence for the area around Galilee paints a sharply contrasting picture of Gentile dominance. A concluding chapter addresses the proverbial 'Galilee of the Gentiles', traditions of Jesus' Gentile contacts, and the cultural atmosphere of Galilee. The study is careful and often persuasive, although, since often the evidence is ambiguous or limited, exhibits a tendency to use this negatively of 'unproven' Gentile presence and positively of 'probable' Jewish presence. Indeed, some may find most striking the indeterminacy of the evidence and the problems of defining many of our terms, 'Jew', 'Gentile', 'pagan', 'culture', 'religion', 'ethnicity', which C. tends to treat as unproblematic.

J. LIEU

CHARLESWORTH, JAMES H. (ed.), *The Hebrew Bible and Qumran* (The Bible and the Dead Sea Scrolls, 1; N. Richland Hills, TX: Bibal Press, 2000), pp. xxxvi + 359 (including 8 pages of drawings and photos). $39.95. ISBN 0-94103756-8.

This first of a projected five-volume series on the Bible and the Dead Sea Scrolls (=DSS) arose out of a symposium in Princeton in 1997. The series aims to be a definitive statement of current research but with students and non-specialists in mind. With this in view, the editor introduces the volume with an essay answering some of the questions that non-specialists might ask. There are also some helpful drawings, photos and maps. The essays are the following: 50 years of discovery and controversy (Charlesworth); Scripture in the first century (J.A. Sanders); revealing invisible scripts digitally (K.T. Knox, R.L. Easton Jr, R.H. Johnston); Qumran and the Enoch groups (G. Boccaccini); the biblical scrolls from Qumran and the canonical text (F.M. Cross); the DSS and the Hebrew scriptural texts (E. Ulrich); the book of Daniel and the DSS (L.T. Stuckenbruck); the rewritten Bible at Qumran (S.W. Crawford); Qumran and a new edition of the HB (R.S. Hendel); the challenge of 4QSam[a] (D.W. Parry); the meaning and function of the three sobriquets of the Wicked Priest, the Synagogue of Satan, and the Woman Jezebel (H. Bengtsson); the biblical and Qumranic concept of war (P.R. Davies); and psalms and psalters in the DSS (P.W. Flint). Unfortunately, there are no indexes.

L.L. GRABBE

CHARLESWORTH, JAMES H., *The Pesharim and Qumran History: Chaos or Consensus?* (Grand Rapids, MI: Eerdmans, 2002), pp. xiv + 171. 12 illustrations. $20.00. ISBN 0-8028-3988-6.

This book serves as a sort of companion to volume 6b of the Princeton Theological Seminary Dead Sea Scrolls Project, *Pesharim, Other Commentaries, and Related Documents* (see p. 23). In it C. relates the evidence of the pesharim first to the archaeological evidence for 'Qumran' history (meaning, of course, the history of the ancient community that occupied the ruins of Khirbet Qumran), and to the other textual evidence (in 'Was Qumran a Celibate Monastary?'), and then examines the historical allusions in the pesharim. The treatment is balanced and unsensational, offering a valuable summary of the evidence. Extensive, and useful, appendixes by L. Novakovic of biblical quotations and text-critical variants encompass a third of the volume. As for the subtitle, the seductive promise of 'chaos', at least, seems to relate more to the attempted 'Sociology of Qumran Hermenuetics' than to any upset to 'consensus'.

D.D. SWANSON

CLAUßEN, CARSTEN, *Versammlung, Gemeinde, Synagoge: Das hellenistisch-jüdische Umfeld der frühchristlichen Gemeinden* (SUNT, 27; Göttingen: Vandenhoeck & Ruprecht, 2002), pp. 368. €82.00. ISBN 3-525-53381-0.

This careful reconsideration of all the evidence for synagogues is a very timely and worthwhile study. The introductory section is a detailed consideration of the history of research on the topic and of the nature of the sources available. The second section contains chapters on the geographical spread of synagogues, on the wide range of terminology associated with them (the term συναγωγή belongs to NT times), on the origins of synagogues, and on their architecture and functions, practices and officials (for which the catacombs of Rome offer much). Although the work is presented to illuminate the synagogues which Paul is supposed to have encountered on his travels, for the most part the NT is suitably kept in the background. Overall C. concludes that the Jewish synagogues of the first century CE are predominantly to be thought of as house-synagogues; Jews gathered principally in private houses. Large synagogue structures are, however, also evident in the diaspora and in Palestine (Gamla, Masada, Herodium, and probably Jerusalem [on the basis of the Theodotus inscription]) before the fall of the temple; these are the exception. From Jerusalem to Rome the early Christians grouped themselves together in small house communities, modelled on their Jewish counterparts, not least with the purpose of marking themselves off from pagan cultic practices.

G.J. BROOKE

DAVIES, PHILIP R., GEORGE J. BROOKE and PHILLIP R. CALLAWAY, *The Complete World of the Dead Sea Scrolls* (London: Thames and Hudson, 2002), pp. 216. 216 illustrations; 84 in colour. £24.95. ISBN 0-500-05111-9.

A stunningly illustrated photographic book, this volume was written and compiled by three recognized experts on the Dead Sea Scrolls and would make a suitable gift for the interested friend. It is produced in the format of a 'coffee table' book, although its size is more manageable than most of its kind. The five chapters cover the following topics: 'The Scrolls Revealed'; 'The Ancient World of the Scrolls'; 'Inside the Scrolls'; 'The Qumran Settlement'; and 'The Meaning of the Scrolls'. There are also the usual appendixes with a helpful 'Further Reading' list of recommended texts. The text is written in a lively and engaging manner and while one can quibble over the inadequate coverage of non-English research on the scrolls (e.g., on the influence of Zoroastrianism in French scholarship), the authors have done a commendable effort in discussing the most important aspects of scrolls research and controversies. *The Complete World of the Dead Sea Scrolls* makes the reading of the dry, often impenetrable, fragments come alive. In this age of images, its collection of photographs, charts and illustrations can also serve as a resource for teaching visually responsive students and the public alike.

T.H. LIM

DAVILA, JAMES R., *Descenders to the Chariot: The People behind the Hekhalot Literature* (JSJSup, 70; Leiden: Brill, 2001), pp. xi + 343. €89.00/$40.00. ISBN 90-04-11541-2; ISSN 1384-2161.

This book marks a significant advance in understanding the background and aims of the groups responsible for producing the Hekhalot literature. It consists principally of a detailed comparison between the social role and practices of these groups and those of the shamans of Siberia, the Arctic and the North American Indians. D. successfully establishes that such cross-cultural study is a key to grasping how the Hekhalot literature functioned in the Jewish society of Late Antiquity and the Early Middle Ages. Against those who have argued that the Hekhalot texts are purely literary creations and do not reflect an actual mystic or magical praxis D. claims to have shown that they preserve 'rituals and adjurations that were meant to be used; that they actually were used in specific social contexts for practical reasons and for named clients; and that the people who produced the rituals correspond to the multifaceted cross-cultural typology of a recognizable intermediary or magico-religious practitioner—the shaman/healer' (p. 304). Through a comparison with the Babylonian magical bowls and amulets he is able to locate in Nippur between the fifth and seventh centuries CE at least one of the groups active in producing the Hekhalot literature. Other parallels suggest the presence of similar groups in Palestine/Syria at the same time, and later in Egypt in the eleventh and twelfth centuries. The composers of the texts are located in scribal groups envious of the power and social status of the rabbis and determined 'to compete with them using their own rituals of power'.

A.P. HAYMAN

DAVIS, STEPHAN K., *The Antithesis of the Ages: Paul's Reconfiguration of Torah* (CBQMS, 33; Washington, DC: Catholic Biblical Association of America, 2002), pp. x + 259. $11.00. ISBN 0-915170-32-9.

This published dissertation explores the issue of Paul's view of the Torah. D. first considers the meaning of Torah in such literature as Sirach, *1 Enoch*, the *Temple Scroll* and *4 Ezra*. He concludes that Torah was no longer merely the Mosaic books considered as the repository of divine wisdom but was elevated to be the 'pre-eminent intermediary between God and the phenomenal world'. He considers this is the relevant context for such Pauline passages as Romans 9–10,

Galatians 3 and 2 Corinthians 3. Not all will be convinced, but this is a closely argued work at a very affordable price.

R.H. MORTIMORE

DELAMARTER, STEVE with a contribution by JAMES H. CHARLESWORTH, *A Scripture Index to Charlesworth's* The Old Testament Pseudepigrapha (London: Sheffield Academic Press, 2002), pp. viii + 99. n.p. ISBN 0-8264-6431-9.

This is an index of all the (Protestant) biblical references (to the OT and NT) that are provided in the margin and the footnotes to J.H. Charlesworth's *Old Testament Pseudepigrapha* (1983, 1985) (*OTP*). Since those two volumes are now irreplaceable for the study of the Jewish literature they contain, so too will this index be an essential volume for all who work on the Pseudepigrapha. The user should be aware that the attention to biblical citations or allusions in *OTP* did not aim to be comprehensive. Anyone therefore, for example, looking in this index for instances where Isaiah 11 informs postbiblical messianism will not be directed to the *Psalms of Solomon* 17.22-24, 29 or to *1 Enoch* 49, even though both passages clearly allude to it. And each pseudepigraphon has an introduction in *OTP* with a section devoted to the 'relation to canonical and non-canonical books' that sometimes contains valuable intertextual data not included in the notes and margins of the text. This too is not included in the index. The user should also know that oddly the volume is in fact two indexes, one for *OTP* 1 and one for *OTP* 2, each of which must be consulted separately.

C.H.T. FLETCHER-LOUIS

DESILVA, DAVID A., *Introducing the Apocrypha: Message, Context, and Significance* (Grand Rapids, MI: Baker Academic, 2002), pp. 428. $29.99. ISBN 0-8010-2319-X.

D. has produced a very comprehensive introduction to the books of the Apocrypha, having adopted 'the widest delineation' of the term, and included 'the more marginal texts' (p. 19) such as *3* and *4 Maccabees*. Following two chapters in which he discusses the value of the Apocrypha, especially from a Christian standpoint, and the historical context in which these books were composed, D. devotes the rest of the book to a detailed treatment of 16 writings. He follows a similar pattern each time: after giving a summary of its structure and contents, he discusses its textual transmission, followed by matters relating to authorship, date and setting. Then he inquires about its genre and purpose and the formative influences upon its author. The greatest space is devoted to its teaching and theology and, finally, attention is paid to its influence upon Jewish and Christian writings. The work is written throughout in a lucid style and one of its features is that even the most elementary terms are explained so that the beginning student could easily cope with it. At the same time, the practised professional can derive much from its comprehensiveness and the individual judgments of its author. Highly recommended.

J.T. WILLIAMS

DOMBROWSKI, BRUNO W.W., *Ideological and Socio-Structural Developments of the Qumran Association*. Part II. *Assorting the Bulk of the Remainder of Scrolls and Fragments found in the Area of Caves I–XI* (Qumran Mogilanensia, 12: Kraków: Enigma Press, 2002), pp. 108. $18.00. ISBN 83-86110-45-7; ISSN 0867-8707.

This work seeks to reconstruct something of the history of the Qumran community (or 'Association') through the study of its ideological developments. Part I, which was reviewed in *B.L.* 1996, pp. 137-38, was concerned mainly with the major texts of Qumran Cave 1, CD and 4QMMT. Part II deals with the rest of the literature found at Qumran, classifying it as follows. (A) Texts used by members of the Qumran Association: (a) authoritative texts, that is, texts offering authoritative definitions or self-evidence of the Association; (b) texts not being constitutive; (c) texts accepted by the Association as being seemingly compatible, though not constitutive, and with uncertain authorship = 'hybrid' texts. (B) Texts having been produced by others or like those of others, yet having been copied or adapted in part by members of the Association. The line of thought is not always easy to follow, and the reader is not helped by the frequent use of awkward syntax which at times makes sentences unintelligible. Much greater care could have been taken in the preparation for publication.

D.M. STEC

DOUDNA, GREGORY L., *4QPesher Nahum: A Critical Edition* (JSPSup, 35; Copenhagen International Series, 8; London: Sheffield Academic Press, 2001), pp. 813. £95.00. ISBN 1-84127-156-X; ISSN 0074-9745.

An unsupervised, unexamined and unrevised Copenhagen dissertation, this lengthy doctoral thesis is more than a critical edition of 4QpNah. Between the two covers of the book are found 813 pages of dense discussion, often in small font, not only of every line, word, lacuna and space of this short, but important, Qumran text but also the fundamental issues of palaeography, carbon 14 dating, and the historical setting of the sectarian commentary to Nahum. Even if only a portion of the numerous arguments, suggestions and assertions is correct, then the basic Qumran textbooks will have to be rewritten. D. advances the hypothesis that 4QpNah was written at the time of Pompey's conquest of Palestine in 63 BCE, arguing that 'the lion of wrath', commonly identified with Alexander Jannaeus, is a reference to the Roman general, and Aristobulus II is a figure known in the pesharim and CD as 'Manasseh', 'the Wicked Priest', 'the Liar', and 'the last priest'. This revolutionary thesis should not be dismissed out of hand, though it suffers from fundamental problems and is ultimately unconvincing. (1) The critical text (apart from certain reconstructions of lacunae) it purports to produce of 4QpNah is not very different from those that are already available. Moreover, in many ways it is often inferior to the one, say, edited by M.P. Horgan. There are transcriptional errors, for instance, in col. 3-4.ii.5 (p. 760); col. 1-2.ii.5a, 8 (p. 756). (2) Vital texts are emended (when there is no indication of error in the original) because they are inconvenient for the historical reconstruction. For instance, the independent plural pronoun, *hēm*, is changed to the singular *hû'* (pp. 762, 515, 519-20, 650 and *passim*) in order to suit his interpretation of Manasseh as a singular individual. Or again, the perfect of 'they did' and 'God gave him' in 1QpHab 9.2 and 10 respectively are contextually altered (pp. 619-20) to the imperfect to fit the alleged future punishment of the Wicked Priest. (3) The historical criticism and reconstruction are inconsistent, highly idiosyncratic and often incongruous. For example, he argues that 'Judah' should be read in a similar or identical sense everywhere in CD (pp. 584-85), yet only one of 'the last priests of Jerusalem' (1QpHab 9.4-5) can be identified with the singular (rather than multiple) figure of the Wicked Priest. (4) The genre of the *Pesher Nahum* as a 'genuine prophecy' (p. 672) rather than a sectarian interpretation of biblical oracle is asserted rather than argued. This is apparently why mass crucifixion is mentioned in the scroll, because the pesherist expected it from Roman practice, when in fact Pompey did not do so. D. himself provides the best summary of his work: 'In the Danish system the disputats is not done under a committee, or under an adviser, but is independent work analogous to the German Habilitation. Accordingly the only questions that I pursued in this study were my own; there were no committee members to whom I reported; there was no control over what I wrote, thought or expressed' (p. 13).

T.H. LIM

EGGER-WENZEL, RENATE (ed.), *Ben Sira's God: Proceedings of the International Ben Sira Conference, Durham, Ushaw College 2001* (BZAW, 321; Berlin: W. de Gruyter, 2002), pp. viii + 393. €98.00. ISBN 3-11-017559-2.

These papers concentrate more on theology and worship than on the philosophical context of Ben Sira's work. They thus refresh Ben Sira studies in valuable ways. They are grouped under four headings. There are four overall thematic pieces: A.A. di Lella's overview on God and Wisdom in the theology of Ben Sira, O. Wischmeyer's study of theology and anthropology in Sirach, J. Coley's essay on God as merciful father in Ben Sira and the NT, and O. Kaiser's comparison of the ethics of Ben Sira with those of Paul. Particular thematic studies are offered by N. Calduch-Benages (on Sir. 43.27-33), P.C. Beentjes (on the root רחם), M. Gilbert (on Sir. 15.11–18.14), F.V. Reiterer (on God and sacrifice), C.T.R. Hayward (on divine names), J. Liesen (on praise), T.R. Brown (on Sir. 44–50), O. Mulder (on Sir. 50), A. Goshen-Gottstein (a canonical reading of the praise of the fathers), U. Wicke-Reuter (on providence in Ben Sira and stoicism), and J.K. Aitken (on divine will and providence). Two studies focus on the Jewish use of Ben Sira: D.S. Levene looks at Ben Sira among the rabbis and S.C. Reif considers prayer in Ben Sira, Qumran and Second Temple Judaism. In an appendage R. Egger-Wenzel provides the text of a short unpublished contribution by A. Altmann with brief comments, E.-M. Becker writes briefly about a Lutheran catechism from 1561, W.T. van Peursen reports on three Leiden projects on the Syriac text of Ben Sira, F.V. Reiterer lists sacrificial terminology used in Ben Sira, and P.C. Beentjes provides a list of corrections to his 1997 edition of Hebrew Ben Sira. The overall quality of these papers is a pleasure to read and the alacrity with which the conference volume has been produced commendable.

G.J. BROOKE

EISSLER, FRIEDMANN, *Königspsalmen und karäische Messiaserwartung: Jefet ben Elis Auslegung von Ps 2.72.89.110.132 im Vergleich mit Saadja Gaons Deutung* (Texts and Studies in Medieval and Early Modern Judaism, 17; Tübingen: Mohr Siebeck, 2002), pp. xxi + 700. €149.00. ISBN 3-16-147706-5.

This Tübingen dissertation (supervisor S. Schreiner) is a study of the late tenth-century Karaite Bible exegete Japheth ben Eli, specifically his commentary on five royal psalms in Judaeo-Arabic. E. has picked these particular psalms because of the messianic interpretation given to them by the Karaites which can be compared with that of Qumran; however, this selection also allows one to see a good sample of Japheth's exegesis and to compare it with contemporary rabbinic exegesis (including that of Saadia Gaon, which E. also looks at). The first part of the book provides a detailed analysis of Japheth's commentary. The second part provides the Judaeo-Arabic text (from Ms hébr. 286 of the Bibliothèque nationale) and a German translation. This is a splendid addition to the small number of works on the Karaites available to the non-specialist.

L.L. GRABBE

ELDRIDGE, M.D., *Dying Adam with his Multiethnic Family: Understanding the Greek Life of Adam and Eve* (SVTP, 16; Leiden: Brill, 2001), pp. xvi + 316. €98.00/$117.00. ISBN 90-04-12325-3.

The *Life of Adam and Eve* and its related literature is beset with difficulties, some of which are tackled in this book, a reworking of the author's doctoral dissertation. Part of its success is due to its focus on the Greek *Life of Adam and Eve*. The book is divided into three sections; the first one ('Laying the Foundations') deals with the usual questions of introduction: date, language, sources, first text form and question of affiliation. The author develops a cautious consensus: he demonstrates the strong Hellenistic elements of the text, narrows down the parameters to offer a suggestion about a date, and re-evaluates Nagel's thesis of the priority of MSS DSV over MSS ATLC. The second part is concerned with the meaning of the text and uses the literary tools of narrative criticism and speech-act theory with success. The questions of Jewish or Christian provenance are tackled in the third part ('The Historical Dimension'). In some ways this is a cautious book, yet one cannot underestimate some of the novelty of its approach in this field. It is clear that the methods developed in this book have far-reaching implications, not least for questions about Jewish proselytism, and the position of Jewish Hellenistic women. This is an important study for anyone interested both in some of these topics and in the literary treatment of pseudepigraphic literature.

A. JEFFERS

ENDO, MASANOBU, *Creation and Christology: A Study on the Johannine Prologue in the Light of Early Jewish Creation Accounts* (WUNT, 2/149; Tübingen: Mohr Siebeck, 2002), pp. xx + 292. €54.00. ISBN 3-16-147789-8; ISSN 0340-9570.

Nearly three-quarters of this work is devoted to the identification and exhaustive study of Jewish creation accounts from about the second century BCE to the first century CE. In the case of each passage investigated, there is discussion of matters relating to its literary context and its main concerns; where necessary, a reconstruction of its text; the influence upon it of key passages from the OT; and, finally, the theological themes propounded by it. No stone appears to be left unturned in the search for parallels and influences upon these texts. Thus this part of the work serves as a comprehensive source book for these creation narratives. Finally, E. 'attempts to find a correspondence between the way the Genesis creation account is referenced in early Jewish tradition and John's attempt to depict the identity of the Son in the Johannine prologue' (p. 206). Included within this part of the work is a textual study of six passages from Deutero-Isaiah (pp. 212-15), which are related to the Genesis creation account in as much as the concept of the divine word in them was expanded in the context of both creation and eschatology in first century CE, apocalyptic literature. E. concludes that the Johannine 'prologue attempted to develop Christology on the basis of the exegetical traditions of the Genesis creation account' (p. 227).The influence of his doctoral supervisor, R. Bauckham, is detectable in his method of arguing for the way Jewish monotheism was carefully preserved throughout this process. Due attention is also paid to the importance of the images of life and light to the prologue in the context of the Jewish writings earlier adduced.

J.T. WILLIAMS

FITZMYER, JOSEPH A., *Tobit* (Commentaries on Early Jewish Literature; Berlin: W. de Gruyter, 2003), pp. xviii + 374. €88.00. ISBN 3-11-017574-6.

This is the first volume to appear in the new series, Commentaries on Early Jewish Literature, edited by Loren T. Stuckenbruck. F.'s skills as a commentator are well known, not only from commentaries on NT books but also on the *Genesis Apocryphon* and the Sefire inscriptions. He is also the editor of the Qumran fragments of Tobit (DJD, 19; *B.L.* 1997, p. 29). This is a solid, reliable commentary of the traditional sort, with close attention given to linguistic matters. Both versions of Tobit are given in translation. Both Greek and Hebrew script are used in the commentary. F. dates Tobit to the period 225 to 175 BCE, probably toward the latter part of that period. A main reason for dating it late seems to depend on the fact that the authoritative status of the Pentateuch was widely accepted. But it seems to me that this does not rule out the late Persian or early Greek period as F. seems to think. The other indicator, though, is the form of Aramaic of the Qumran fragments, which F. believes is no earlier than that of Daniel. This is indeed a worthy volume to inaugurate this new commentary series.

L.L. GRABBE

FLETCHER-LOUIS, CRISPIN H.T., *All the Glory of Adam: Liturgical Anthropology in the Dead Sea Scrolls* (STDJ, 42; Leiden: Brill, 2002), pp. xii + 546. €140.00/ $163.00. ISBN 90-04-12326-1; ISSN 0169-9962.

'This is the development of a footnote in my published doctoral dissertation' (p. xi)! F. attempts to demonstrate that the angelic liturgy in the *Songs of the Sabbath*

Sacrifice assumes a transformed, angelic humanity as the worshipping community. The book tries to prove that early Jewish thought took it for granted that humanity in either its original or redeemed state is divine (and/or angelic) and that this is conceptually and experientially grounded in temple worship. F. traces this 'high' anthropology from priestly traditions, sometimes linked with kings or Moses, but especially with priests themselves, and so argues that when it is encountered in community texts at Qumran it is not sectarian. After three introductory chapters, one of which considers Noah, the Qumran scrolls are analysed: first, their general anthropological statements are investigated (what they say about Moses, and about priests, especially the high priest and his breastplate), and secondly the *Songs of the Sabbath Sacrifice* are looked at in detail in four chapters. The cultic matrix of the concept is endorsed through its presence in texts which are liturgical or closely associated with the cult: parts of the *Hodayot*, 4Q380-81, the *Songs of the Sabbath Sacrifice*, the *Words of the Heavenly Lights*, 1QSb, the *Songs of the Sage*, the *War Rule*, 4Q392, 4Q393, 4Q408. In other texts the exalted anthropology is linked with the descriptions of priests or priestly heroes: 1QapGen, *1 Enoch* 106, 11QMelch, *Jubilees*, 4QTAmram, 4QTLevi. F. accounts for the absence of a temple-as-microcosm theology in the Qumran sectarian texts on the grounds that the community had taken itself away from the Jerusalem temple and so sought other ways of describing its cultic views. This is a significant study for challenging pictures of the world-view of the Qumran community and Jews more generally as a kind of dualism in which humans are inevitably earthy and earthly, but F. leaves unresolved the dichotomy between the hardships of daily life and the supposed sublimations of Jewish worship.

G.J. BROOKE

GROSSMAN, MAXINE L., *Reading for History in the Damascus Document: A Methodological Study* (STDJ, 45; Leiden: Brill, 2002), pp. xiii + 255. €68.00/$79.00. ISBN 90-04-12252-4; ISSN 0169-9962.

This exercise in postmodern historiography builds on notions of textual indeterminacy and the reader's construction of meanings. The 'history' sought does not lie *behind* a text but is *produced by the text*, through its reading by a particular audience, individual or collective. Chapter 1 first compares modern readings for history in the Damascus Document (D) and then points to the problem of an 'authoritative' Qumran text engendered by the dynamic process of composition, editing and interpretation. Chapter 2 presents two 'test cases' of the 'new history': gender in D (Were women part of the community? In reality or in theory?) and the Halakhic Letter, 4QMMT (Is it a letter? Intracommunal?). Different readings are not only possible today but always were, at different times with different readers (or editors). In Chapters 3 and 4 G. analyses the presentation of history in D, arguing that whether they are experienced or constructed (or both) is impossible to determine. The complex history of a text's composition and reception do make determinate meaning hard to aim at, and such a meaning is methodologically contingent if not open-ended. A postmodern, even somewhat deconstructive thesis, and the conclusion in many respects persuasive: 'To the extent that our evidence reflects potentially multivalent constructions of past historical events, it follows that our own historical narratives must be understood as individual mobilizations of meaning, and interpretive constructions of history' (p. 228). These arguments and conclusions apply, of course, equally well to the HB itself.

P.R. DAVIES

HABEL, NORMAN C. and VICKY BALABANSKI (eds.), *The Earth Story in the New Testament* (The Earth Bible, 5; London: Sheffield Academic Press; Cleveland, OH: The Pilgrim Press, 2002), pp. xx + 225. £18.99. ISBN 0-8264-6060-7; 0-8298-1501-5 (USA and Canada).

The final volume (see *B.L.* 2002, pp. 77, 163-65) in a series in which scholars from four continents seek to establish a new understanding of Earth based on six eco-justice principles and in the spirit of von Rad who wrote of an 'inner law' of creation and 'a secular understanding of the world'. The whole project reflects trends in contemporary hermeneutics, in this case predominantly the NT, though several of the 15 contributions have reference to the OT. In an essay on 'Swords into Ploughshares', for example, linking Micah with Q/Luke 9.62, A.H. Cadwallader acknowledges the importance of the plough as a tool of production but then goes on to explore it also as a tool of manipulation, symbol of male colonization of women and a continuation of the war simply using different rapiers. Beginning with Luke (peace on earth), M. Trainor goes back to Abraham and Moses to answer the question as to whether earth is throne or footstool; he decides that it is both but further complicates matters by concluding that both images have negative and positive consequences. In an essay on 'Human Anxiety and the Natural World' A.M. Leske begins with the Sermon on the Mount which treats the natural order in a positive manner reflecting the underlying theme of interconnectedness in Jesus' teaching on anxiety (Mt. 6.25-34) and then proceeds to examine its roots in relation to wisdom literature and the prophets, Isaiah in particular. All in all, OT specialists will find little of interest though those with a sense of wholeness may find it helpful as a way of completing the picture. Something seems to have gone wrong with Hebrews in the index.

A. GILMORE

HECKEL, ULRICH, *Der Segen im Neuen Testament: Begriff, Formeln, Gesten, mit einem praktisch-theologischen Ausblick* (WUNT, 150; Tübingen: Mohr Siebeck, 2002), pp. x + 431. €39.00. ISBN 3-16-147847-9; ISSN 0512-1604.

This Tübingen *Habilitationsschrift* was motivated in part by the practical concerns of Christian ministry and the questions about blessing which arise there. The conclusions are largely directed at Christian practice: on the basis of NT texts there are reflections on how blessing becomes christologically centred, on how blessing plays a role in making the churches part of Israel's salvation history, on the soteriological and eschatological significance of blessing, particularly as these involve the holy spirit and tend towards a trinitarian expression, and on how blessing involves ethical consequences. The NT uses of blessing show continuities with the OT and early Judaism (though H. somewhat downplays these), and also developments in new directions. Readers of the *B.L.* should note that what has been produced is a thorough reassessment of the concept in all its diversity and the first chapter is an effective updating of the relevant word study in *TDNT*, with the relevant citation and examination of OT and other textual counterparts. References to OT and early Jewish material also occur throughout the book; the most detailed comments on the Qumran sectarian uses of blessing feature in the section on the combination of blessings and curses.

G.J. BROOKE

HEDNER ZETTERHOLM, KARIN, *Portrait of a Villain: Laban the Aramean in Rabbinic Literature* (Interdisciplinary Studies in Ancient Culture and Religion, 2; Leuven: Peeters, 2002), pp. x + 214. €34.00. ISBN 90-429-1033-X.

This competent dissertation, supervised by H. Trautner-Kromann of Lund University and A. Shinan of the Hebrew University of Jerusalem, sets out to explain how the image of Laban is presented in midrashic and targumic literature and how this relates to the original biblical texts, the rabbinic understanding of Scripture, and certain aspects of the religious philosophy of postbiblical Judaism. The researcher carefully defines the nature of the midrashic method before making a close study of Laban, Jacob and Esau in the biblical and pre-rabbinic sources, comparing Deut. 26.5 with Gen. 31.22-25, and analysing all the relevant texts of the midrashim and targumim. She demonstrates a sound awareness of both traditional and modern literature, paying particular attention to the literary theories of D. Boyarin, M. Riffaterre and W. Iser. Her conclusion is that 'the negative image of Laban may have emerged simply as a result of rabbinic hermeneutics and the identification of Jacob with the people of Israel, without any identification between Laban and a historical enemy necessarily being made' (pp. 184-85). This assessment of the rabbinic image of Laban as an interaction exclusively with the biblical text, rather than any reflection of Jewish clashes with other cultures, is ultimately perhaps a trifle severe.

S.C. REIF

HELYER, LARRY R., *Exploring Jewish Literature of the Second Temple Period: A Guide for New Testament Students* (Downers Grove, IL: InterVarsity Press, 2002), pp. 528. $20.00. ISBN 0-8308-2678-5.

This is a commendably up-to-date introduction to early Jewish literature designed for the Christian beginner in the field. Arranged in a fashion very similar to that found in G.W.E. Nickelsburg's *Jewish Literature between the Bible and the Mishnah* (1981), H.'s volume has the advantage of including chapters on Philo, Josephus and the Mishnah itself. The constant cross-references to the NT some-times intrude unhelpfully by saying more than really can be said, but overall they should prod the Christian reader to see that it too is part of early Jewish literature, as H. himself points out (p. 23). Occasional substantial quotations from the relevant documents assist in familiarizing the reader with the primary material itself. The books of the apocrypha and several of the Dead Sea Scrolls are well described, but the pseudepigrapha are under-represented: only the *Letter of Aristeas, 1* and *2 Enoch, 4, 5* and *6 Ezra*, the *Testament of Moses*, the *Psalms of Solomon*, and *Sibylline Oracle 5* are discussed. Surely, the *Testaments of the Twelve Patriarchs* merit a place and are of more significance for understanding the NT than *2 Enoch*.

G.J. BROOKE

HEMPEL, C., A. LANGE and H. LICHTENBERGER (eds.), *The Wisdom Texts from Qumran and the Development of Sapiential Thought* (BETL, 159; Leuven: University Press; Peeters, 2002), pp. xi + 502. €80.00. ISBN 90-5867-243-3 (University Press); 90-429-1010-0 (Peeters).

The majority of the papers in this collection were originally given at a Research Seminar held in Tübingen in 1998 devoted to the Qumran wisdom texts, the remaining contributions were added to cover topics not dealt with at the Seminar. The volume is divided into six sections. (1) A. Lange provides a general introduction to the Qumran wisdom texts, J. Strugnell examines the relationship of 4QInstruction to the other wisdom texts from Qumran, primarily through an analysis of the vocabulary, and A. Schoors studies the language of the Qumran sapiential texts. (2) E.J.C. Tigchelaar and H. Lichtenberger deal with specific texts, the former providing a reconstruction of the beginning of 4QInstruction (4Q416 1 + par.), the latter a new edition of 4Q185. (3) H.-P. Müller, whose contribution is not directly concerned with the Qumran texts, analyses the different elements in Job and compares them with parallel texts from Babylon, and H. Niehr compares *Ahikar* with 4QInstruction. (4) H.-J. Fabry writes on the beatitudes in the Bible and in the Qumran wisdom texts, and G.J. Brooke on the way Scripture is used in these wisdom texts. (5) The greatest number of papers is devoted to analyses of specific texts from the late Second Temple period. P.S. Alexander traces the origins of Jewish interest in natural science back to *1 Enoch*, particularly to the *Astronomical Book*. L.T. Stuckenbruck examines, and rejects, the claim that 4QInstruction is dependent on Enochic traditions. D.J. Harrington compares Sirach and 4Qinstruction under the four rubrics: genre; traditions; world-view; community. C. Hempel considers whether there are any sectarian elements in the Qumran wisdom texts, and whether there are any wisdom elements in the Rule Books. C. Böttrich analyses the wisdom character of *2 Enoch* and, briefly, compares the book with 4Qinstruction, 4QMysteries, and 4QBeatitudes. J.H. Charlesworth discusses the question how the *Odes of Solomon* are influenced by Jewish wisdom traditions. J. Dochorn provides a detailed discussion of the use of Gen. 3.18a and 4.12b in 4Q423 2 3 (DJD 1, 2 and 3) and in Greek *Life of Adam and Eve* 24. (6) Finally, J. Frey considers the origin of Paul's negative use of 'flesh' against the background of usage in Jewish texts and particularly in the Qumran sapiential texts, and A. Klostergaard Petersen considers the construction of the others in 4QMysteries and in 1 Corinthians 1–2. This is an interesting and helpful collection that should materially assist in the understanding and interpretation of a group of texts that has only lately begun to receive detailed attention, and it is only to be regretted that it was so long in press.

M.A. KNIBB

HORST, PIETER W. VAN DER, *Japheth in the Tents of Shem: Studies on Jewish Hellenism in Antiquity* (Contributions to Biblical Exegesis and Theology, 32; Leuven: Peeters, 2002), pp. iv + 272. €35.00. ISBN 90-429-1137-9.

This is the second published collection of H.'s essays on the cultural milieu of the NT, again focusing especially on the interaction of Judaism and Christianity. Of the 15 essays, 13 are republished (sometimes with revision), and the topics display the author's impressive range of expertise, ranging chronologically over six centuries or so and covering Christianity, Judaism, Samaritanism and 'paganism'. They include a number of specialized studies, such as on Papyrus Egerton 5, claimed as a Jewish liturgical prayer, the distinctive vocabulary of *Contra Apionem*, or the 'First Female Jewish Author', (not Moses' sister Miriam, but Maria Alchemista, c. second century CE) and Greek synagogue prayers in the *Apostolic Constitutions* Book 7. There are also two essays on Samaritans and one on the last Jewish Patriarchs and Graeco-Roman medicine. But of particular interest to the less specialized reader (including the OT/HB scholar) will be the many treatments of major themes: Greek in Jewish Palestine, Sabbath worship in the synagogue before 70 CE, Jews and Christians in Antioch, celibacy in early Judaism, antediluvian knowledge, tombs of the prophets in early Judaism and sacred books as oracles in late antiquity. The overt mastery of primary and secondary sources makes the entire collection a fascinating, stimulating and instructive read, even if the conclusions themselves deliver fairly few surprises.

P.R. DAVIES

ILAN, TAL, *Integrating Women into Second Temple History* (Peabody, MA: Hendrickson, 2001), pp. xiii + 296. $24.95. ISBN 1-56563-547-7.

This is the third volume in a trilogy on Jewish women in the Second Temple and rabbinic periods. It consists of a collection of ten studies which are presented in three parts: 'Women and Sects'; 'Women and Sources'; and 'Women and the Judaean Desert Papyri'. Half these studies have previously been published in various places between 1992 and 1996, the remainder were written for this volume. I. draws on archaeological and epigraphic remains along with narrative, historiographic and legal texts as she sets about rewriting Jewish women's history. The studies all relate to the period from Hellenistic Judaism through to the second century CE and deal with subjects as diverse as misogyny in Ben Sira, skeletal remains in relation to gender and social issues, the dating of Esther, Judith and Susanna and their purpose as propaganda for the reign of Queen Shelamzion in 76 BCE, and a bill of divorce from a woman to her husband dated 135 CE. I.'s feminist insights are clearly expressed throughout these studies and there is no doubt about her agenda. She engages with a wide range of Jewish scholars and presents her arguments clearly. Relevant texts are cited in English translation on the whole, although the disputed *get* text is also presented in Hebrew. This is a useful and accessible volume for anyone studying that period of history and the place of women in Jewish society.

J.E. TOLLINGTON

ILAN, TAL, *Lexicon of Jewish Names in Late Antiquity*. Part I. *Palestine 330 BCE–200 CE* (TSAJ, 91; Tübingen: Mohr Siebeck, 2002), pp. xxvi + 484. €159.00. ISBN 3-16-14731-2; ISSN 0721-8753.

This valuable collection covers the main part of the 'Greek' period, that is, the period when Jews were under Greek influence. It is both an onomasticon (collecting all the names used by Jews in Palestine during the stated period) and a prosopography (a listing of the people who bore the names, as far as they are known). All names collected, including doubtful ones, come to 3595; of these 2826 are thought to be certain enough to use for statistical purposes. Six lists are included: (1) biblical names, (2) Greek names, (3) Latin names, (4) Persian names, (5) other Semitic names in the Hebrew alphabet, and (6) other Semitic names in the Greek alphabet. For each entry, there is information on orthography, a description of the person, where found (mainly relevant for names found in an archaeological/epigraphic context), source, exceptions (doubtful names, nicknames, second names and so on) and dating. Unfortunately, all this information is not always available, in which case the particular section of the entry is left blank. With names occurring in a variety of forms and alphabets (including Cyrillic and Coptic), not to mention the huge number of sources containing Jewish names, this has been a Herculean work. I. notes that another volume is needed for names of Jews in the Diaspora, and a further volume for the end of the 'Greek' period, including talmudic literature (from 200 to 650 CE), projects which she hopes to carry out. In the meantime, we can be grateful for an extremely useful collection.

L.L. GRABBE

JACKSON, GLENNA S., *'Have Mercy on Me': The Story of the Canaanite Woman in Matthew 15.21-28* (JSNTSup, 228; Copenhagen International Seminar, 10; London: Sheffield Academic Press, 2002), pp. xiv + 197. £60.00. ISBN 0-8264-6148-4.

Based on a dissertation for Marquette University, this slim volume is a study of the Matthaean form of the healing of the Canaanite woman's daughter (Mt. 15.21-28). Connecting with recent debates as to the 'Jewish' nature of the Matthaean community, and its attitude to Gentiles, the book argues that the story, with its pattern of a fourfold request, thrice met by rejection, the last time met with acceptance, conforms to a ritual pattern for a female proselyte. The volume bears many of the characteristics of a dissertation, with a somewhat discursive style, discussions of other scholarly views, and a review of the Canaanites and of Tyre and Sidon in biblical tradition, whose strict relevance is not always clear. Surprisingly, the argument for a proselyte pattern explores the Psalms and the Book of Ruth but only make passing reference to some (not all) relevant rabbinic texts, and does not address debates about the dating and origins of formal patterns for the admission of proselytes. While the book usefully draws attention to some of the distinctive and problematic characteristics of the Matthaean redaction, the proposal invites a more sustained argument and analysis than is offered.

J. LIEU

JIMÉMENZ BEDMAN, FRANCISCO, *El misterio del Rollo de Cobre de Qumrán: Análisis lingüístico* (Biblioteca Midrásica, 25; Estella: Editorial Verbo Divino, 2002), pp. 269. €20.00. ISBN 84-8169-507-6.

The largest section of this monograph is the presentation of the text of the Copper Scroll in transcription with a Spanish translation and with all the significant readings of J.M. Allegro, F. García Martínez and E.J.C. Tigchelaar, J.K. Lefkovits, B. Luria, J.T. Milik, P. Muchowski, B. Pixner, É. Puech and A Wolters. Surprisingly in this endeavour, J.B. uses Lefkovits' dissertation rather than its published form (Leiden: Brill, 2000). Two chapters precede the transcription and translation: in the first J.B. describes the history of the investigation of the Copper Scroll in three phases (up until the appearance of the *editio princeps*; from Milik to Puech; since Puech); in the second he gives a palaeographic analysis of the scroll (first century CE), mentioning the possibility of multiple copyists, but then only considering each letter as a single entity. For the transcription and translation the key to many of J.B.'s preferred understandings rests in using the phrases and idioms of other known texts including those from Qumran. A brief chapter considers some important conflicting readings, after which a comprehensive chapter is a thorough linguistic analysis of the scroll. Such analysis naturally depends in some measure upon how the scroll is read, but there are helpful comments on grammar and vocabulary in relation to biblical antecedents, rabbinic Hebrew, Aramaisms and Greek loanwords, as well as consideration of eight distinctive terms. An attempt is made at suggesting how the scroll reflects linguistic realities in first century Palestine; its affinities with rabbinic Hebrew are given pride of place and its Greek loanwords used to assert its urban origins, so that if it is Essene, it is probably Jerusalem Essene rather than Qumran Essene.

G.J. BROOKE

KNITTEL, THOMAS, *Das griechische 'Leben Adams und Evas': Studien zu einer narrativen Anthropologie im frühen Judentum* (TSAJ, 88; Tübingen: Mohr Siebeck, 2002), pp. xiv + 349. €99.00. ISBN 3-16-147712-X.

The last decade has witnessed a resurgence of interest in the numerous problems associated with the *Life of Adam and Eve*, and a number of studies of this writing have been published; the present work, a revised and abbreviated version of a Leipzig dissertation—like that of Eldridge (see above, p. 166)—is further evidence of this renewed interest. The author's main aim is to examine the anthropology of the Greek version of the *Life*, and to this end he provides a detailed exegetical study of substantial portions of the text under the four rubrics 'Creation and Image of God: The Origin of Mankind'; 'Victim and Culprit: The "Fall" of Mankind'; 'Sickness, Hardship, and Discord: The Present of Mankind'; and 'Death and

Resurrection: The Future of Mankind'. In the absence of a critical edition of the Greek *Life*—in fact one is currently in preparation—he has reconstructed the text of the passages he studies; his reconstruction is based on the work of Nagel, but his text differs in some respects from that provided by Nagel for the *Concordance* of A.M. Denis that is also used in the G. Anderson/M. Stone synopsis. K. gives a translation of each of the passages he reconstructs and discusses their literary structure, the sources and traditions that they use, their theology and, finally, the way the pericope is treated in the other four primary versions (Latin, Armenian, Georgian, Slavonic). This exegetical study takes up some two-thirds of the book; it is preceded by a discussion of the problems associated with the interpretation of the *Life of Adam and Eve* and a survey of previous research. The author's main conclusions, based on his study of the Greek *Life* as an outline of a narrative anthropology, are that the work is a unity, but incorporates a wide range of diverse traditions that give it something of the character of a compendium; that priority is to be accorded to the Greek version of the *Life*; that it is a Jewish work, probably from the diaspora, and was composed in Greek; and that it dates from the first, or possibly the early second, century CE. His conclusions are solidly based and would, at least in part, be shared by others, but the possibility cannot be absolutely excluded that the *Life of Adam and Eve* is a Christian work from a slightly later date.

M.A. KNIBB

KUGEL, JAMES L. (ed.), *Shem in the Tents of Japhet: Essays on the Encounter of Judaism and Hellenism* (JSJSup, 74; Leiden: Brill, 2002), pp. ix + 286. €80.00/ $93.00. ISBN 90-04-12514-0; ISSN 1384-2161.

Papers from two conferences, at Bar Ilan University in 1998 on Jewish Writings in Greek, and at Harvard University in 1999 on Hellenism and Judaism, are here brought together under the subheadings, 'Issues of Language'; 'Hellenism in Jewish Writings'; 'The Reception of Judaism by the Greek Fathers'. The authors are all notable authorities on their subjects: A. Baumgarten on how the Greeks differed from other imperial powers, and on 'Bilingual Jews and the Greek Bible'; N. Cohen on 'Greek Words for Jewish Concepts in Philo'; C. Holladay on 'Resonance and resistance' in the attitude to Hellenism on Hellenistic Jewish authors; J.J. Collins on apocalyptic eschatology in the Wisdom of Solomon; D. Winston on the fusion of Jewish and Hellenistic perspectives in Philo and the Wisdom of Solomon on creation, revelation and providence; D.T. Runia on eudaimonism in Hellenistic–Jewish literature, and on the 'Christian Reception of Philo the Jew in Egypt'; C. Milikowsky arguing for links between Josephus's chronology, drawn from previous sources, and rabbinic traditions, especially the *Seder 'Olam*; A. van den Hoek on Philo's influence on Origen; N. Constas on Proverbs, Song of Songs and, especially, Ecclesiastes in Origen and the Gregorys. An overview and introduction by the editor would have been a valuable addition to a useful, albeit disparate, collection of essays, and might have asked how they contribute to debates about the somewhat tired epithets, 'Hellenistic/Jewish'.

J. LIEU

LEHNARDT, ANDREAS, *Qaddish: Untersuchungen zur Entstehung und Rezeption eines rabbinischen Gebetes* (TSAJ, 87; Tübingen: Mohr Siebeck, 2002), pp. xiv + 386. €89.00. ISBN 3-16-147723-5.

The Qaddish is one of the prayers of the rabbinic synagogue. In this Free University of Berlin dissertation (P. Schäfer) L. sets out to investigate its text and history on the basis of manuscript evidence which is carefully collected and catalogued here in separate chapters on rabbinic liteature, hekhalot literature, Gaonic literature and mediaeval writings. There are five versions that differ in minor ways among themselves, arising in part from the different contexts in which the Qaddish is used. The earliest manuscripts are from the Cairo Genizah, dating during the ninth to the eleventh centuries CE. The language is an Aramaic-Hebrew mixture characteristic of much rabbinic literature. The argument that it was derived from a Hebrew original that was translated into Aramaic is not supported by L.'s investigation. More than one social context is also possible for its development, including both the synagogue and the Bet-Midrash (*pace* J. Heinemann). Its origin is not associated with a specific rabbinic figure, but it seems to have developed in a long process of expansion and reuse, perhaps originally from a short doxological formula. It is only a guess whether this expansion took place in Babylonia or Palestine. This is an important contribution to the study of Jewish liturgy.

L.L. GRABBE

LUDLOW, JARED W., *Abraham Meets Death: Narrative Humour in the Testament of Abraham* (JSPSup, 41; London: Sheffield Academic Press, 2002), pp. x + 209. £50.00. ISBN 0-8264-6204-9.

The result of a dissertation project for the University of California at Berkeley and the Graduate Theological Union, this book is a study of the (different) narrative strategies of the two main recensions (A and B), where L. compares the 'major differences...in plot structure and characterization' in order to 'determine why these two recensions are different and which one may have come first' (p. 2). L. is chiefly interested in the narrative form and features of this text, an aspect overlooked in previous studies. He acknowledges previous studies that identified comic and satirical elements of the text and proceeds to compare the comic elements used in recension A with their almost complete removal from recension B. He also considers the 'more original' narrative ordering of A against the 'more original' vocabulary of B. The book contains seven chapters and two appendixes. Chapter 1 is introductory and L. gives a brief history of the textual tradition, the few scholarly studies of this work and a description of the goals of each chapter. Chapter 2 addresses the problem of genre, while in Chapters 3, 4 and 5, he discusses the characterization of Abraham, Michael and Death. In Chapter 6 L. explores and compares the plot of A and B, with seven diagrams clarifying his argument. A comparison of the Greek MSS follows in Chapter 7, with a concluding chapter (8) where he concludes that A represents the original form of the tale—a comic tale with an unexpected treatment of the three major characters: Abraham, Michael and Death, while B is an abridged form of the tale, which has removed most of the comic elements and was probably intended for a more conservative audience, hence the fact that A appears in Greek and Romanian, while B is found in Greek, Slavonic, Rumanian, Coptic, Arabic and Ethiopic. He supports the view that the tale originated in Egypt. Appendix 1 lists the 54 narrative units found in the text, while Appendix 2 presents in parallel columns the citations of three MS families, Bb, Be and A. All in all, this is a useful as well as entertaining book which offers a positive and much-needed contribution to narrative studies of ancient literature.

R. ALLAN

MAIER, HARRY O., *Apocalypse Recalled: The Book of Revelation after Christendom* (Minneapolis, MN: Fortress Press, 2002), pp xvi + 271. 1 illustration. $18.00. ISBN 0-8006-3492-6.

As the author points out the genre of apocalypse has constantly influenced Christian audiences and still today shapes popular Christian attitudes and lifestyles. M. reads the book of Revelation from his personal reading site, using autobiographical detail to give new meaning to the biblical text. His approach links the NT book both with its OT roots and with early Christian writings. He uses both OT texts such as Isaiah, with its divine warrior imagery, OT themes such as Jerusalem as holy city, and modern literary criticism, such as that of Foucault and Kristeva, as intertextual resources for his own readings. Drawing on subjects such as narratival time, orality, irony and parody, M. constructs an interpretation of Revelation which reflects the work of other modern commentators—with the addition of his personal analysis of the significance of apocalyptic today.

M.E. MILLS

MATTHEWS, SHELLY, *First Converts: Rich Pagan Women and the Rhetoric of Mission in Early Judaism and Christianity* (Contraversions: Jews and Other Differences; Stanford, CA: Stanford University Press, 2001), pp. xvi + 164. $45.00/ £30.00. ISBN 0-8047-3592-1.

There has been recently a renewed interest in the questions of mission at the turn of the first millennium. As its title indicates, *First Converts* proposes to study the question of mission in early Judaism and Christianity. The underlying thesis is that the criteria used to define mission are by far too narrow, leading to a flawed picture, hence the importance of using material relating to Hellenistic religious propaganda. But this is much more than a revival of Georgi's thesis: the author makes a strong case for broadening the idea of mission of course, and achieves it by including insights provided by feminist models of historical reconstruction. The contribution of the author is to highlight the diversity of material among Graeco-Roman authors concerning 'elite' women's participation, and patronage, in foreign cults. The material analysed in the four chapters focuses on Josephus's *Antiquities* 18 and on Acts 16. Both stress the role of women in missionary religions, and unearth the dialectic concerning women from the lower classes. This is a book of interest to anyone looking at Jewish and Christian mission; its methodology and the rhetorical analysis it employs, along with extensive notes and useful bibliography contribute to making this book a useful tool.

A. JEFFERS

MORRAY-JONES, C.R.A., *A Transparent Illusion: The Dangerous Vision of Water in Hekhalot Mysticism: A Source-Critical and Tradition-Historical Inquiry* (JSJSup, 59; Leiden: Brill, 2002), pp. xiii + 322. €89.00/$104.00. ISBN 90-04-11337-1; ISSN 1384-2161.

This book examines the accounts in the hekhalot literature of the vision of water, in fact the vision of the firmament which Ezekiel saw separating the throne from the four fiery creatures. M.-J. argues that H. Zutarti preserves pre-rabbinic ascent midrashim, passages which are both exegetical and also concerned with mystical ascent. Only those who understand the ascent know the hidden meaning of the biblical text. The earliest hekhalot literature derived from ancient esoteric traditions which existed in tension with those of the classical rabbinic texts. This book is important for students of the OT; it is essential reading for anyone engaged in study of the NT and the early Church.

M. BARKER

MURPHY, CATHERINE M., *Wealth in the Dead Sea Scrolls and in the Qumran Community* (STDJ, 40; Leiden: Brill, 2002), pp. xxi + 672. 10 plates. €150.00/$174.00. ISBN 90-04-11934-5; ISSN 0169-9962.

This comprehensive dissertation consists of seven chapters topped and tailed with an introduction and concluding summary. M. goes way beyond a consideration of shared property to look at as much evidence as possible for systems of production and distribution at Qumran and elsewhere. Chapter 2 assesses the *Damascus Document*: wealth plays a part in every redactional stage of the composition and in every sub-genre; it was instrumental in spawning the community and in shaping its identity on scriptural principles. Chapter 3 considers the *Rule of the Community*: again, wealth plays a part at every redactional stage and M. argues that its discussion reflects actual community practices. Chapter 4, on *Instruction*, highlights the popularity of the work at Qumran and notes suitably that the sayings about agricultural economics and married life might suggest that the community there was more engaged with the surrounding world than often supposed. Chapter 5 notes that nothing on wealth in other literature found at Qumran contradicts the attitudes and practices discernible in the core constitutional compositions. Chapter 6 considers the archaeological evidence for wealth at Qumran and in its vicinity: the religious community at Qumran was economically open, especially through barter, and was concerned with a social asceticism characterized by lack of need rather than by poverty as such. Chapter 7 evaluates other documentary materials from the Judaean desert and shows how they highlight by contrast the special economic circumstances prevailing at Qumran. The testimonies of Philo, Josephus and Pliny the Elder to Essene economic practices are evaluated positively in Chapter 8; the descriptions of Essenes in these classical authors cohere with the Qumran community. The 130 pages of appendixes and bibliography provide data used in the discussion. A wealth of detail is presented cautiously and convincingly.

G.J. BROOKE

NEUSNER, JACOB, *Contemporary Views of Ancient Judaism: Disputes and Debates* (Academic Studies in the History of Judaism; Binghamton, NY: Global Publications, 2001), pp. xix + 349. $50.00. ISBN 1-58684-114-9.

There is much to learn from this book. First, one must be inspired by the industry and prodigious energy of N. who seems to compose an informed, critical review of everything that he reads—and he reads a lot. Second, this book contains a useful list of publications in the field of postbiblical Jewish studies, which have been produced in English over the last ten or so years, and in German since 1945. N.'s reviews of these works form the bulk of the book. Although final judgment on this scholarship must await the test of time, it is probably an honour to be included in this book, and thus worthwhile for the scholar to consult these publications, especially in the light of N.'s remarks. N. does not discuss trivia, and in spite of his frequent harsh criticisms—it often seems that only authors *en passant* merit his praise—nevertheless the scholar whose work is analysed here should, on the whole, feel more happiness than hurt. An interesting antidote to N.'s extrovert style can be found in a recent work by I. Kalimi, *Early Jewish Exegesis and Theological Controversy* (Netherlands: Royal Van Gorcum, 2002), which includes an analysis of the opinions of R.P. Knierim on the theology of the HB, with which the author of this book profoundly disagrees. The discussion is informed and impersonal, calm and controlled. The result is persuasive, and a lesson for us all.

N.L. COLLINS

NEUSNER, JACOB, *Development of a Legend: Studies on the Traditions Concerning Yohanan Ben Zakkai* (Classics in Judaic Studies; Binghamton, NY: Global Publications, 2001), pp. xviii + 316. $50.00. ISBN 1-58684-120-3.

This is a reprint of N.'s 1970 book of the same title, originally published by E.J. Brill. The book is a good example of N.'s earlier work, examining and sorting the sources and traditions of rabbinic literature, and as such is valuable for understanding the present historical and literary approaches to the subject.

J.K. AITKEN

NICKELSBURG, GEORGE W.E., *1 Enoch 1: A Commentary on the Book of 1 Enoch, Chapters 1–36; 81–108* (Hermeneia; Minneapolis, MN: Fortress Press, 2001), pp. xxxviii + 617. $46.40. ISBN 0-8006-6074-9.

The appearance of this commentary is timely, coinciding as it does with ever-increasing scholarly awareness of the central importance and influence of the Enochic writings in the Second Temple period. Already distinguished as a student of *1 Enoch*, N. offers a thoughtful and carefully considered synthesis of his learning in a format which will be familiar to readers of the Hermeneia series. This volume does not, however, deal with the *Book of Parables* and the *Book of the Luminaries*: these sections will be treated separately in a further publication. The remainder of *1 Enoch* is supplied with a comprehensive 134-page introduction, covering a description of N.'s method in the commentary and a short account of *1 Enoch*; a detailed discussion of textual witnesses, manuscripts and ancient versions; the literary structure of *1 Enoch* and the genres represented therein; and a discussion of the world-view represented by apocalyptic thought. The 'theology' of the corpus is examined at length in a section headed 'God and Humanity'; and this leads to a wide-ranging investigation of probable sources for ideas found in the writing, where N. is able to summarize many of his earlier arguments concerning the *Sitz-im-Leben* of the material. In particular, N. emphasizes the testamentary character of much of *1 Enoch*, and is disposed to find a greater degree of coherence in its various parts than some other students. A section on the reception of Enochic material within Judaism and early Christianity concludes with a survey of modern scholarship on the texts, and an agenda for future study. The commentary proper presents English translation of the text in bold type, with the textual apparatus immediately beneath; verse-by-verse commentary follows, with user-friendly foot-notes as opposed to endnotes. Excursuses appear at significant points within the commentary: these are sometimes constructed, and may indeed be read, as separate articles, treating of such key matters as the Watchers and the Holy Ones; the *Book of Giants* and *1 Enoch*; Babylonian and early Greek cosmographies; traditions about a religious awakening in the Hellenistic period; and the image of the plant in Israelite literature. These in particular contrive to make the volume rather more than a commentary, and demonstrate how impressive is N.'s understanding of this complex and difficult text.

C.T.R. HAYWARD

OTZEN, BENEDIKT, *Tobit and Judith* (Guides to Apocrypha and Pseudepigrapha; London: Sheffield Academic Press, 2002), pp. xiii + 162. £14.99. ISBN 0-8264-6053-4.

This book is well set out. O. claims in the preface that he offers more historical research than several others do in this series. He also shows how the authors have adapted material from biblical and non-biblical sources always with the aim of using it as a teaching tool for the Israelite community. This is demonstrated very competently in the discussion of both books. O. engages with the positions of other scholars pertaining to the material and he makes clear at the end of the debate his own opinion about each particular issue. The book has been well researched, though there seems to be a couple of contradictory statements. In O.'s discussion of the use of sources in the book of Judith, he says that it is 'more important to observe similarities between the book of Judith and Exodus on a more general level' (p. 75). However, in a similar discussion in Tobit he suggests that a weak point in Deselaers' catalogue of parallels is one specific point lacking in a list of 33 (p. 21). This seems inconsistent. A chapter on feminist and narrative approaches in the Judith section of the book is welcome; a similar chapter is needed for Tobit. The suggested reading at the end of each section and O.'s overt discussion about the theological issues within each book are especially commendable. This is an excellent resource as a guide to the books of Tobit and Judith.

A. GRANT-HENDERSON

PAO, DAVID W., *Acts and the Isaianic New Exodus* (Biblical Studies Library; Grand Rapids, MI: Baker Academic, 2002), pp. x + 311. $29.99. ISBN 0-8010-2496-X.

In this 'literary-critical' study P. supplies 'a systematic study of the use of the Isaianic New Exodus' (p. 17) in the Lukan writings, and especially in Acts. He first of all identifies the themes in Isa. 40.1-11 which are developed in the rest of Deutero-Isaiah. Included among them are allusions to the Exodus paradigm, which in Deutero-Isaiah is transformed by the prophetic eschatology into an essential ingredient of his message of salvation. He argues that 'these themes not only give structure to the narrative of Acts', but 'also become keys for understanding the meaning of the narrative' (p. 45). In addition, 'the use of the *hodos* terminology in an ecclesiological sense is also dependent upon the context of Isa. 40.3-5' and 'is used to evoke the Isaianic tradition to establish the identity of the early Christian movement' (p. 45), which is seen to be 'now the legitimate heirs of the ancient Israelite traditions' (p. 77). Indeed, 'the continuation of the story of the people of God is central to the Lukan program' (p. 89). The beginning of the process of the restoration of Israel is confirmed by Acts 1.8 and 'is portrayed through the model of the Isaianic New Exodus in which the salvation of the Gentiles becomes part of the program of the reconstitution of Israel' (p. 96). A chapter is devoted to the role of the undefeated Word of God in Acts, which is considered in the context of the Exodus traditions as transformed in Isaiah 40–55. Isaiah also provides the context for the anti-idol polemic in Acts, idols being symbols of 'those who oppose the Lord of the early Christian movement' (p. 182). Finally, the New Exodus programme in Acts is seen to transcend that in Isaiah through its focus on the Gentiles in that its emphasis on the equality of Jews and Gentiles moves beyond what is found in Isaiah. Of special interest to readers of this *B.L.* will be the detailed treatments of selected texts from Isaiah itself together with the excurses at the end of four of the chapters on postexilic Jewish topics.

J.T. WILLIAMS

PINNICK, AVITAL, *The Orion Center Bibliography of the Dead Sea Scrolls (1995–2000)* (STDJ, 41; Leiden: Brill, 2001), pp. viii + 228. €50.00/$59.00. ISBN 90-04-12366-0; ISSN 0169-9962.

This bibliography is the successor to F. García Martínez and D.W. Parry, *A Bibliography of the Finds in the Desert of Judah 1970–95* (STDJ, 19; Leiden: Brill, 1996). It lists over 3000 items, of which approximately 600 are book reviews. It is the book form of what has been made available weekly through the website of the Orion Center for the Study of the Dead Sea Scrolls and Associated Literature at the Hebrew University (orion.mscc.huji.ac.il) and in most issues of *Revue de Qumrân*.

Entries are listed alphabetically, by author and title, with reviews appearing as 'r'; users should note that often further books and articles are listed after the reviews. Compared with STDJ, 19, the smaller font allows for many more items per page. The indexes of texts and subjects are comprehensive. The editor is to be congratulated on making such a useful tool available so swiftly.

G.J. BROOKE

PUMMER, REINHARD, *Early Christian Authors on Samaritans and Samaritanism: Texts, Translations and Commentary* (TSAJ, 92; Tübingen: Mohr Siebeck, 2002), pp. xiv + 518. €129.00. ISBN 3-16-147831-2; ISSN 0721-8753.

Because the native Samaritan sources are mostly late, usually mediaeval at the earliest, our knowledge of the earlier history of the Samaritan sect depends primarily on Christian writings. This valuable collection will make use of these sources much more convenient, since some of the relevant writings have not been easily accessible. P. has included all passages mentioning the Samaritans (though not necessarily all those mentioning Samaria when they make no addition to knowledge of the sect), with the exception of those credited to Simon Magus and Menander, since it has not been well demonstrated that the Simonian movement is connected to the Samaritans of Mt Gerizim. Drawing on the best critical editions, P. gives the original text (usually Greek or Latin, but also Syriac, Georgian, Coptic, Ethiopic, and Arabic; an exception is Eusebius's Chronicle, where J. Karst's German translation is given instead of the Armenian text) and an English translation. An introduction is given to each writer, with a critical discussion of the information on the Samaritans provided in each case. P.'s contributions to Samaritan studies are already well known; he now puts us in his debt with another important addition to the small but growing number of works for a proper study of the Samaritans.

L.L. GRABBE

RAJAK, TESSA, *Josephus: The Historian and his Society* (London: Duckworth, 2nd edn, 2002), pp. xviii + 261 (including 1 map). £14.99 (paper). ISBN 0-7156-3170-5.

This oft-cited work first appeared in 1983 and has stood the test of time as an important introduction to Josephus and his contemporary background. The basic text has not been revised for the new edition, but it has a new preface, new introduction, and a four-page guide to literature that has appeared since 1983. These help to update the reader on some of the main debates in the past 20 years, though one cannot help wishing that a fully revised text was being presented to us.

L.L. GRABBE

RAJAK, TESSA, *The Jewish Dialogue with Greece and Rome: Studies in Cultural and Social Interaction* (AGJU, 48; Leiden: Brill, 2001), pp. xix + 579. €156.00/ $182.00. ISBN 90-04-11285-5; ISSN 0169-734X.

These 27 studies illustrate the problems of disentangling Hellenism as a cultural force from Judaism and of understanding group interaction and cultural change (p.

viii), themes well exemplified in the three new studies. In 'Judaism and Hellenism Revisited' (pp. 3-10) R. balances M. Hengel's emphasis on hellenization in Judaea and the Diaspora against Millar's highlighting of 'Jewish exceptionalism', arguing that 'both sides are right in their own terms' (p. 5) (cf. also her critique of Millar's *Roman Near East 31 BC–AD 337*, pp. 503-509). In 'Ethnic Identities in Josephus' (pp. 137-46), R. points out that in Josephus we meet no Jewish hellenizers in Judaea between the Hasmonaeans and 70 CE, 'only...the exact opposite—the Greek judaizers of the cities of Syria (*BJ* II. 463)' (p. 145). Josephus's later writings show an increasing awareness of the challenge of Greek culture; one wonders, was Paul well ahead of him? 'Jews, Pagans and Christians in Late Antique [*sic*] Sardis: Models of Interaction' (pp. 447-62) usefully challenges the 'glowing portrayal of [Jewish and Gentile] co-existence' presented by the accepted interpretation of archaeological findings. (Discussing donors' inscriptions, p. 457-58, R. surprisingly ignores the Jewish origin in 1 Chron. 29.14 of the 'we offer yours from yours' formula.) Essays on history in Jewish intertestamental writing (pp. 11-37; 1986) and 'Hasmonaean kingship and the invention of tradition' (pp. 39-60; 1996) will interest historiographers; a study of Josephus and the Essenes (pp. 219-40; 1994), where R. argues that 'on the one hand, Josephus knew a fair amount about the Essenes while, on the other, he drew on Greek models', will interest Qumran devotees. A stimulating, but demanding, collection.

J.R. BARTLETT

RAPP, HANS A., *Jakob in Bet-El: Gen 35, 1–15 und die jüdische Literatur des 3. und 2. Jahrhunderts* (Herders Biblische Studien, 29; Freiburg, Herder, 2001), pp. xi + 348. €50.00. ISBN 3-451-27558-9.

This monograph examines the traditions surrounding Jacob's journey from Shechem to Beth-El as reflected in various Second Temple texts. In his introduction (Part I), R. stresses that the biblical version of this story (Gen. 35.1-15) is itself only one facet of what must have been a much larger body of literature. Later texts should not be regarded as merely creative exegeses of the Pentateuch, but as independent compositions that utilize the biblical version alongside a variety of extrabiblical traditions. Part II comprises an analysis of the main pericope in Genesis 35 and related biblical passages. R. then identifies various aspects of the Beth-El tradition as evidenced in later texts such as the *Temple Scroll*, the *Aramaic Levi* Documents, the *Testament of Levi*, 4Q537, the *Prayer of Joseph*, genealogical texts from Qumran, and *Jubilees* (Part III). Two phenomena are especially significant: first, the interpretation of God's appearance to Jacob at Beth-El as containing God's central covenantal promise to the patriarchs; and second, the connection of the journey to Beth-El with Levi's election as the forerunner of the priesthood. Before a concluding summary, other Second Temple conceptions of Israel's history are examined, in order to demonstrate that the emphasis on Jacob and Beth-El was limited to one particular priestly group (Part IV). R.'s judicious textual analysis and his recognition of the sophistication with which Second Temple authors reworked their sources (biblical and otherwise) make this a valuable contribution to the study of Jewish literature in the Hellenistic period.

M. ZAHN

REIF, STEFAN C. (ed.), *The Cambridge Genizah Collections: Their Contents and Significance* (Cambridge University Library Genizah Series, 1; Cambridge: Cambridge University Press, 2002), pp. xiv + 239. 22 plates. £45.00/$60.00. ISBN 0-521-81361-1.

This book originated in two courses of lectures in Cambridge, the first taking advantage of the presence in Cambridge in 1994 of four scholars from the Hebrew University of Jerusalem, and the second held to mark the centenary in 1998 of the presentation of the Genizah Collection to Cambridge University Library. The nine lectures are presented here in updated form, and prefaced by a magisterial introductory survey by the editor. The volume is dedicated to the memory of one of the contributors, Professor Michael Klein. While the whole volume is of interest to the wider field of Hebrew studies, readers of the *B.L.* will be most interested in the contributions of Klein (Targumic Studies and the Cairo Genizah) and Menahem Kahana (The Tannaitic Midrashim), as well as in the section on Bible in the editor's survey (A Centennial Assessment of Genizah Studies). A comprehensive list of biblical references in the Index of Subjects and Sources will enable scholars to see at a glance whether there is any material relevant to a particular passage. This is an excellent book, and a worthy tribute to the importance of the Genizah Collections and of the work done in the Genizah Research Unit at Cambridge University Library.

A. GELSTON

ROWE, ROBERT D., *God's Kingdom and God's Son: The Background to Mark's Christology from Concepts of Kingship in the Psalms* (AGJU, 50; Leiden: Brill, 2002), pp. xvii + 435. €109.00/$127.00. ISBN 90-04-11888-8; ISSN 0169-734X.

This erudite book studies the relationship between the kingship of God and messianic kingship within a Jewish context as a means for understanding Mark's portrayal of Jesus, who proclaims the good news of God's kingship and is celebrated as the Messiah who suffers and is vindicated. A meticulous and carefully documented analysis develops, first, the two themes and their inter-relationship in the psalms and the later chapters of Isaiah; secondly, the kingship of God in postbiblical Jewish literature and in Mark's Gospel; and, finally, messianic thought in early Judaism (Qumran, Josephus and the zealots) and in Mark. It is in the latter section that the study comes together as the Isaiah chapters and significant psalms are presented as structuring the thought and development of Jesus according to Mark. The author sees some of the psalms and the servant of Isaiah as implicitly messianic from the start, and also weaves into this nexus 'Son of God' and 'Son of Man'; he also feels confident in moving from what is not explicitly Markan redaction to Jesus' own filial and messianic self-consciousness. The resultant picture is thus a familiar one but one that seems to bypass a number of recent alternative constructions of Jewish variety. The book betrays its origins as a 1990 thesis in method and annotation, and in its major dialogue-partners, although it has been updated in bibliography, footnotes and some references in the body of the text.

J. LIEU

RUNIA, DAVID T., *Philo of Alexandria: On the Creation of the Cosmos according to Moses: Introduction, Translation and Commentary* (Philo of Alexandria Commentary Series, 1; Leiden: Brill, 2001), pp. xviii + 443. €103.00/$120.00. ISBN 90-04-12169-2.

This is the first volume of a new series, the aim of which is to address a significant lacuna in Philonic studies today, namely, the lack of critical commentaries on the major treatises of Philo of Alexandria. On a number of other levels also this volume is a first: it is the first English translation of *De Opificio Mundi* for 70 years, and it is the first ever English commentary on this work. Containing an introduction (pp. 1-45), translation (pp. 47-95) and extensive commentary (pp. 96-391), R. has annotated the various sections of the work thoroughly with biblical references, detailed footnotes and suggestions for further reading as appropriate. He has also developed a significant number of excurses on various aspects, each one following his excellent commentary on the specific paragraphs in question. These include, for example, an excursus after §§1-6 entitled 'Law, cosmos and nature', another after §§7-12 devoted to 'Recent interpretations of Philo's argument' and another exploring 'Philo's attitude towards women and sexuality' after §§151-152. An extensive bibliography of 20 pages, followed by five separate indexes (one each for biblical texts, Philo's works, other ancient texts, a subject/name index and an index of Greek terms) constitute useful resources for both student and scholar alike, and complement the wealth of detail contained in the entire volume. Particularly pleasing is the way in which the Philonic text itself has been translated and presented. As R. explains, he has taken care 'where possible to render terms consistently, for example, always translating νοῦς by "intellect" and διανοία by "understanding", but in some cases (notoriously in the case of ἀρχή and λόγος), this kind of correspondence is quite impossible to maintain' (p. 44). In terms of layout, R.'s choice of bold type to signal words and phrases in Philo's text which correspond verbally to the biblical text, and bold italics for those alluding to or based on the biblical text, but do not share the same lexical or grammatical form, makes Philo's use of the biblical text visually very clear. Scholars and graduate students not only working on Philo, but also in the wider fields of Hellenistic Judaism, Greek Bible versions, patristics and middle Platonism will need to have ready access to this volume. This is truly a very valuable book (the first in what promises to be a most valuable series). What a pity that it does not also include the Greek text of Philo!

C. MCCARTHY

SAMELY, ALEXANDER, *Rabbinic Interpretation of Scripture in the Mishnah* (Oxford: Oxford University Press, 2002), pp. xi + 481. £55.00. ISBN 0-19-827031-3.

In S.'s own words, this book aims 'to provide a comprehensive catalogue of hermeneutic components, that is, a full hermeneutic profile of the Mishnah'. To this end, he is concerned especially to provide a description of what takes place when a verse or 'segment' of Scripture is employed by the Mishnah; and his description of this hermeneutic exercise is couched 'in the rich and diversified conceptual apparatus supplied by academic discourses on linguistics, reading, and philosophy of language'. A glossary of technical terms used by those discourses is provided, though in fact S. communicates quite clearly, and often wittily, what he has to say. S. speaks of Scripture as a 'resource', or indeed 're-source', for the Mishnah, manifesting itself in six 'hermeneutic or linguistic categories' (word constitution and semantics; syntax/text structures; subject matter; analogical procedures; narrative; and pragmatics), each of which includes various 'families' of interpretation. The precise definition of these 'families' is set out in 'Appendix I: The Hermeneutic Configuration of the Mishnah: An Overview of Resources' (pp. 399-417), which the reader needs constantly to keep in view. Each and every scriptural passage utilized in the Mishnah S. has catalogued, describing as precisely as possible the particular 'family' and hermeneutic strategy it represents; indeed, he has devised a sophisticated system of sigla for this purpose, which are also used as descriptors in his *Database of Midrashic Units in the Mishnah*, available from http://www.art. man.ac.uk/mes/samely/. With the exception of the first and the last, each chapter is introduced by a short summary to guide the reader through technicalities. For example, Chapter 9, 'Taxonomic and Paradigmatic Extensions: Logical Constants', immediately explains itself as dealing with the Mishnah's treatment of scriptural terms by extending their potential or by supplementing them with similar items: 'in such interpretations, ready-made Mishnaic lists of items (paradigms) play an important role, as well as verses which contain a group of co-ordinated terms'. By such methods S. ensures that the reader is able to follow him through the necessary wealth of detailed illustrations of the Mishnah's hermeneutics. This is quite the most important contribution towards an understanding of the Mishnah's interpretative strategies to have appeared in recent years; and as S. points out, its method might be usefully adopted in other fields of hermeneutical endeavour.

C.T.R. HAYWARD

SCHÄFER, PETER, *Mirror of His Beauty: Feminine Images of God from the Bible to the Early Kabbalah* (Jews, Christians, and Muslims from the Ancient to the Modern World; Princeton, NJ: Princeton University Press, 2002), pp. xv + 306. 16 figures. $29.95. ISBN 0-691-09068-8.

The *Sefer ha-Bahir* is one of the most enigmatic works of Jewish mysticism. Gershom Scholem, who, beginning with his doctorate, devoted a lifetime of study to the work, dated it to twelfth-century Provence, and assigned it a pivotal role in the emergence of the Spanish Qabbalah. Though he made some effort to relate its innovative ideas to mediaeval Catharism and Albigensianism, he was not impressed by the parallels, and instead argued that the *Bahir* essentially represents the surfacing into the light of day of a Jewish Gnosticism which had originated in the east in the Talmudic era, and been transmitted by subterranean channels, including the circles of the Rhineland Hasidei Ashkenaz, to southern France. S. suggests that

Scholem, when considering a possible mediaeval context for the distinctive doctrines of the *Bahir*, may have been looking in the wrong place. One of the *Bahir*'s most striking ideas is enshrined in its claim that a personified feminine entity within the Godhead (which the author calls by the traditional name Shekhinah) functions as a mediator between heaven and earth and plays a redemptive role in the divine economy. S. demonstrates that there is a remarkable convergence between this doctrine and Christian Mariology of the same period, and suggests that there must be some link. This is not an easy thesis to prove. He first surveys the concept of a female deity in Judaism from biblical Wisdom through Ben Sira, Wisdom of Solomon, Philo, the Gnostics, and the Talmudic concept of the Shekhinah, to the mediaeval Jewish philosophers, in order to show that antecedent tradition does not wholly account for the *Bahir*'s peculiar views. He then expounds the development of the doctrine of Mary in Christianity to illustrate the parallels. A chapter follows on traditional negative Jewish images of Mary in Talmudic sources, in the *Toledot Yeshu* and *Sefer Zerubbabel*. The argument is rounded out with a nuanced methodological discussion of what models of influence may account for the parallelism. This is an important book, which will doubtless provoke controversy. As S. himself ruefully remarks: 'Woe to the historian of Judaism who happens to be a Christian (Roman Catholic no less) and to "discover" that the Christian veneration of Mary might have had an impact on the feminine manifestation of God in the Kabbalah!' (p. 15). But it dovetails neatly with other recent research which suggests that the 'parting of the ways' should never be seen as final and absolute: Christianity and Judaism have remained, with fluctuating degrees of intensity, in a dynamic dialectic from the first century to the present day.

P.S. ALEXANDER

SCHREINER, J., *Jesus Sirach 1–24* (Die Neue Echter Bibel Altes Testament, 38: Würzburg: Echter Verlag, 2002), pp. 134. €17.40/SwF 31.80. ISBN 3-429-02355-6.

S. has sensibly divided his commentary on Ben Sira's work into two volumes, the first of these containing an introduction to the whole book. The introduction deals succinctly with the main features of the work: authorship, literary form, time of writing and aim. The aim is seen to be linked closely with the building up of Jewish self-confidence just before the Hellenistic reform which was at the time of writing just around the corner. S. deals briefly with the textual situation, complicated by the manuscripts from the Cairo Genizah, Qumran and Masada. The commentary is workmanlike, filling in the background prior to the explosion of Greek ideas in the Hellenistic reform. S. continually compares Ben Sira's work with earlier wisdom literature, thus bringing out clearly Ben Sira's own contribution to the wisdom movement. Brief textual comments discuss the complications of the divergent readings in Greek, Syriac and Hebrew texts. The commentary itself covers several verses at a time in blocks rather than taking it verse by verse—this makes it sometimes rather difficult to locate comments on a particular verse. Ben Sira's superb knowledge of the HB is illustrated by the many cross-references and shows him clearly relating traditional values to the new Greek situation. This commentary will help every reader to appreciate how Ben Sira was, in his own words, a 'grapegatherer' of the harvest of the OT.

J.G. SNAITH

SCHWARTZ, SETH, *Imperialism and Jewish Society, 200 BCE to 640 CE* (Jews, Christians, and Muslims from the Ancient to the Modern World; Princeton, NJ: Princeton University Press, 2001), pp. xiii + 320. £27.95. ISBN 0-691-08850-0.

This book investigates the Jewish response to imperialism during the Second Temple period and the Roman period to the Islamic conquest; however, the main investigation really begins with the Maccabean period, so that the study is primarily a study of the Jews under Roman imperialism. The first section covers the period to 70 CE. Imperial support for the national Jewish institutions led to temple and Torah becoming the chief symbols of Jewish corporate identity. This was a period of integration in which more and more Jews came to define themselves around these two symbols (even apocalyptic literature included material centred on temple and Torah). The next main period is 135–350 CE which is a period of disintegration. Much of the reconstruction of this period has been based on rabbinic literature (which represents only a minority movement at this time), but archaeology and other sources tell a somewhat different story, one of a 'shattered' Judaism: 'for most Jews, Judaism may have been little more than a vestigial identity, bits and pieces of which they were happy to incorporate into a religious and cultural system that was essentially Greco-Roman' (p. 15). The next main period (350–640 CE) is Judaism under a Christianized Roman empire. Because Jews had a special status under Christian Roman law, Judaism had a revival into a Torah- and synagogue-centred religious community. This was not a product of the rabbinic influence, though the rabbinic movement benefited from it (and eventually came to dominate Judaism in the mediaeval period). S. has some trenchant criticisms of earlier scholarship. I leave it to specialists to judge his treatment of the later periods, but for the Second Temple period (despite an occasional sharp disagreement), I think he is spot on. This is an important contribution to Jewish studies.

L.L. GRABBE

SCOTT, JAMES M., *Geography in Early Judaism and Christianity: The Book of Jubilees* (SNTSMS, 113; Cambridge: Cambridge University Press, 2002), pp. viii + 337. £45.00. ISBN: 0-521-80812-X.

The subtitle of this stimulating study is only the beginning of the story: building on some of his previous studies, S., after a careful analysis of the rereading of Genesis 10 in Jubilees, traces its continuing influence in Luke–Acts, in the Jewish–Christian source preserved in Ps.-Clement, *Recognitions* 1.27-51, in Theophilus of Antioch and in Hippolytus of Rome. A final chapter explores the influence on mediaeval *mappae mundi* of Graeco-Roman, Jewish and Christian traditions, and raises the possibility that the confluence of the first two may have been achieved by Cypros, wife of Agrippa I, and, according to a first-century epigrammist, the weaver of a map of the world—the subject of the opening chapter of the book. The author writes authoritatively, interacting with an impressive range of scholarship in the fields he covers. Although readers may not always be persuaded by details of the argument, this is more than a fascinating exercise in scholarly detective work, or even a further demonstration of the influence of the pseudepigrapha on Christian tradition. For scholars who are now increasingly drawing on the geographical as well as on the socio-cultural dimensions of the world of our ancient texts, it emphasizes the need to engage not with how we map the world but with how they did.

J. Lieu

Scott, James M. (ed.), *Restoration: Old Testament, Jewish, and Christian Perspectives* (JSJSup, 72; Leiden: Brill, 2001), pp. xiii + 600. €155.00/$180.00. ISBN 90-04-11580-3; ISSN 1384-2161.

This volume is dedicated to the late O.H. Steck, whose final published work features in it. The 17 essays are divided up into four categories. In the 'Formative Period', J.G. McConville offers a nuanced 'canonical' study of the theme of 'Restoration in Deuteronomy and the Deuteronomic Literature', K. Schmid and O.H. Steck present a systematization and diachronic analysis of salvific expectations in the prophetic books of the HB. Finally, L.L. Grabbe casts a historian's eye over the tales of restoration in Ezra–Nehemiah, identifies three or four foundation legends and critically discusses them. 'The most trustworthy source is probably the Nehemiah Memorial' (p. 102). In the 'Greco-Roman Period', S. Talmon looks at similar material to Grabbe, tracing a shift from 'inspiration' to 'interpretation'. This is alleged to become 'a distinctive feature of the conceptual universe of the sages' and to open the door 'to diversification within Second Temple Judaism' (p. 142). D.E. Aune and E. Stewart outline the eschatological conceptions found in Jewish apocalyptic literature under six themes: land, kingship, regathering the people, Jerusalem and Temple, paradise lost and regained, and restoration of the cosmos. J. Tromp argues that the expectation of a Davidic Messiah emerged around 100 BCE as part of the rhetoric of opposition to the Hasmonaeans. More controversially he contends that this hope did not feature in the early days of Persian rule over Judaea. L.H. Schiffman discusses the concept of restoration in the Dead Sea Scrolls and finds three points of view: most texts regarded the Second Temple period as one of continuous exile and still looked for eschatological restoration, some narrow down the focus of restoration from 'Israel' to the 'sectarians', and some have 'a utopian vision that claims to be a return to the past, but is in actuality the creation of a new future' (p. 220). Finally, L.H. Feldman examines how Josephus portrays Zerubbabel, Ezra and Nehemiah and finds evidence of editorial activity in the preoccupation with the Temple and the representation of them as loyal, law-abiding citizens. The third and fourth sections of the collection are categorized according to tradition rather than period. In 'Formative Judaism', C. Milikowsky studies the *Seder 'Olam*, which connects Elijah's return to the messiah and the day of God. He argues that this evinces a tradition that has influenced the Christian presentation of John the Baptist as the Elijah who precedes Jesus (p. 276). S.C. Reif investigates the notion of restoration in early rabbinic prayers, especially the daily *'amidah*.

G.G. Porton analyses the various perceptions of Ezra in rabbinic literature, and B. Chilton looks at the themes of the temple restored and the temple in heaven in Targumim of Isaiah and the Prophets. The final part of the book concentrates on 'Early Christianity'. J.P. Meier argues for the historicity of Jesus' choice of 'Twelve' and regards this as the basis for further work on Jesus' understanding of restoration. S. Freyne's study of the geography of restoration identifies a fault-line between Judaeans and Galileans that is based on two distinct models of ethnicity and restoration, and which underlies the emergence of the early Christian movement. R. Bauckham looks at the theme of the restoration of Israel in Luke–Acts: Luke sees that 'there is a future for Israel with Jesus the Messiah', but leaves open how the prophecies of Scripture will be fulfilled (p. 486). In similar vein S. focuses on Rom. 11.26, and finds that Paul's hopes fit within wider Jewish expectations: 'all Israel' refers to 'the whole nation, including all twelve tribes' (p. 525). The final essay by F.S. Jones looks at the Pseudo-Clementine *Recognitions*, which are a rare witness to the expectations of a Jewish-Christian group who had a clear 'attachment to "the land"' (p. 547). This volume provides a companion to the similar collection, also edited by S., entitled *Exile: Old Testament, Jewish, and Christian Conceptions* (JSJSup, 56; Leiden: Brill, 1997; *B.L.* 1998, p. 132). S. hopes that they will 'provide a useful point of departure for further interdisciplinary study' on these connected themes (p. 1). They certainly go a long way towards achieving that goal—I found much overlap between different periods and traditions. Equally it was fascinating to engage with the great diversity of approaches possible to such 'elastic' subject material.

D.J. BRYAN

SMITH, DAVID E., *The Canonical Function of Acts: A Comparative Analysis* (Collegeville, MN: Liturgical Press, 2002), pp. 136. $15.95. ISBN 0-8146-5103-8.

The authority and subsequent canonicity of the book of Acts was virtually undisputed in the early church. S. accounts for this not only because of the association of its author with the apostle Paul, but also because of its content. He examines patristic attitudes towards Acts, especially in the works of Irenaeus and Tertullian in the late second and early third centuries, and Cyril of Jerusalem and John Chrysostom in the fourth. He concludes that each of these writers found Acts very useful because it could be interpreted to support the growing claims to hermeneutical authority by the bishops of the catholic church. Moreover, Acts functioned as a unifying factor in the developing views about the canon. This was because its teaching about the Holy Spirit linked past revelations of God through the prophets (and indeed the whole OT) and through Jesus with those made through the Jerusalem apostles and through Paul. Because of the content of Acts, particularly its record of the provision of bishops to succeed the generation of the apostles, the Catholic bishops could assert against their gnostic and Marcionite rivals their right to supply the only accurate interpretation of the gospel message. S. briefly analyses various apocryphal books of Acts and shows that they did not supply such a link, and then ends with a short application of his views to various contemporary issues. The book is interesting, well written, and pleasingly free from typographical errors, but its relevance to OT studies is minimal.

D.J. CLARK

SNYDER, H. GREGORY, *Teachers and Texts in the Ancient World: Philosophers, Jews and Christians* (Religion in the First Christian Centuries; London: Routledge, 2000), pp. xv + 235. ISBN 0-415-21766-0 (paper); 0-415-21765-2 (cloth).

This little volume marks a real contribution to an ongoing and fruitful debate as to how valid the model of the 'school' is for understanding Judaism and Christianity in late antiquity. S. demonstrates that how texts were 'performed' in the Greek philosophical schools (Stoic, Epicurean, Peripatetic and Platonist) can be closely paralleled by how they were 'performed' in early Judaism (Qumranic and Rabbinic) and in the Christian Church. He continues the recent and welcome trend towards breaking down the boundaries between palaeography, textual and literary criticism, and social history, and treating texts in their physical wholeness as cultural arte-facts. The role they played, the levels of literacy they imply, the way they were written, read and taught, all illuminate the communities which used them and help to contextualize those communities within the world of their day. What emerges is how easily Judaism and Christianity could cross the divide into the pagan world and find a place on the Graeco-Roman cultural map as philosophical sects within the School of Moses. Even the ritual sides of Christianity and Judaism (already minimal for Diaspora Jews before the destruction of the Temple, compared with adherents of the pagan city cults) can be paralleled to a degree in the Graeco-Roman philosophical communities. It is interesting, too, that the earliest clear attestation of this form of Judaism should be found in the Dead Sea Scrolls. This lively study will prove particularly attractive to students.

P.S. ALEXANDER

STANTON, GRAHAM, *The Gospels and Jesus* (Oxford: Oxford University Press, 2nd edn, 2002), pp. xiv + 324. £15.99. ISBN 0-19-924616-5.

This is a revised edition of a work first published in 1989 and it includes new material in most chapters as well as a new bibliography. In Part I, S. offers a fuller discussion of literary approaches to the gospels in the light of recent developments in scholarship and the work of the Jesus Seminar. The discussion of the *Gospel of Thomas* is also more extensive. In Part II, the sections dealing with Jewish evidence regarding Jesus of Nazareth, the Dead Sea Scrolls and archaeological evidence have been updated and there is now a discussion of 4Q521 in relation to the Son of Man on pp. 253-54. S. says nothing distinctively new about passages from the OT but he has again produced a work that is remarkable for the clarity of its argument and the breadth of its scholarship.

J.E. TOLLINGTON

TIGCHELAAR, EIBERT J.C., *To Increase Learning for the Understanding Ones: Reading and Reconstructing the Fragmentary Early Jewish Sapiential Text*

4QInstruction (STDJ, 44; Leiden: Brill, 2001), pp. xv + 267. €84.00/$98.00. ISBN 90-04-11678-8; ISSN 0169-9962.

This volume is a detailed study of the text of 4QInstruction, which nevertheless modestly claims to be less than a full-scale analysis of the material (p. 245). The first part deals with reconstructing the text and the second with themes and vocabulary. There is a comprehensive index and bibliography. T. compares the text to similar materials and suggests which material may have been incorporated from older sources. He concludes with a general observation that would be appropriate to any wisdom text: that all creation has its divinely alloted place. This minutely argued book is very much scholar talking to scholar, and shows clearly both the skill of such practitioners, and also the large element of guesswork involved in the process. All the conclusions must necessarily hang by a slender thread.

M. BARKER

TORIJANO, PABLO A., *Solomon the Esoteric King: From King to Magus, Development of a Tradition* (JSJSup, 73; Leiden: Brill, 2002), pp. xiv + 333. €104.00/$121.00. ISBN 90-04-11941-8; ISSN 1384-2161.

The declared aim of this study is 'to understand the development of the figure of Solomon and the different characterizations it acquired throughout history and to ask what were the social, religious and historical settings that could lead to them'. According to T., Solomon is depicted as a Hellenistic monarch in the LXX, Eupolemus and Josephus; as a Hermetic sage in the Wisdom of Solomon; as the (messianic) Son of David in the *Psalms of Solomon*; and as a horseman on amulets from the third century CE onwards. But the main emphasis is on texts dealing with astrology, exorcism and magic: the first-century CE apocryphal psalm scroll from Qumran (11QpsAp^a); the Greek *Testament of Solomon* (probably fourth century); the various versions of the *Hygromanteia* (probably of Byzantine provenance); the Mandaean *Ginza*; the Syriac Zosimus (probably fourth century); the Nag Hammadi tractate *On the Origin of the World*; the *Selenodromion of David and Solomon*; and the Hebrew *Sepher ha-Razim* (probably late fourth century). A synopsis of four MSS of the *Hygromanteia* and a translation of one of them (*Monacensis* 70) are given in appendixes. The interest of these texts is, however, in the information they offer about auspicious times and the procedures effective for removing demons (exorcism) or compelling angels to do one's bidding (magic). Solomon is invoked merely to show that the material is traditional, tried and tested. T. has put in a lot of work on the documents but has not been able to tell us much about the settings in which they were produced.

R. TOMES

VELTRI, GIUSEPPE, *Gegenwart der Tradition: Studien zur jüdischen Literatur und Kulturgeschichte* (JSJSup, 69; Leiden: Brill, 2002), pp. xxvii + 319. €103.00/$120.00. ISBN 90-04-11686-9; ISSN 1384-2161.

V. is known mainly for his contribution to rabbinic studies. Here he reproduces 15 studies published between 1987 and 1997. Only one of these originally appeared in English; the rest first appeared in German and are reprinted here with only minor corrections: the 'canon formula' about not adding to or taking from the words written, canon development and the Yavne legend, speech philosophy and translation theory about 'holy speech', whether a targumic translation arose in the time of Ezra, the Greek 'targum' of Aquila, Justinian's novelle 146 *Peri Hebraiōn*, the origin of the LXX in the Jewish historiography of the Middle Ages, whether there was a fast day because of the LXX, the womb motif in the *Papyri Graecae Magicae* and the Cairo Genizah, the ordeal for the woman suspected of adultery in the Jewish Middle Ages, Platonic myths and rabbinic exegetical developments, the concept of 'good fortune' in ancient Judaism, the mediaeval imitation of wisdom texts, on the Jewish and Christian appraisal of the Aggada, and Azariah de Rossi's critique of Philo (this last originally published in English in *Jewish Studies Quarterly* 2 [1995], pp. 372-93).

L.L. GRABBE

WIRE, ANTOINETTE CLARK, *Holy Lives, Holy Deaths: A Close Hearing of Early Jewish Storytellers* (Studies in Biblical Literature, 1: Atlanta, GA: SBL, 2002), pp. x + 420. $49.95 ISBN 1-58983-022-9.

This book is an example of the current vibrant interest in orality among scholars of the Bible (so far more of NT than OT) and of Jewish literature in general. The bulk of the book relates stories clustered around four themes—'prophecy at birth', 'wondrous provisions', 'prophets' signs', and 'martyrdom and vindication'—and draws its material from a wide spectrum of Jewish literature: OT and NT (here regarded as Jewish literature), extra-canonical works, Josephus and the Talmud. The purpose of the work is to utilize folklore methodology in 'some ways to get access to the creative performance' (p. 10) that takes place in the stories which we now only know as texts. This goal is pursued in brief commentaries on the stories and more extensive reflections on each of the themes. Methodologically the most interesting part of the book is, however, the—regrettably short—introduction, which briefly outlines relevant folklore scholarship and its appropriation in biblical/ Jewish studies and also specifies the author's own approach: adaptation of work by two famous folklorists, A. Dundes and D. Ben-Amos. The book is lucidly written, creative and original in its perspective and comprehensive in its knowledge of the relevant texts. Where more could be expected is in deepening, and updating, the initial discussion on method and providing more references to it throughout the book. However, even as it stands the book is an interesting and valuable contribution to the study of orality in biblical and related texts.

A. NAHKOLA

10. PHILOLOGY AND GRAMMAR

CHIESA, BRUNO, *Filologia storica della Bibbia ebraica*. I. *Da origene al medievo* (Studi Biblici, 125; Brescia: Paideia Editrice, 2000), pp. 237. €20.00. ISBN 88-394-0596-8.

CHIESA, BRUNO, *Filologia storica della Bibbia ebraica*. II. *Dall'età moderna ai giorni nostri* (Studi Biblici, 135; Brescia: Paideia Editrice, 2002), pp. 247-501. €20.00. ISBN 88-394-0644-1.

This learned and illuminating pair of volumes traces attitudes to, and scholarship on, the text of the HB from Origen down to modern times. Volume 1, in five chapters, takes the reader up to the early Middle Ages, with an emphasis on the East: thus it includes excellent coverage of Saadia Gaon and al-Qirqisani, as well as of Syriac exegesis. In the four chapters in Volume 2, special attention is given to developments in the sixteenth century and to those in the seventeenth/eighteenth centuries (J. Morin, L. Cappel, R. Simon, J. LeClerc). The final chapter, on text history and text criticism, highlights some basic differences in contemporary academic approaches to the biblical text. This is an important and splendidly stimulating work; it is richly annotated (the bibliography runs to over 40 pages), and well indexed. It certainly ought to be translated into English.

S.P. BROCK

KALTNER, JOHN and STEVEN L. MCKENZIE (eds.), *Beyond Babel: A Handbook for Biblical Hebrew and Related Languages* (SBLRBS, 42; Atlanta: SBL, 2002), pp. xiii + 241. $29.95 (paper). ISBN 1-58983-035-0.

After an overview of the Semitic languages (J. Huehnergard), this volume gives a survey of some of the main Semitic languages: Akkadian (D. Marcus), Ammonite, Edomite and Moabite (S.B. Parker), Arabic (Kaltner), Aramaic (F.E. Greenspahn), Hebrew: Biblical and Epigraphic (J.A. Hackett), Hebrew: Postbiblical (B.A. Levine), Phoenician (C.R. Krahmalkov), and Ugaritic (P.L. Day). There are also chapters on Egyptian (D.B. Redford) and Hittite (H.A. Hoffner Jr). This is a useful collection, though it is not clear why there are no chapters on Epigraphic South Arabian and Ethiopic (the editors do briefly comment on why they omitted Sumerian). Naturally, in a short volume some things will be omitted or overlooked. For example, there are three volumes of *Ras Shamra Parallels*, not just two. R. Blachère *et al.*, *Dictionnaire arabe-français-anglais* could have been usefully added to the Arabic lexicons. The Wadi Daliyeh papyri have now been published in D.M. Gropp, *Wadi Daliyeh II: The Samaria Papyri from Wadi Daliyeh (B.L.* 2002, pp. 28-29). Some important Aramaic grammars have been missed: M.L. Folmer, *The Aramaic Language in the Achaemenid Period* (1995; *B.L.* 1998, p. 216); T. Muraoka, and B. Porten, *A Grammar of Egyptian Aramaic* (1998; *B.L.* 1999, p. 202). To Aramaic dictionaries, one can now add M. Sokoloff, *A Dictionary of Jewish Babylonian Aramaic* (2002). No indexes are included.

L.L. GRABBE

LONG, GARY A., *Grammatical Concepts 101 for Biblical Hebrew: Learning Biblical Hebrew Grammatical Concepts through English Grammar* (Peabody, MA: Hendrickson, 2002), pp. xvii + 189. £14.99. ISBN 1-56563-713-5.

This book is designed to complement the standard teaching grammars. It aims at the student who is beginning to learn biblical Hebrew and who has little formal knowledge of grammar. It is divided into three sections: Part I: Foundations, which covers sound production (consonants and vowels), the syllable and translation; Part II: Building Blocks, which explains grammatical categories such as gender, number, conjunction, noun, pronoun, adjective, adverb, participle, gerund, tense, aspect, mood, voice; and Part III: The Clause and Beyond, which includes discussion of subject, predicate, semantics and discourse analysis. In each case L. begins by explaining the relevant English grammatical category, then he compares those of biblical Hebrew, pointing out both the similarities and dissimilarities. The language used is simple, sometimes even simplistic. The book is easy to read with plentiful and clear illustrations in both English and Hebrew. The explanations become increasingly complex, especially when discussing the Hebrew verb. The detailed description of the English verbal system is beyond what would normally be required for a basic grammar, but it becomes necessary to the subsequent explanation of the Hebrew verb. This is where the method comes into question. Does it help the student to learn a list of labels for grammatical categories in English and then remember where biblical Hebrew is the same or different? This is, nevertheless, an interesting read and a good basic guide to grammatical concepts.

S.A. GROOM

NICCACCI, ALVIERO, *Sintaxis del Hebreo biblico* (Instrumentos para elestudio de la Biblia, VIII; Estella: Editorial Verbo Divino), pp. 236. €30.00. ISBN 84-8169-479-7.

My translation of N.'s *Sintassi del verbo ebraico nella prosa biblica classica (B.L.* 1987, p. 123) appeared in 1990 as *The Syntax of the Verb in Classical Hebrew Prose (B.L.* 1991, p. 154) and included extensive additions and revisions by the author. The present translation into Spanish, prepared by Guadalupe Seijas de los Ri'os-Zarzosa, is from the revised Italian original, with some changes in the text, notes and examples and with additional tables. The principal change is the addition of an appendix that provides a full syntactical analysis of Joshua 1–5. In general, the layout is more generous than in the English edition, so that in the examples the (vocalized) Hebrew text and translation are now side by side. This updated edition is very welcome.

W.G.E. WATSON

SHIMASAKI, KATSUOMI, *Focus Structure in Biblical Hebrew: A Study of Word Order and Information Structure* (Bethesda, MD: CDL Press, 2002), pp. xvi + 314. $38.00. ISBN 1-883053-62-5.

Whereas the few previous studies of word order in biblical Hebrew treat verbal and nominal clauses separately, S., in his revised doctoral thesis, based on text-linguistics and functional grammar, applies information-structure analysis to both types of clause. He engages with the views of other scholars (F.I. Andersen, J. Hoftijzer, T. Muraoka, A. Niccacci, E. Revell and so on) and builds on their work, though he is prepared to be courteously critical where necessary. He is particularly concerned with defining the term 'focus' ('to focus is to mark an item as informationally prominent', p. 42) and differentiating it from terms such as 'emphasis', 'contrast', 'new information' and the like. Three types of structure are identified, depending on whether the focus is on the predicate, the argument or the clause (Chapters 3–6). He also discusses these types in terms of parallelism and lists. The last two chapters deal with problems and exceptions. Much of the theory is quite technical, yet by means of clear explanations, simple examples, tables and judiciously placed summaries, the author has succeeded in making his new approach intelligible to most readers. There are three appendixes: a list of nominal clauses, a list of verbal clauses and a clause-by-clause analysis of Deut. 4.44–11.32 in terms of focus structure, in effect an application of his theory to a continuous text. These are followed by a bibliography, and indexes of biblical passages and of topics. S. has undoubtedly advanced our understanding of word order in classical Hebrew.

W.G.E. WATSON

ZEVIT, ZIONY (ed.), *Hebrew Studies: A Journal Devoted to Hebrew Language and Literature*, vol. 42 (University of Wisconsin, Madison, WI: National Association of Professors of Hebrew in American Institutions of Higher Learning, 2001), pp. 412. $40.00 p.a. ISSN 0146-4094.

ZEVIT, ZIONY (ed.), *Hebrew Studies: A Journal Devoted to Hebrew Language and Literature*, vol. 43 (University of Wisconsin, Madison, WI: National Association of Professors of Hebrew in American Institutions of Higher Learning, 2002), pp. 372. $40.00 p.a. ISSN 0146-4094.

This journal covers all phases of Hebrew; only those articles likely to be of interest to most readers of the *B.L.* will be listed here. As well as articles, each issue has more than 100 pages of book reviews. Volume 42 has the following: the coherence of Prov. 30.11-33 and the unity of Proverbs 30 (A.E. Steinmann); Rabbi Abraham Ibn-Ezra's contribution to mediaeval Hebrew grammar (L. Charlap); אולי from Biblical to Modern Hebrew (Z. Livnat); exegetical implications of the Masoretic cantillation marks in Ecclesiastes (M. Carasik); the nineteenth-century

Jewish exegete S.D. Luzzatto (Shadal) on *pashat* exegesis (S. Vargon); Hebrew Philological Notes II: on Prov. 30.4, צלמות, Gen. 38.25, Exod. 32.18, Prov. 22.19 (G.A. Rendsburg); the third person masculine singular pronominal suffix -*h* in Hebrew biblical texts (I. Young); the movement from *qal* to *piel* in Hebrew and the disappearance of the *qal* internal passive (S.E. Fassberg); imperative and second person indicative forms in biblical Hebrew prose (A. Shulman); a review article of M.J.A. Horsnell, *A Review and Reference Grammar for Biblical Hebrew* (P.J. Gentry). Volume 43 has the follow articles: Hebrew Philological Notes III: Zech. 3.7, Ps. 22.17, the number 75, 1 Kgs 20.15, the origin of the personal name Ruth (Rendsburg); Greek evidence for the meaning of 'buy' for לקח (A. Yadin). There is also a symposium on the modern Hebrew play *Murder* by Hanoch Levin.

L.L. GRABBE

BOOKS ALSO RECEIVED OR RECEIVED TOO LATE FOR REVIEW IN 2003

The books in the following list have also been received; if directly related to the interests of the *Book List* they will be reviewed in the *Book List* for 2004.

BECKER, MICHAEL, *Wunder and Wundertäter im frührabbinischen Judentum: Studien zum Phänomen und seiner Überlieferung im Horizont von Magie und Dämonismus* (WUNT, 2/144; Tübingen: Mohr Siebeck, 2002), pp. xviii + 534. €74.00. ISBN 3-16-147666-2; ISSN 0340-9570.

CHISHOLM, ROBERT B. JR, *Handbook on the Prophets: Isaiah, Jeremiah, Lamentations, Ezekiel, Daniel, Minor Prophets* (Grand Rapids, MI: Baker Academic, 2002), pp. 512. $32.99. ISBN 0-8010-2529-X.

CIRAOLO, LEDA and JONATHAN SEIDEL (eds.), *Magic and Divination in the Ancient World* (Ancient Magic and Divination, 2; Leiden: Brill/Styx, 2002), pp. xii + 152. €59.00/$69.00. ISBN 90-04-12406-3; ISSN 1566-7952.

COLAUTTI, FEDERICO M., *Passover in the Works of Josephus* (JSJSup, 75; Leiden: Brill, 2002), pp. xii + 277. €78.00/$91.00. ISBN 90-04-12372-5; ISSN 1384-2161.

DAVIES, PHILIP R. (ed.), *First Person: Essays in Biblical Autobiography* (The Biblical Seminar, 81; London: Sheffield Academic Press, 2002), pp. 168. £55.00/ $105.00. ISBN 1-84127-320-1.

DECLAISSÉ-WALFORD, NANCY L., *Biblical Hebrew: An Introductory Textbook* (St Louis, MO: Chalice Press, 2002), pp. vii + 280. $39.99. ISBN 0-8272-0231-8.

DEMPSEY, CAROL J., *Hope Amid the Ruins: The Ethics of Israel's Prophets* (St Louis, MO: Chalice Press, 2000), pp. x + 160. $19.99. ISBN 0-8272-1439-1.

DUBE, MUSA W., *Postcolonial Feminist Interpretation of the Bible* (St Louis, MO: Chalice Press, 2000), pp. ix + 221. $32.99. ISBN 0-8272-2963-1.

GÓIS, DAMIÃO DE, *O Livro de Eclesiastes: Reprodução em Facsímile da edição de Stevão Sabio* (Veniza, 1538), critical edition and introduction by T.F. Earle (Lisbon: Fundação Calouste Gulbenkian, 2002), pp. xi + 189. 65 plates. n.p. ISBN 972-31-0964-6.

HOMAN, MICHAEL M., *To Your Tents, O Israel!: The Terminology, Function, Form, and Symbolism of Tents in the Hebrew Bible and the Ancient Near East* (Culture and History of the Ancient Near East, 12; Leiden: Brill, 2002), pp. xxvi + 229. 64 plates. €69.00/$81.00. ISBN 90-04-12606-6; ISSN 1566-2055.

HOPKINS, DENISE DOMBKOWSKI, *Journey through the Psalms* (St Louis, MO: Chalice Press, rev. edn, 2002), pp. vii + 176. $26.99. ISBN 0-8272-1714-5.

KAMANO, NAOTO, *Cosmology and Character: Qoheleth's Pedagogy from a Rhetorical-Critical Perspective* (BZAW, 312; Berlin: W. de Gruyter, 2002), pp. xvi + 308. €88.00. ISBN 3-11-017242-9.

KRISPENZ, JUTTA, *Literarkritik und Stilstatistik im Alten Testament: Eine Studie zur literarkritischen Methode, durchgefürt an Texten aus den Büchern Jeremia, Ezechiel und 1 Könige* (BZAW, 307; Berlin: W. de Gruyter, 2001), pp. x + 251. €84.00. ISBN 3-11-017057-4.

LAURENT, FRANÇOISE, *Les biens pur rien en Qohéleth 5,9-6,6 ou La traversée d'un contraste* (BZAW, 323; Berlin: W. de Gruyter, 2002), pp. xii + 281. €78.00. ISBN 3-11-017498-7.

LEVIN, CHRISTOPH, *Fortschreibungen: Gesammelt Studien zum Alten Testament* (BZAW, 316; Berlin: W. de Gruyter, 2003), pp. 360. €98.00. ISBN 3-11-017160-0.

LIM, JOHNSON T.K., *Grace in the Midst of Judgement: Grappling with Genesis 1-11* (BZAW, 314; Berlin: W. de Gruyter, 2002), pp. xii + 262. €68.00. ISBN 3-11-017420-0.

LIM, TIMOTHY H., *Pesharim* (Companion to the Qumran Scrolls, 3; London: Sheffield Academic Press, 2002), pp. 106. £50.00/$95.00 (hardback); £13.99/$29.95 (paperback). ISBN 1-84127-325-2 (cloth); 1-84127-273-6 (paper).

LÜDEMANN, GERD, *Paul: The Founder of Christianity* (Amherst, NY: Prometheus Books, 2002), pp. 292. $22.00. ISBN 1-59102-021-2.

MCCORMICK, CLIFFORD MARK, *Palace and Temple: A Study of Architectural and Verbal Icons* (BZAW, 313; Berlin: W. de Gruyter, 2002), pp. x + 221. €68.00. ISBN 3-11-017277-1.

MATTHEWS, VICTOR H., *A Brief History of Ancient Israel* (Louisville, KY: Westminster John Knox Press, 2002), pp. xvi + 171. £12.99. ISBN 0-664-22436-9.

MATHEWSON, DAVID, *A New Heaven and a New Earth: The Meaning and Function of the Old Testament in Revelation 21.1–22.5* (JSNTSup, 238; London: Sheffield Academic Press, 2003), pp. xii + 282. £60.00. ISBN 0-8264-6226-X.

MILLAR, WILLIAM R., *Priesthood in Ancient Israel* (Understanding Biblical Themes; St Louis, MO: Chalice Press, 2001), pp. viii + 126. $18.99. ISBN 0-8272-3829-0.

NEAGOE, ALEXANDRU, *The Trial of the Gospel: An Apologetic Reading of Luke's Trial Narratives* (SNTSMS, 116; Cambridge: Cambridge Univeristy Press, 2002), pp. xiv + 253. £40.00. ISBN 0-521-80948-7; ISSN 0074-9745.

NOLL, K.L., *Canaan and Israel in Antiquity: An Introduction* (The Biblical Seminar, 83; London: Sheffield Academic Press, 2001), pp. 331. 36 figures. £60.00/$115.00. ISBN 1-84127-318-X (cloth).

RAPOPORT-ALBERT, ADA and GILLIAN GREENBERG (eds.), *Biblical Hebrew, Biblical Texts: Essays in Memory of Michael P. Weitzman* (JSOTSup., 333, The Hebrew Bible and its Versions, 2; London: Sheffield Academic Press, 2001), pp. 528. £75.00/$145.00. ISBN 1-84127-235-3.

RAPP, URSULA, *Mirjam: Eine feministisch-rhetorische Lektüre der Mirjamtexte in der hebräischen Bibel* (BZAW, 317; Berlin: Walter de Gruyter, 2002), pp. xvi + 434. €108.00. ISBN 3-11-017384-0.

REITERER, FRIEDRICH V. (ed.), *Zählsynopse zum Buch Ben Sira* (Fontes et Subsidia ad Bibliam pertinentes, 1; Berlin; W. de Gruyter, 2003), pp. xii + 247. €68.00. ISBN 3-11-017520-7.

RICHTER, SANDRA L., *The Deuteronomistic History and the Name Theology: ľšakkēn šᵉmô šām in the Bible and the Ancient Near East* (BZAW, 318; Berlin: W. de Gruyter, 2002), pp. xiv + 246. €68.00. ISBN 3-11-017376-X.

RIEDE, PETER, *Im Spiegel der Tiere: Studien zum Verhältnis von Mensch und Tier im alten Israel* (OBO, 187; Freiburg: Universitätsverlag; Göttingen: Vandenhoeck & Ruprecht, 2002), pp. xi + 364. 23 figures. SwF 98.00. ISBN 3-7278-1407-1 (Universitäsverlag); 3-525-53044-7 (Vandenhoeck & Ruprecht); ISSN 1015-1850.

RO, JOHANNES UN-SOK, *Die sogenannte „Armenfrömmigkeit" im nachexilischen Israel* (BZAW, 322; Berlin: W. de Gruyter, 2002), pp. xii + 238. €68.00. ISBN 3-11-017471-5.

RUNIONS, ERIN, *Changing Subjects: Gender, Nation and Future in Micah* (Playing the Texts, 7; London: Sheffield Academic Press, 2001), pp. 295. £18.99/$25.00. ISBN 1-84127-270-1 (paper).

SCOBIE, CHARLES H.H., *The Ways of Our God: An Approach to Biblical Theology* (Grand Rapids, MI: Eerdmans, 2003), pp. xviii + 1038. $45.00/£32.00. ISBN 0-8028-4950-4.

SORENSEN, ERIC, *Possession and Exorcism in the New Testament and Early Christianity* (WUNT, 2/157; Tübingen: Mohr Siebeck, 2002), pp. xiii + 295. €49.00. ISBN 3-16-147851-7; ISSN 0340-9570.

SPAWN, KEVIN L., *"As It Is Written" and Other Citation Formulae in the Old Testament: Their Use, Development, Syntax, and Significance* (BZAW, 311; Berlin: W. de Gruyter, 2002), pp. xviii + 301. €94.00. ISBN 3-11-017161-9.

TERRIEN, SAMUEL, *The Psalms: Strophic Structure and Theological Commentary* (Eerdmans Critical Commentary; Grand Rapids, MI: Eerdmans, 2003), pp. xix + 971. $95.00/£65.00. ISBN 0-8028-2605-9.

WIMBUSH, VINCENT L., *The Bible and African Americans: A Brief History* (Facets; Minneapolis, MN: Fortress Press, 2003), pp. xii + 98. $6.00. ISBN 0-8006-3574-4.

INDEX OF AUTHORS

INDEX OF REVIEWERS

INDEX OF SERIES

INDEX OF PUBLISHERS

The Society for Old Testament Study is a British Society for Old Testament Scholars. Candidates for membership, which is not confined to British subjects, must be nominated by two members of the Society. All correspondence concerning membership and domestic affairs of the Society should be sent to:

Dr John Jarick
St Stephen's House
16 Marston Street
Oxford OX4 1JX
England

The Society has a website where further information can be obtained:
http://www.trinity-bris.ac.uk/sots